UNIVERSITY OF MICHIGAN PUBLICATIONS

HISTORY AND POLITICAL SCIENCE
VOLUME XIX

The Right to Counsel in American Courts

The
Right to
Counsel in
American
Courts

WILLIAM M. BEANEY

GREENWOOD PRESS, PUBLISHERS
WESTPORT, CONNECTICUT

The Library of Congress has catalogued this publication as follows:

Library of Congress Cataloging in Publication Data

Beaney, William Merritt, 1918-
   The right to counsel in American courts.

   Original ed. issued as v. 19 of University of
Michigan publications. History and political science.
   Bibliography: p.
   1. Right to counsel--United States. I. Title.
II. Series: Michigan. University. University of
Michigan publications. History and political science,
v. 19.
KF9646.B4 1972   347'.73'05   72-5275
ISBN 0-8371-5725-0

Originally published in 1955 by the University of Michigan
Press, Ann Arbor

Reprinted with the permission of the University of Michigan
Press

Reprinted by Greenwood Press, Inc.

First Greenwood reprinting 1972
Second Greenwood reprinting 1977

Library of Congress catalog card number 72-5275
ISBN 0-8371-5725-0

Printed in the United States of America

PREFACE

THIS study of the right to counsel in American courts has been undertaken in the belief that a detailed analysis of the cases and other relevant literature might convey to lawyers, judges, and students of our judicial system a more accurate knowledge of the present content of the right to counsel and of its possible future development.

An examination of the cases and the literature is not enough, however, to give one an understanding of how a right is extended in practice, and, so far as time and financial resources have permitted, I have observed court proceedings and have interviewed lawyers, trial judges, and members of prosecutors' staffs in order to gain insights which the printed page inevitably denies. I wish here to record my appreciation to the Princeton University Research Committee for a grant which made possible a widening of the "live" research program.

No project of this kind can be accomplished without help. The staff of the law library at the University of Michigan, Mr. Frank Hudon, of the United States Supreme Court Library, the staff of the State Law Library, Trenton, New Jersey, and of the Firestone Library, Princeton University, gave freely of their professional services, for which I am most grateful.

Of the many judges, prosecutors, and lawyers who coöperated, Judge James A. Breakey, Jr., Judge J. Louis Comerford, Hon. Frank P. Ashemeyer, and Messrs. Lewis E. Boess and Charles Symmes were particularly helpful, and exceedingly generous with their time.

My father, and several lawyer friends of long standing, Messrs. Shubrick T. Kothe, John R. Chapin, Robert O. Hancox, Neil McKay, and John Stoddert, made it possible to interview many of those who are actively participating in the judicial system, and gave me aid and comfort in other forms.

A debt of quite a different nature is owed Miss Alice B.

McGinty and Miss Grace E. Potter, of the University of Michigan Press, whose efforts to convert a "first" manuscript into a readable book can be fully appreciated only by me.

My wife, with a loyalty which far transcends any marital obligation, cheerfully undertook so many tasks connected with this work, such as typing, arrangement of tables, and the like, that adequate words of thanks are impossible.

Finally, I want to express my deepest gratitude to Professor Harold M. Dorr, of the University of Michigan, who encouraged this study from its inception, and who, in spite of many heavy professional obligations, has attempted to save me from some of the more grievous faults of style and substance.

Needless to say, the responsibility for all errors and conclusions is mine.

W. M. B.

PRINCETON, NEW JERSEY
August, 1953

TABLE OF CONTENTS

vii

ABBREVIATIONS USED IN THE CITATIONS

A.B.A.J.—American Bar Association Journal
Annals—Annals of the American Academy of Social and Political Science
Calif. L. Rev.—California Law Review
Chi-Kent L. Rev.—Chicago-Kent Law Review
Col. L. Rev.—Columbia Law Review
Corn. L. Rev.—Cornell Law Review
F.R.D.—Federal Rules Decisions
H. C. Deb.—House of Commons Debates
Ill. B. J.—Illinois Bar Journal
Ind. L. J.—Indiana Law Journal
Iowa L. Rev.—Iowa Law Review
J. Amer. Judic. Soc.—Journal of the American Judicature Society
J. Crim. L. and Crim.—Journal of Criminal Law and Criminology
J. Crim. L., Crim. and Pol. Sci.—Journal of Criminal Law, Criminology
   and Police Science (formerly, J. Crim. L. and Crim.)
Legal Aid Rev.—Legal Aid Review
Marq. L. Rev.—Marquette Law Review
Mich. L. Rev.—Michigan Law Review
Minn. L. Rev.—Minnesota Law Review
Mo. St. L. J.—Missouri State Law Journal
Nat. B. J.—National Bar Journal
Neb. L. Rev.—Nebraska Law Review
N.J.L.J.—New Jersey Law Journal
N. Y. U. L. Rev.—New York University Law Review
So. Calif. L. Rev.—Southern California Law Review
Stanford L. Rev.—Stanford Law Review
Temp. L. Q.—Temple Law Quarterly
Tex. L. Rev.—Texas Law Review
Univ. of Chic. L. Rev.—University of Chicago Law Review
Univ. of Pa. L. Rev.—University of Pennsylvania Law Review
U.S.C.A.—United States Code Annotated
Va. L. Rev.—Virginia Law Review
Vanderbilt L. Rev.—Vanderbilt Law Review
Yale L. J.—Yale Law Journal

CHAPTER I

INTRODUCTION

THE very strength of legal institutions—their adherence to basic principles and traditions—becomes a hindrance when a procedure long employed proves undesirable in modern practice. Unfortunately, the right of a defendant in criminal trials to retain counsel and, more especially, his right to have counsel appointed if he is indigent, received a definition at English common law which, though broadened over the years, fails in many respects to accord with our concept of fairness. Yet, this right to counsel might well be considered crucial—a right by which virtually all other rights are protected in practice. Whenever the judicial process unfolds, whether against the unlicensed orator in a public park, the protagonist of unpopular religious beliefs, or the citizen accused of assault or murder, the trial and its result give us in practice whatever meaning the rule of law possesses. It is obvious, too, that in order for a trial to achieve substantial justice there must be a fair and full presentation of the case for and against the accused. "His day in court" is an idle expression if the defendant lacks the assistance of able, courageous, and zealous counsel. The present study has resulted from an attempt to learn whether the right to counsel, which is vital in criminal cases, is enjoyed as consistently and widely in the United States as the needs of justice require.

Moreover, since 1937 the Supreme Court has relegated economic rights to a subordinate position in its hierarchy of constitutional rights, and has emphasized the First Amendment rights of speech, press, religion, and assembly and, in lesser degree, the procedural guarantees contained in the Bill of Rights. This "double standard" of the Court, as one observer has described it,[1] promises to endure for the discernible future, and

[1] C. Herman Pritchett, *The Roosevelt Court* (New York: Macmillan, 1948), p. 92.

thus it casts upon students of the Court the duty to describe more fully the precise nature and scope of each of the personal rights with which the Court is, and will be, concerned.

Until recently the literature dealing with the right to counsel was fragmentary, and even now, no single comprehensive treatment exists.[2]   Conversations with judicial officials and members of the bars of several states have revealed considerable confusion about the legal and practical problems involved in extending the right to counsel.   Most of these persons, whose comments must remain anonymous in this book unless their words and conduct are part of an official record, believe that a comprehensive treatment of the counsel problem would be of some value to those charged with the administration of justice.   It is hoped that this work may, in spite of its defects, help to fill that need.

A discussion of the right to counsel is also timely and important because there are so many problems related to it which have not been solved.   Each new volume of the sectional or state reporters and of the federal reports contains its quota of counsel cases, and important cases have been presented to the Supreme Court in almost every term since 1945, with many more petitions for certiorari denied.[3]   This condition affects the popular evaluation of courts.   If a newspaper recounts a story of a policeman who treats a prisoner with lack of concern for his rights, or if a "confession" is induced by an overzealous prosecutor, we may be offended, but we usually attribute such deviations to haste, overwork, or anger on the part of the official.   But when a reviewing court holds that a trial court has denied some element of the right to counsel, we find it more difficult to rationalize the error, since one of the most persistent myths of the layman is

---

[2] Shortly after the preparation of the original draft of this study in 1950, two excellent articles appeared by the well-known writer on constitutional subjects, Professor David Fellman, of the University of Wisconsin: "The Constitutional Right to Counsel in Federal Courts," 30 *Neb. L. Rev.* (May, 1951), 559, and "The Federal Right to Counsel in State Courts," 31 *Neb. L. Rev.* (Nov., 1951), 15.   In addition, there was published in 1951 a thorough study by Professor Francis H. Heller, of the University of Kansas: *The Sixth Amendment* (Lawrence, Kan.: Univ. Kansas Press, 1951); Chap. VI treats the right to counsel.

[3] In the four terms 1946–50, forty-seven of the 145 constitutional cases decided involved criminal procedure.   See John P. Frank, "Court and Constitution: The Passive Period," 4 *Vanderbilt L. Rev.* (April, 1951), 400–401.   This trend continued in the 1950–51, 1951–52, and 1952–53 terms.

that in every trial counsel is furnished. And although it is true that courts have been handicapped by insufficient or vague legislative provision concerning counsel or by legislative unwillingness to allow the courts to act through their rule-making power, the major blame will attach to them.

Furthermore, all members of a civilized society should be concerned with the means whereby any one of their number loses his liberty. The repulsive act of criminal violence should not blind us to any element of unfairness in the procedure by which "justice" is done, for each of us is threatened by an official act of injustice, which requires only acceptance and repetition to become part of our practical jurisprudence. There is no need to be maudlin about the "poor convict" in the penitentiary, but interest is justified if inadequate and dangerous procedures are being employed by our courts when defendants, both the innocent and the guilty, come before them. The essence of trial in the Anglo-American system of law is to determine guilt or innocence in a fair proceeding. But the fairness of the proceeding is unquestionably more important, if we adhere to a long view of judicial objectives, than the result in this or that specific case. The public irritation with the legal "technicality," although occasionally justified, is in most instances a purely emotional response to situations understood only vaguely, if indeed understood at all. Thus the fact that the counsel issues have been raised by men who have been convicted of crime should neither blind us to the general importance of the issues nor affect the answers which we give.

There are two other factors justifying a more than academic interest in the counsel problem which deserve mention here. First, modern criminologists and penologists offer as the ultimate purposes of their sciences both the prevention of crime and the rehabilitation of those who violate the criminal law. Experience frequently shows that a "bitter" prisoner is one who feels that he suffered an injustice as the result of a defective trial procedure, and while it is true that there are men for whom no procedure would prove completely satisfying, it is equally true that a fair procedure would satisfy the majority of men and reduce the resentment toward society which they might otherwise harbor. Secondly, there is a constant pressure upon our state and our national governments, as there is on governments every-where, to undertake an increasing variety of functions and to regulate a great number of activities which were formerly mat-ters of private concern. In order for them to execute these social purposes, it has become customary to attach criminal liability to a host of activities formerly devoid of legal significance. At the same time, there is a tendency to eliminate wrongful intent as an ingredient of the legally defined "wrong." The inevitable result of these trends will be to add tremendously to the burden on our courts.

To enable the courts to deal satisfactorily with this growing volume of cases it is even more necessary than in the past to re-examine our judicial procedures and to correct those features which are found defective. Stated more simply, as the courts face increasingly difficult problems and heavier burdens they must develop suitable safeguards for liberty and more efficient techniques with which to dispense equal justice under law. Representation of the accused, as will be shown, deserves a cen-tral position in this undertaking.

Before beginning a detailed analysis of the origin and devel-opment of the right to counsel it would seem wise to indicate where and how the question of counsel arises. When the 1931 report of the Wickersham Commission outlined the essential characteristics of American criminal proceedings, it made no specific reference to counsel. Summarized, the features of a criminal procedure which it indicated were:

1. The accused is brought before or within the power of the proper tribunal.
2. A preliminary investigation is made to insure that the crime is one which should be prosecuted.
3. Notice is given to the accused of the offense charged against him.
4. Opportunity is given the accused to prepare for trial, procure witnesses, and make such investigation as he deems necessary.
5. The accused is given a speedy trial.
6. The accused is given a fair trial before an impartial tribunal.

7. A review of the case by a suitable appellate tribunal is available where warranted.[4]

These steps sketch in the role of the accused and indicate the presence of a properly constituted tribunal. It is implied further that an official, the prosecutor, will undertake a preliminary investigation, and from our own knowledge we can add that official to the picture. It is also clear that after receiving "notice" the defendant is to be given an opportunity to prepare a defense with certain legal powers to aid him, and then is to receive a speedy and "fair" trial. Significantly, this outline of criminal procedure does not define the accused's right to counsel, and it leaves unanswered many pertinent questions—for example, Is the accused to defend himself? A consideration of this question and other related issues will indicate the precise contours of the whole counsel problem.

It is generally known that the accused can retain a lawyer, and the layman has a dim conception that every defendant has or is given counsel in any case involving the possibility of imprisonment. But several phases of this right require clarification—among them, the legal protection of the desire to retain a lawyer and the practical effectiveness of this guaranty, the time at which the accused can first obtain the aid of a lawyer, the defendant's ability to gain a postponement if the attorney is not immediately available, the right to change lawyers if the defendant becomes dissatisfied, the amount of time the lawyer is allowed for his preparation, the right of the defendant to consult his attorney out of court before trial and during trial, the effect of counsel's absence at any stage during trial, and the limits, if any, that the court can place on counsel's efforts in court on behalf of his client.

All of the previously stated problems which arise in connection with the service of retained counsel suggest themselves again when counsel is appointed for the defense of an indigent accused, and, in addition, a wholly new set of questions arises. Must the poor defendant forego the assistance of a trained lawyer if he is unable to retain one? If the court furnishes a lawyer who will

[4] National Commission on Law Observance and Enforcement, *Report on Criminal Procedure* (Washington, D.C.: Government Printing Office, 1931), p. 16.

serve without cost to the defendant, by what authority does the court make the appointment? Is it the court's duty to appoint counsel in all cases and for all defendants, or are there limited categories where this action is necessary? Is appointment of counsel a discretionary power or a duty? Furthermore, if the states do not have identical procedures respecting appointments is there any limitation arising from the United States Constitution which affects a state's procedure concerning counsel for indigents? How do judges select the attorneys who are appointed and how are they paid, if at all? Once appointed, must a counsel serve regardless of his and the defendant's wishes, or can new appointments be requested? What is the standard of service which counsel must furnish, whether retained or appointed? Finally, it is important to ascertain whether a defendant can obtain an adequate review by the appellate courts of his claim of denial of one or more aspects of the right to counsel. If he must use a collateral attack through habeas corpus or *coram nobis,* what are the particular hazards to be faced?

The answers to these questions are complicated because we must deal not only with the separate criminal procedures of forty-eight states, but at the same time we must observe what occurs in the federal court system, whose criminal jurisdiction has grown impressively with the increase in federal activities. This is not all, for the United States Supreme Court has assumed, in addition to its burdensome duty of supervising the criminal procedure of the lower federal courts, the delicate task of scrutinizing the state-court decisions involving criminal trials and of testing their validity by the due-process clause of the Fourteenth Amendment. An examination of the cases resulting from this review function is essential.

The method followed in the present study in essaying answers to these problems has been to sketch the historical background of the right to counsel in English and early American law, to examine the process by which the Sixth Amendment counsel provision has been applied in federal courts, and to survey the state constitutional and statutory provisions and the great mass of cases in which they have been applied. In addition, it has been necessary to analyze the interpretation by the United States Supreme Court of the due-process clause of the Fourteenth

Amendment as a limitation on state procedure in respect to counsel. Finally a review of the practical problems which courts face in furnishing counsel is presented, followed by a summary and conclusions.

Underlying the whole discussion are the assumptions that judicial procedure is important and that criminal procedure is at least as important as that involving civil matters. Further, it is assumed that most defendants in criminal proceedings are not legally trained and would welcome professional assistance if it were obtainable. The final assumption is that a wealthy nation which has devoted much attention to egalitarian theory and implemented it by extensive economic, political, and social legislation can afford decent treatment for its indigent members who face a danger of losing either life or liberty in a criminal proceeding. These assumptions explain whatever bias may be revealed in the analysis that follows. It is hoped, however, that the information presented and the positions taken reflect a thoughtful consideration of alternative views and of the available evidence, rather than a wishful sentimentalism. Any change which might seem desirable in this or any other element of our criminal procedure should come as the result of a careful and critical analysis of the condition which exists and the alternatives proposed. It is hoped that this short study will assist those who attempt such an analysis of the right to counsel in American courts.

CHAPTER II

RIGHT TO COUNSEL IN ENGLISH AND EARLY AMERICAN LAW

RIGHT TO COUNSEL IN ENGLAND BEFORE 1836

Since so many elements of our substantive and procedural law have an English ancestry, it is natural to assume that there were precedents in early English law concerning the right to appear with counsel in criminal cases. Although Parliament and the courts threw their protection around the right to trial by jury, which dated from the period of Bracton in the mid-thirteenth century and attained its more modern form by the middle of the fifteenth century,[1] they showed little interest in extending the statutory right to retain counsel to all criminal proceedings until 1836.

Illogically, in the least serious cases, English law had granted recognition of the accused's right to retain counsel and to make a defense with his assistance.[2] In these minor cases, or misdemeanors, examples of which were libel, perjury, battery, and conspiracy,[3] the state's interest was apparently deemed so slight that it could afford to be considerate toward defendants.[4]

In addition, there was a group of misdemeanors for which the common law did not provide any punishment, or provided punishment that was regarded as insufficient. Such acts (frequently of a political nature) which the Crown chose to notice, although less serious than sedition or treason, were triable before the court of Star Chamber. Here the presence of counsel was

[1] Sir James F. Stephen, *A History of the Criminal Law of England* (London: Macmillan, 1883), I, 260–265.

[2] *Ibid.*, p. 341.

[3] William Blackstone, *Commentaries on the Laws of England,* 12th ed. (London: T. Cadell, 1795), IV, 5n(2).

[4] Stephen, *op. cit.*, I, 397–399, stresses the advantages which the Crown claimed in other criminal trials.

8

not only permitted but was mandatory, because the defendant was required to have his answer to the charge signed by his counsel. His failure to obtain this signature was taken as a confession that the information was true.[5] In view of this consideration for defendants in minor cases, one might assume that where more serious charges were brought before King's Bench, such as larceny, robbery, murder, and treason, the accused would at least have the right to retain counsel, and possibly might receive some greater safeguard from the state. Such, however, was not the situation, for, except in cases of treason, defendants in felony cases had no legal right to appear with counsel.

Before 1695 one accused of treason or misprision of treason had no right to retain counsel, but in that year Parliament chose to create a preferred position for such defendants. By statute, not only was the accused permitted to retain counsel, but it was provided that the court must appoint counsel, not exceeding two, upon the request of the accused.[6] This gesture was one result of the frequent alternations in political power which characterized seventeenth-century England and which made treason a likely concomitant of a political career for many who felt themselves "loyal" and decent citizens. Members of Parliament were all "political" figures, and the reform in 1695 reveals in eloquent terms their ideas of a fair judicial proceeding in a case where they might be involved personally.

In all other felonies the accused was not permitted counsel in the fullest sense until 1836, and it should be remembered that most felonies of the seventeenth and eighteenth centuries were capital offenses, for which the possible (and likely) punishment was death. Thus the incongruous practice existed that in cases where death might be the penalty, an accused was denied the right to retain counsel, while in cases involving a fine or, at most, brief imprisonment, the courts afforded him this right. This situation was made tolerable only because in many cases the court of its own volition, and without pretending to change the rule, permitted counsel to argue points of law.[7]

[5] *Ibid.*, p. 341.
[6] 7 and 8 W. 3, c. 3, s. 1 (1695).
[7] See comment by Thomas M. Cooley, *Constitutional Limitations,* 1st ed. (Boston: Little, Brown, 1868), pp. 330–338.

Sir James F. Stephen, the outstanding authority on the history of English criminal law, indicates a further relaxation of the rule dating from about 1750. A practice emerged by which counsel was allowed to perform an increasing number of the functions associated with the defense until, by the end of the eighteenth century, he could do everything necessary for the defendant except address the jury at the conclusion of the evidence, a privilege of the king's counsel.[8] Because there was no statutory basis for this practice, variations were frequent. In 1752, for example, in the trial of Mary Blanding for the poisoning of her father, the defendant was allowed to retain counsel who conducted both the direct examination and the cross-examination.[9] Yet one year later, in the trial of John Barbot, an attorney, on a charge of murder, when the accused asked for the right to make full defense by counsel and cited two precedents, king's counsel purported to be shocked at the suggestion, and only after some argument did the court agree to permit counsel to assist on points of law. It is notable, however, that the counsel who appeared in the case went further and conducted the direct examination and the cross-examination,[10] which forces one to conclude that the courts were rather broad in their interpretation of what constituted "legal questions." The generosity of the courts is illustrated again in 1755, at the trial of McDaniel and others as accessories before the fact to robbery, when the court assigned counsel to argue legal matters for the prisoners who appeared without counsel. The appointee was not particularly pleased, apparently, since he prefaced his argument with the following apology: ". . . I could not have been prevailed upon to have been counsel for such a set of rogues, had I not been appointed by your lordships."[11]

This increasingly relaxed attitude of the courts in permitting counsel to appear coincided with the general change in English criminal procedure. It became very objective toward both the state and the accused because of the fact that in the period following the Revolution prosecutions were instigated primarily by

8 Stephen, op. cit., I, 424.
9 Cobbett's State Trials, comp. T. B. Howell (London: T. C. Hansard, 1813), XVIII, 1117.
10 Ibid., p. 1230.   11 Ibid., XIX, 790.

private persons, rather than by the state, and thus by the mid-eighteenth century the judge could look upon himself as a disinterested referee between two contestants, rather than as an essential arm of Crown power.[12]   This supposedly neutral position of the judge furnished an excuse, however, for continuing the practice of denying counsel in felonies, and the reason commonly given was that the judge was impartial and looked with equal suspicion on both sides in a criminal action, with the further explanation that a criminal proceeding was so simple that any man could understand what was being done.[13]   Another reason, though certainly not stated openly at the time, was the view that the defendant, having been indicted as an enemy of the king, was at least half guilty and that all aids should be furnished to the king, whose security, at any rate during the seventeenth century, was more important than that of the individual accused.[14]

Blackstone severely attacked this illogic in the English legal system, inquiring: "Upon what face of reason can that assistance [of counsel] be denied to save the life of a man, which is yet allowed him in prosecutions for every petty trespass?"[15]   He observed that the judges themselves had been aware of this irony, because they of their own volition had permitted most counsel to deal with the factual as well as the legal issues of a case.[16]

The movement for reform which began after 1800 resulted in great changes in the law by 1850.   Aided by the efforts of Bentham and others who aimed at substantial changes in the procedural as well as in the substantive law, it brought about in 1836 a legislative grant of the right to retain counsel in all cases.[17] Parliament specifically provided that "all persons tried for felonies should be admitted, after the close of the case for the prosecution, to make full answer and defence thereto, by counsel learned in the law, or by attorney in courts where attornies practice as counsel."[18]   At that late date the right to counsel in prose-

---

[12] Stephen, *op. cit.*, I, 418–419.

[13] Theodore F. Plucknett, *A Concise History of the Common Law*, 3rd ed. (London: Butterworth, 1940), pp. 385 ff.

[14] Stephen, *op. cit.*, I, 397–399.

[15] Blackstone, *op. cit.*, IV, 355.   [16] *Ibid.*

[17] See Leon Radzinowicz, *A History of the English Criminal Law* (London: Stevens, 1948), pp. 399–601, for a detailed account of this movement.

[18] 6 and 7 W. 4, c. 114, s. 1 (1836).

cutions for felony was placed on the same basis as the right previously enjoyed in cases involving misdemeanors.

RIGHT TO COUNSEL IN ENGLAND AFTER 1836

The striking feature of the treason act of 1695 was its provision for the appointment of counsel for the prisoner if he were unable to retain counsel and requested such appointment.[19] It would have been a substantial advance on the existing rule if merely the right to retain counsel in treason cases had been granted, but by giving the right to appointed counsel Parliament showed a tenderness for defendants which it was not to exhibit again for two centuries, since the act of 1836 did not go so far as the 1695 act.[20] The act of 1836 simply permitted persons accused to appear and defend with counsel retained by them. This did not mean, of course, that indigents never had counsel in felony cases, for in murder cases it was common for distinguished advocates to come forward to defend them without cost, and it is probable that in lesser crimes some counseling would be given when a town character ran afoul of the law. In rural villages the method of payment of counsel was frequently so flexible that legal aid was virtually free. Moreover, the inherent power of the courts was broad enough to permit the appointment of counsel for indigents who were minors or who appeared mentally deficient. It was not, however, until the Poor Prisoners' Defence Act of 1903 that provision was made in English law for the appointment of counsel in all felonies.[21]

Under the act of 1903 the committing magistrate or the judges of assize were empowered to appoint a solicitor and a counsel in all indictments when the defendant's means were insufficient to enable him to obtain counsel, *and* when it appeared from the nature of the defense set up, as disclosed in evidence given or statements made before the committing magistrate, that justice required such an appointment.[22]

Two features of this act are striking. First, it required the

19 7 and 8 W. 3, c. 3, s. 1 (1695).
20 6 and 7 W. 4, c. 114, s. 1 (1836).
21 3 Edw. 7, c. 38, s. 1 (1903).
22 Halsbury's *Laws of England* (London: Butterworth, 1909), Vol. IX, "Criminal Law and Procedure," Pt. V, par. 684.

prisoner to reveal his defense, since he could not otherwise obtain appointed counsel.   Secondly, the judge, upon hearing the prisoner's version of the events, which might be far less convincing than the same set of facts presented by an experienced counsel, might decide that counsel should not be appointed and might thus, in effect, decisively prejudge the case.   The existence of these two elements made the 1903 act of little value to the prisoner, and it was rarely used except in the trial of very serious crimes, such as murder.[23]   In the average case the defendant was not given legal aid because English judges felt assured of their personal ability to dispense justice.[24]

When it had become apparent that the 1903 act was an inadequate solution in situations in which an indigent accused had no counsel, the Poor Prisoners' Defence Act of 1930 was passed.[25] The chief improvement brought about by this act is that when an indigent is charged with murder, counsel must be assigned. In other felonies, however, appointment of counsel is discretionary, depending on whether "by reason of the gravity of the charge or of exceptional circumstances, justice requires such an appointment." [26]   In practice the act has proved less satisfactory than was anticipated.[27]   Relatively few prisoners have learned of their rights under it, and an extremely small number of defendants have had legal aid at the preliminary examination which led to commitment because the magistrate passed the duty of appointment on to the judges.   Furthermore, a large number of applications for appointment have been rejected.[28]

(Beginning in 1945, there was a general nonpolitical movement in Parliament to improve the position of indigent litigants, both civil and criminal.   This effort culminated in the Legal

[23] Lester B. Orfield, *Criminal Procedure from Arrest to Appeal* (New York: New York Univ. Press, 1947), p. 362, n. 72.   This valuable treatise contains useful brief references to the right to counsel.

[24] See Thomas Leaming, *A Philadelphia Lawyer in the London Courts* (New York: Holt, 1912), p. 159, for an interesting reaction to the English procedure.

[25] 20 and 21 Geo. 5, c. 32 (1930).

[26] *Ibid.*, s. 2.   This quoted portion was repealed by 12 and 13 Geo. 6, Pt. II, s. 18(2)(a) (1949).

[27] Richard M. Jackson, *The Machinery of Justice in England* (Cambridge, England: Cambridge Univ. Press, 1940), pp. 123-125, 253.

[28] Orfield, *op. cit.*, pp. 363-364.

Aid and Advice Act, 1949, which became law on July 30, 1949.[29]

Unfortunately, the act is designed primarily as a civil legal-aid measure and contains few provisions which alter directly the rights of an accused under the Poor Prisoners' Defence Act of 1930.[30] The principal changes introduced are the requirement that doubts concerning the appointment or allowance of counsel "where justice requires" are to be resolved in favor of the prisoner, and the provision that an accused can apply at an early stage, before arraignment, for the allowance of counsel.[31]

It seems reasonable to assume, nonetheless, that an accused in a criminal case will be treated more generously in the future. It would be ironic if, in spite of the improved civil-litigation features of the act, judges and magistrates were to persist in their hitherto narrow attitude toward the indigent criminal defendant. The probability is that the availability of free legal advice at an early stage will become generally known and that the plea of the criminal defendant will be received only after advice has been given. For the accused, however, any benefit to be had in the future must depend, as it did in the past, on the attitude of the judges and magistrates when the absence of counsel is noted.

RIGHT TO COUNSEL IN PRE-REVOLUTIONARY AMERICA

A scholarly controversy has long been waged as to the relative influence of English common law in its substantive and procedural aspects upon colonial American law. One group, headed by Roscoe Pound, limits the practical effect or impact of English law to the post-Revolutionary period. The stress is laid by this group on the "native" elements, the "frontier" influence, by virtue of which colonial law, like other phases of colonial life, developed along lines markedly more primitive than, and noticeably different from, English law.[32]

29 See Reginald H. Smith, "The English Legal Assistance Plan," 35 *A.B.A.J.* (June, 1949), 453. The act is reprinted in VI *Briefcase* (Dec., 1948), 82. The official citation is 12 and 13 Geo. 6, c. 51 (1949).

30 R. H. Smith, 35 *A.B.A.J.* (June, 1949), 453, 456.

31 Part II, s. 15–18. See remarks in the Commons debates, 459 *H. C. Deb.* 1241 and 465 *H. C. Deb.* 1389, on the changes in the criminal procedure. The second of these references indicates some dissatisfaction with the actions or lack of action by judges and magistrates under the 1930 act.

32 J. Goebel and T. R. Naughton, *Law Enforcement in Colonial New York* (New York: Commonwealth Fund, 1944), p. xix, n. 5, contains a list of Pound's writings on this theory, which the authors oppose.

A second group, headed by Julius Goebel, refutes the Pound thesis by showing that English law had a firm reception in this country at a much earlier period. It further points out that the colonial statutes which wrought changes in the existing English law give a false picture of the development of American law if they are separated from the context of the law in which they were passed. ⸝ Colonial records are produced to demonstrate that a deliberate and conscious effort was made in colonial America to copy English substantive and procedural rules.[33]

In respect to the right to counsel there appears to be evidence from which each group might derive some comfort. On the one hand, in accordance with Pound's analysis, it seems to be agreed that the shortage of legally trained judges and trained lawyers made some procedural improvisation necessary in the earlier colonial period. To be sure, there was a tendency to rely on statutes because the more subtle common law was either unknown or imperfectly understood,[34] but there were a number of statutes, as will be shown presently, which undertook to improve the position of the accused, or at least to confirm in statutory form rights which in England remained subject to the discretion of the judge. On the other hand, intensive examination of colonial court records in New York and Virginia has convinced Goebel and Naughton that the right to counsel in those states was no greater in actual practice than in England.[35] An observer might well conclude that the typical "reception" statute found in the original state constitutions rather accurately reflects the true status of the law in declaring that the common law and the statutes of England, as received in the colony, along with acts of the colonial legislature composed the body of law in each colony in 1776 or in later years, when state constitutions were adopted.

With the knowledge of the English rule and practice in mind it is now necessary to survey legislative provisions in the colonies before 1776 in order to obtain at least a rough comparison. One must remember, however, that a statute tells us nothing of the practice under it. The paucity of studies in the field of colonial

---

[33] *Ibid.* The introduction contains a brilliant critique of Pound's theory.
[34] Oliver Chitwood, *A History of Colonial America* (New York: Harper, 1931), pp. 191–192.
[35] Goebel and Naughton, *op. cit.*, p. 574; see also Arthur P. Scott, *Criminal Law in Colonial Virginia* (Chicago: Univ. Chicago Press, 1930), pp. 76–80.

criminal procedure makes any final judgment at this time impossible.[36]

There was no statutory provision for the appointment of counsel in criminal cases in Connecticut before 1818, when the first state constitution was adopted. Yet the custom of appointing counsel if the accused requested this assistance apparently existed after 1750. In addition, the court usually advised the prisoner of his right to have counsel, and appointed one without request where the accused seemed to labor under some handicap.[37] The fact that this judicial practice was established at an early date and was of such broad scope would go far to explain the lack of any counsel cases under the 1818 Connecticut constitutional provision regarding counsel. It would tend to show that when a court chooses to exercise its power to provide adequate counsel the absence of a statute makes little difference.

In Pennsylvania the Frame of Government of 1683 had contained this clause concerning counsel: "In all courts all persons of all persuasions may . . . personally plead their own cause themselves, or if unable, by their friend . . . ." [38] Further provision was made in the Charter of Privilege of 1701 to the effect that "all criminals shall have the same Privileges of Witnesses and Council as their Prosecutors." [39] (A statute of 1718 declared, in addition, that treason trials should be conducted as in England, which meant that counsel should be assigned, and then went even further by listing a large number of capital crimes and by stating that "upon all trials of the said capital crimes, lawful challenges shall be allowed, and learned counsel assigned to the prisoners."[40] Since so many felonies were capital crimes in this period, it was a notable advance when counsel for indigents accused of serious crimes was provided by statute.

In the Delaware charter of 1701 the principle was similarly laid down that "all criminals shall have the same Privileges of

---

36 The studies by Scott and by Goebel and Naughton stand alone. A few isolated collections of court records from other states have been published, but they yield little of value. Official court records usually omitted reference to counsel even where counsel may have appeared.

37 Zephaniah Swift, *A System of the Laws of Connecticut* (Windham, Conn., 1795), II, 392, cited in *Powell* v. *Alabama*, 287 U.S. 45 at 62–63.

38 Par. VI.

39 Par. V.

40 3 *Statutes at Large of Pennsylvania* (Busch, 1896), 199.

Witnesses and Council as their Prosecutors." [41] (The Pennsylvania procedure was adhered to again when in 1709 a statute was adopted with a provision which required the appointment of counsel in cases involving capital offenses.[42])

South Carolina extended substantially the same right by an act passed on August 20, 1731, which gave to one accused of treason, murder, felony, or other capital offense, the right "to make his and their full defence, by council learned in the law . . . . And in case any person . . . shall desire council, the court . . . is hereby authorized and required, immediately, upon his or their request, to assign . . . such and so many council not exceeding two, as the person or persons shall desire, to whom such council shall have free access at all reasonable times." [43]

In Virginia it is not clear that there was any broadening of the English rule. (An act of 1734 permitted the accused in all capital cases to defend by counsel upon request to the court.[44]) But this apparent gain was nullified because the courts interpreted it to mean little more than did the English practice which permitted counsel to argue points of law.[45] An earlier act, interestingly enough, had allowed slaveowners to make a full defense of slaves accused of a capital offense, causing Scott to comment, with justifiable cynicism, "Slaves were too valuable to be hanged without due deliberation." [46])

A Rhode Island act of March 11, 1660, expressed in clear terms the reason why any accused needs counsel: "Whereas it doth appear that any person . . . may on good grounds, or through mallice and envie be indicted and accused for matters criminal, wherein the person that is so [accused] may be innocent, and yett, may not be accomplished with soe much wisdom and knowledge of the law as to plead his own innocencye, &c. Be it therefore inacted . . . that it shall be accounted and owned from henceforth . . . the lawful privilege of any man that is indicted, to procure an attornye to plead any poynt of law that

---

[41] First Article, § V.
[42] I *Laws of Delaware, 1700–1797* (S. and J. Adams, 1797), p. 66.
[43] XLIII *Laws of the Province of South Carolina* (Trott, 1736), pp. 518–519.
[44] IV *Statutes-at-Large of Virginia* (Hening, 1823), p. 404.
[45] Scott, *op. cit.*, pp. 76–80.
[46] *Ibid.*, p. 79.

may make for the clearing of his innocencye." [47] It can be seen
that this is hardly more than an early statutory embodiment of
the English procedure, although it did have the effect of limiting
judicial discretion.   No statutory provision existed in the other
colonies.

(Before the Revolution, then, one can say that in four colonies
there was a definite advance over the English procedure of the
period.   In Pennsylvania, Delaware, and South Carolina there
was a statutory recognition of a right which went beyond the
English practice to the extent that courts appointed counsel
where a capital crime was charged and the accused requested it,
and in Connecticut the practice was even more generous.   In
Virginia and Rhode Island there was at least a statutory recognition of a right which in England rested on judicial discretion.
In the remainder of the colonies the English procedure seems to
have prevailed, because no statutory provisions can be found and
no evidence exists of any broader right arising from the practices
of the courts.\ It is probably true that the English rule combined with the early shortage of lawyers in the colonies made it
inevitable that an accused should defend himself in most cases.[48]
Yet the general tendency of the new state constitutions ratified in
1776 and in the succeeding years to include a provision granting
the right to counsel suggests that in all American courts the practice of permitting counsel to perform more and more of the functions involved in a criminal defense under a broad interpretation of what constituted "legal questions" was well established
by the year 1776.

RIGHT TO COUNSEL UNDER EARLY STATE CONSTITUTIONS

\ With the exception of Connecticut and Rhode Island, which
continued to use their seventeenth-century charters, the states
adopted constitutions, beginning in 1776.[49]   An examination
of these constitutions and of legislative enactments immediately
following 1776 will indicate the interest which the legislatures,

---

[47] II *Rhode Island Colonial Records 1664–77* (Bartlett, 1857), p. 239.

[48] On the shortage of lawyers in colonial America, see Charles Warren,
A History of the American Bar (Boston: Little, Brown, 1911), Chaps. II–VI.

[49] Benjamin F. Wright, *A Source Book of American Political Theory* (New
York: Macmillan, 1929), p. 116.

congresses, or conventions had in the right to counsel when they met and framed their lists of rights to be protected.)

Georgia had no provision in its Constitution of 1776 concerning counsel, although the English procedure had been followed at least since the reorganization of government in Georgia after 1754.[50] The recognition of the right to defend by counsel came finally in the Constitution of 1798: "No person shall be detained from advocating or defending his cause before any court or tribunal, either by himself or counsel or both." [51]

Virginia similarly had no provision in the Constitution of 1776, and has failed to include one in its later constitutions. In the Bill of Rights of the Constitution of 1776 the only applicable clause is one to the effect that prosecutions should be in accordance with the "law of the land." However, in 1786 Virginia enacted a statute which allowed the accused to retain counsel to assist him at the trial.[52]

South Carolina, which had extended a very broad right to retain counsel and to have counsel appointed as early as 1731, required in its Constitution of 1778 merely that criminal proceedings be in accordance with the "law of the land." [53]

North Carolina had no constitutional clause regarding counsel until 1868, but an act of 1777 declared that "every person accused of any crime or misdemeanor whatsoever, shall be entitled to council, in all matters which may be necessary for his defence as well as to facts as to law." [54] By statute, then, North Carolina confirmed the best English practice of this period and removed the subject from judicial discretion.

The other seven of the original states and the Independent Republic of Vermont placed some provision in their constitutions.[55] A brief survey will reveal the nature of the right extended.

The Delaware Constitution of 1776 proclaimed that all acts

---

[50] Warren Grice, *The Georgia Bench and Bar* (Macon, Ga.: Burke, 1931), I, 40.

[51] Art. III, § 8.

[52] XII *Statutes-at-Large of Virginia* (Hening, 1823), p. 343.

[53] Par. XLI.

[54] XCIV *Laws of North Carolina* (Iredell, 1791), p. 317.

[55] Vermont was not admitted to the Union until 1791.

and statutes then in force were to continue in force.[56]   This
maintained the previously established right to retain counsel in
all felonies less than capital, and the right to have counsel appointed in capital cases.   The Constitution of 1792 provided:
"In all criminal prosecutions the accused hath a right to be heard
by himself and his counsel." [57]

In the Pennsylvania Constitution of 1776 the right was
phrased in similar terms,[58] and the right, previously enjoyed,
continued.

The New York Constitution of 1777 simply stated that "in
every trial or impeachment for crimes or misdemeanors, the party
impeached or indicted shall be allowed counsel, as in civil actions." [59]   In this state, it will be remembered, the English practice had prevailed, so that the clause marked a significant advance.

In the New Jersey Constitution of 1776 the right was phrased
differently.   New Jersey, which had previously had no statutory
provision and had followed the English rule, now extended a
guarantee that "all criminals shall be admitted to the same privileges of witnesses and counsel, as their prosecutors are, or shall
be entitled to." [60]   This apparently was not deemed sufficient,
for an act of 1795 authorized and required the courts in all cases
of indictment "to assign to such person, if not of ability to procure counsel, such counsel, not exceeding two, as he or she shall
desire." [61]   This, it can be seen, was a tremendous advance over
English rule and procedure.

The Massachusetts Constitution of 1780 declared that "every
subject shall have a right to . . . be fully heard in his defense
by himself or his counsel, at his election." [62]

The Maryland Constitution of 1776 was hardly less explicit
in its provision that "in all criminal prosecutions, every man hath

---

[56] Art. 24.

[57] Art. I, § 7.

[58] Declaration of Rights, IX.

[59] Par. XXXIV.

[60] Par. XVI. A brief discussion of the practice under the English rule is
contained in Preston W. Edsall, ed., *Journal of the Courts of Common Right and
Chancery of East New Jersey* (Philadelphia: American Legal History Society,
1937), p. 130.

[61] *Acts of the General Assembly,* 1791–96, p. 1012.

[62] Pt. I, Art. XII.

a right . . . to be allowed counsel . . . ." [63]   Thus both Massachusetts and Maryland improved on the English rule.

The New Hampshire Constitution of 1784 stated that "every subject shall have a right . . . to be fully heard in his defence by himself, and counsel," [64] and an act of 1791 broadened the right by providing that one indicted for crimes punishable by death "shall at his request have counsel learned in the law assigned him by the court, not exceeding two, and . . . shall have liberty to make his full defence by counsel and by himself . . . ." [65]

The Independent Republic of Vermont in its Constitution of 1777 declared simply that "in all prosecutions for criminal offenses, a man hath a right to be heard, by himself and his counsel . . . ." [66]

The pattern is confused, as can be seen.   When Justice Sutherland stated confidently in *Powell* v. *Alabama* that the English rule was rejected by the colonies, he was correct only insofar as the colonies all confirmed by some statutory provision a right which was extended after 1750 in England by a generous judiciary.   A few states went further, but we have as yet no proof that the actual judicial practice in many of the colonies was more liberal than the English practice.   Also, it is evident that no uniform practice existed throughout the colonies at any time before, or soon after, the Revolution.   Where provision was made for the appointment of counsel, it was done in most states only for capital offenses.   As late as 1800 it seems probable that only in New Jersey, by statute, and in Connecticut, by practice, did the accused enjoy a full right to retain counsel, and to have counsel appointed if he were unable to afford it himself.   Excluding these two states, the right to counsel meant the right to retain counsel of one's own choice and at one's own expense.

Diversity of policy thus seems to be the outstanding characteristic of colonial and early state provisions regarding the right to counsel.   Those who have looked to the English rule and disregarded the English practice after 1750 have also ignored the

[63] Declaration of Rights, XIX.
[64] Pt. I, Art. XV.
[65] *Laws of New Hampshire* (Melcher, 1792), p. 247.
[66] Chap. I, par. X.

early American practice while overemphasizing the early American statutory provisions. The greater distrust of government which the colonists had, along with their greater opportunity to indicate that distrust in legislative form, may go far to explain the widespread statutory concern in the colonies over the right to counsel and the absence of any substantial change in actual judicial procedure. As yet we have insufficient evidence upon which to base any claim that the American practice was in sharp contrast to the English. Advance there was, but in many ways it was a technical advance. To the narrowly legalistic such an advance is a source of much satisfaction. For those interested in the practical aspects of procedure something more is needed.

RIGHT TO COUNSEL IN THE CONSTITUTION OF 1787

In seven of the state conventions called to ratify the Constitution of 1787 demands arose for the addition of amendments, with special emphasis on the need for a bill of rights.[67] In only two states, however, did a right-to-counsel provision appear on the suggested list of "rights," and one state included it as a "condition" of ratification.

One of the two states, Virginia, proposed a list of twenty rights when it ratified the Constitution on June 27, 1788; the eighth of these contained this clause: "In all criminal and capital prosecutions a man hath a right to . . . be allowed counsel in his favor . . . ."[68] Significantly, Virginia had no similar clause in its own constitution, although its judicial practice had been in accordance with English procedure. This suggests that it was the right to retain counsel which was to be protected.

North Carolina, which by statute of 1777 had confirmed the most advanced English practice of the period, copied the bill of rights proposed by Virginia, including the eighth provision, in identical form.[69] But, since ten states had already ratified the Constitution, North Carolina circularized its proposals to Congress and the other states, and the ratifying convention adjourned

---

[67] According to Madison, 126 were proposed. See M. Farrand, *Records of the Federal Convention of 1787* (New Haven, Conn.: Yale Univ. Press, 1928), III, 489.

[68] J. Elliot, *Debates on the Federal Constitution*, 2nd ed. (Philadelphia: Lippincott, 1901), III, 658.

[69] *Ibid.*, IV, 243.

on August 2, 1788, without accepting or rejecting the Constitution.[70]

New York submitted a list of rights but did not include a provision concerning counsel. It did condition its ratification by the formally expressed "assumption" that certain rights would not be abridged by the new government, and "the right to the assistance of counsel" was one of these "assumed" rights.[71] The practice in New York, it will be recalled, had been substantially like that in England.

Little, if any, significance can be drawn from the fact that Virginia and North Carolina were the only states to propose a bill-of-rights provision concerning the right to counsel. The logical inference to be drawn is that the states were satisfied with their existing criminal procedure and assumed that most criminal prosecutions would continue to be undertaken by state governments. Hence other rights seemed of greater importance and more worthy of demand.

In the first session of Congress on July 2, 1789, Madison, in introducing in the House a series of amendments which he wished to see incorporated at appropriate places within the body of the Constitution, included the provision that "in all criminal prosecutions, the accused shall enjoy the right . . . to have the assistance of counsel for his defense" as part of Article I, Section 9.[72] A select committee reported this as part of number thirteen of seventeen proposed amendments,[73] and it was retained by the Senate as number eight of twelve amendments drawn up on the basis of the House suggestions,[74] in which form it was accepted by both houses on September 25, 1789. The available debates on the various proposals throw no light on the significance or the interpretation which Congress attributed to the right to counsel.[75] Although there was considerable debate on the other proposals, affecting the basis of representation,[76] religious freedom,[77]

[70] *Ibid.,* pp. 251–252.
[71] *Ibid.,* I, 327.
[72] I *Annals of Congress* (1789 repr. 1834), 440.
[73] *House Journal,* 1st Congress, 1st Session (1789 repr. 1826), 85–86.
[74] *Senate Journal,* 1st Congress, 1st Session (1789), 77.
[75] The Senate met in secret session throughout this period. No report is available.
[76] I *Annals of Congress* (1834), 747–757.
[77] *Ibid.,* pp. 757–760.

free speech and free press,[78] instruction of representatives,[79] and the right to bear arms,[80] there was a dearth of discussion when on August 21 the House considered the clause containing the "right to have the assistance of counsel." [81]

On December 15, 1791, when the eleventh state ratified, the "right to have the assistance of counsel" became part of the Constitution, as a clause in the sixth of ten amendments.[82]

It is extremely difficult, if not impossible, with the available material to reach any positive conclusion concerning the intention of Congress in proposing the clause or the interpretations given it by the states at the time of ratification. Lack of discussion usually means that there is general agreement, but in view of the varying statutory and judicial practices in the states, the question may well be asked, To what did the states agree? Each state could accept the proposal as guaranteeing a right similar to that which the citizen already possessed against his own state government. But whether an individual would be allowed to interpret it to mean more than the right to retain counsel would depend on the state in which he resided. It was left to the courts to decide the scope of the clause, with a minimum of guidance from the events and the comments accompanying its adoption.

SUMMARY AND CONCLUSIONS

The early identification of Crown interests with criminal prosecutions in England had an unfortunate influence upon the scope of a criminal defendant's right to defend himself by counsel. Those accused of felony enjoyed no legal right to retain counsel, while those prosecuted for lesser offenses had a right as broad as that extended in civil litigation. It was not until 1836 that persons charged with felonies attained a position equal to that of misdemeanants. The saving feature of the English procedure was the tendency of judges to permit counsel to argue points of law and, by an ever more generous interpretation of what constituted "legal questions," to broaden the rights of an accused in practice, while in theory these rights were nonexistent.

78 *Ibid.*, pp. 759–761.   80 *Ibid.*, pp. 778–781.
79 *Ibid.*, pp. 761–776.   81 *Ibid.*, p. 796.
82 Sol Bloom, ed., *Formation of the Union under the Constitution* (Washington, D.C.: Government Printing Office, 1937), p. 62.

The right to counsel in the American colonies deviated from the English right in certain respects. Some type of statutory provision was the general rule, rather than relegation of the matter to judicial discretion. Connecticut in its practice far surpassed the English custom, and its court appointed counsel in all cases where an accused needed and could not retain counsel. Three colonies, Pennsylvania, South Carolina, and Delaware, went part way, and stated that in capital cases an accused should have counsel upon request. In those colonies which permitted only the privilege of retaining counsel, it is far from clear that the defense by retained counsel was any broader in scope than it was in England under the court-evolved rules followed there. There does seem to have been a greater awareness in American courts that an accused who was undefended was at a serious disadvantage, and this awareness became keener as the number of lawyers increased in colonial America.

After the Revolution most states included a clause respecting counsel in their new constitutions.   In the majority of instances, however, it appears that they created no greater right than the accused had been enjoying in practice, although by statute certain states made advances.

The importance of grasping the varying scope of the right from colony to colony will be evident when we attempt to explain the present variations in the right to counsel throughout the forty-eight states. A people can no more escape from its judicial history than from any other phase of its past experience.

The provision in the Sixth Amendment to the Constitution emerged in an atmosphere of silence concerning the intentions which produced it. Since there was a general understanding that the federal courts would have jurisdiction of an insignificant number of criminal proceedings, the logical assumption is that no great thought was given to the precise nature of the federal right to counsel. In such circumstances the judges were left free to shape the right as they thought best.

Perhaps the strongest conclusion which can be derived from the English development in its entirety and from early American practices is that the courts, and not the legislatures, had within their hands the capacity and the power to shape the right to counsel into whatever mold seemed best.   To the courts, then, must be assigned the largest share of whatever praise or blame is due.

(We have seen how England has attempted to provide a method by which an accused might obtain counsel regardless of financial ability.   The acts of 1930 and 1949 made it mandatory that counsel be appointed in murder cases, but in all others the appointment rests in the discretion of the judge.   With the English example in mind, and the early American precedents available, it is now possible to turn to the modern American doctrines respecting the right to counsel.)

CHAPTER III

RIGHT TO COUNSEL UNDER THE SIXTH AMENDMENT

DEVELOPMENT OF THE LAW, 1789 TO 1938

THE data available indicate that no comment or controversy accompanied Congressional proposal of the Sixth Amendment to the Constitution, and the proceedings at the three state ratifying conventions in which counsel provisions were demanded reveal nothing concerning the contemporary meaning of the right to counsel. The lack of comment could be attributed to the general feeling in this formative period that the important processes of criminal law in the future would be those of the states.[1] Thus rival counsel in the leading cases involving the Sixth Amendment have freely speculated about its correct historical interpretation, advocating whatever position coincided with their clients' interests.[2]

The Supreme Court has seemingly avoided the problem of historical analysis in dealing with the counsel provision of the Sixth Amendment, in contrast to its extensive historical discussion when the Fourteenth Amendment due-process requirement of counsel was at issue. This appears strikingly when one compares *Johnson* v. *Zerbst*,[3] dealing with the Sixth Amendment right, with the Fourteenth Amendment cases of *Powell* v. *Alabama*[4] and *Betts* v. *Brady*.[5]

---

[1] See Homer Cummings and Carl McFarland, *Federal Justice* (New York: Macmillan, 1937), pp. 464–475.

[2] For an outstanding example of such historical "reconstruction," see Brief for Petitioner, pp. 20–28, *Walker* v. *Johnston*, 312 U.S. 275, 61 S. Ct. 574, 85 L. Ed. 830 (1941).

[3] 304 U.S. 458, 58 S. Ct. 1019, 82 L. Ed. 1461 (1938).

[4] 287 U.S. 45, 53 S. Ct. 55, 77 L. Ed. 158 (1932).

[5] 316 U.S. 455, 62 S. Ct. 1252, 86 L. Ed. 1595 (1942).

Congress itself has furnished the most illuminating clues concerning the original meaning of the counsel provision of the Sixth Amendment. In the Judiciary Act of 1789, signed by Washington on September 24, the day before the Sixth Amendment was proposed by both houses of Congress, the following clause was inserted: "In all the courts of the United States, the parties may plead and manage their own causes personally or by the assistance of such counsel or attorneys at law as by the rules of the said court . . . shall be permitted to manage and conduct causes therein." [6]

If Congress had thought that the proposed Sixth Amendment counsel provision embodied a startling change from this statutory rule, some discussion concerning the proposal would undoubtedly have occurred on the floor.

The second clue is an act of April 30, 1790, passed seven months before the ratification of the Sixth Amendment, stating: "Every person who is indicted of treason or other capital crime, shall be allowed to make his full defense by counsel learned in the law; and the court before which he is tried, or some judge thereof, shall immediately, upon his request, assign to him such counsel not exceeding two, as he may desire, and they shall have free access to him at all reasonable hours." [7]

If the proposed Sixth Amendment counsel provision included a guaranty of appointed counsel in all felony cases, why did Congress pass this halfway measure? It is logical to conclude that Congress passed the act because the Sixth Amendment was irrelevant, in its view, to the subject of appointment of counsel, and because it intended by this act of 1790 to match the English treason act of 1695, and to include, in addition, all capital cases. It placed the right to counsel in federal courts on the same basis as statutes had placed the right to counsel in the state courts of Delaware, Pennsylvania, and South Carolina, where the constitutions merely gave the right "to be heard by counsel."

The ratification of the Sixth Amendment was not followed by statutory changes, and the acts of 1789 and 1790 remained the sole guides to the legal import of the Sixth Amendment until 1938. Story described the right contained in the Sixth Amend-

[6] 1 Stat. 73, § 35 (1789).
[7] 1 Stat. 118 (1790).

ment as "the right to have counsel employed for the prisoner," [8] and Cooley permitted the phrase to stand as Story had written it.[9] If there had been any general understanding that federal courts were required by the Sixth Amendment to appoint counsel in other than capital cases, which were covered by the 1790 act, it seems remarkable that these two astute observers failed to say so.

Nor does the Fifth Amendment due-process clause furnish any guidance on this subject. Apart from the logical difficulty in arguing that a broader right to counsel should be included under the vague term "due process," when a more explicit provision was available, the concept of due process was limited, at least until 1850, to its historic meaning "law of the land"; the law of the land, as Cooley explained, required procedural safeguards comparable to those extended at common law.[10] As has been shown in Chapter II, there was no common-law precedent which called for the appointment of counsel except in treason cases. Thus, the requirement that due process of law be observed could add nothing to the right to counsel granted by the Sixth Amendment.

It should not be concluded from this brief outline of the original content of the Sixth Amendment provision that counsel were never appointed by the federal judges in felonies less serious than capital crimes. Acting on their inherent power over their own procedure and officers, the federal courts, apart from constitutional or statutory requirements, developed a practice of making appointments of counsel in serious cases which were less than capital.[11] As counsel for the government conceded in *Johnson* v. *Zerbst*, the most important case involving the Sixth Amendment provision, although denying any duty of the federal

---

[8] Joseph Story, *Commentaries on the Constitution*, 3rd ed. (Boston: Little, Brown, 1858), II, 599.

[9] *Ibid.*, Thomas M. Cooley, ed., 4th ed. (1873), II, 551.

[10] *Ibid.*, p. 547. See E. S. Corwin, *Liberty against Government* (Baton Rouge, La.: Louisiana State Univ. Press, 1948), pp. 89–91.

[11] See Alexander Holtzoff, "Right to Counsel under the Sixth Amendment," 20 *N. Y. U. L. Rev.* (June, 1944), 1. In addition to Holtzoff's article, there are two other important and more recent treatments of the Sixth Amendment right: David Fellman, "The Constitutional Right to Counsel in Federal Courts," 30 *Neb. L. Rev.* (May, 1951), 559; Francis H. Heller, *The Sixth Amendment* (Lawrence, Kan.: Univ. Kansas Press, 1951).

courts to appoint counsel in noncapital cases: "The Government recognizes that the practice has become established on the part of bench and bar to see that those defendants shall not go unrepresented who, being indigent and not electing to defend in person, make a timely request and showing for the assignment of counsel." [12]   The word which needs emphasis is "practice." A typical rule found in many federal courts stated: "It shall be the duty of every attorney to act as such without compensation whenever he is appointed by the court to act for any person accused of crime who has no other attorney." [13]   Some federal courts, less willing to coerce their attorneys, used the formula: "The court will compile a list of attorneys who are willing to defend indigent defendants in criminal cases without compensation.   Application for appointment of counsel should be made in advance of the day of arraignment and trial." [14]

Although the content of the counsel provision of the Sixth Amendment was not to be ascertained by the Supreme Court until 1938, there were several previous cases in which claims were raised under that clause.   In an 1898 case, *Andersen v. Treat,* the Supreme Court had touched upon the problem of counsel. The trial judge had, on his own motion, severed the defense of codefendants when he discovered a conflict of interests and had appointed counsel for Treat, who wished to be defended by the one counsel retained by all the defendants.[15]   In a unanimous opinion the Supreme Court upheld this appointment, on the technical ground that habeas corpus, a collateral proceeding, could not be used to attack the judgment, but it implied that on the merits of the case it would have rejected the petitioner's claim, because no timely objection to the appointment of counsel was shown.[16]

---

12 *Johnson* v. *Zerbst*, 304 U.S. 458, 58 S. Ct. 1019, 82 L. Ed. 1461 (1938), Brief for United States, p. 26.

13 Rules of Practice of the United States District Court, N. D. Cal., 1926, No. 24.

14 Rules of the District Court of the United States, District of Md., 1933, Rule 66. There has never been any federal statutory provision for payment of counsel appointed by the court. In *Nabb* v. *Lawless*, 1 Ct. Cl. 173 (1863), the court of claims denied that any contract, express or implied, existed as the result of such an appointment.

15 *Andersen* v. *Treat*, 172 U.S. 24, 19 S. Ct. 67, 43 L. Ed. 351 (1898).

16 172 U.S. 24 at 30–31, 43 L. Ed. 351 at 353–354.

The other cases before 1938 dealt with rather limited aspects of the right to counsel, and can be summarized briefly. It had been held that the requirement of a fee for filing an appearance by counsel was not a limitation on the right to counsel,[17] nor was the practice by which federal judges personally conducted the *voir dire* examination of jurors.[18] And, where counsel for one of several codefendants was absent during the impaneling of the jury, his acceptance of the panel upon his return cured any defect which otherwise might have existed.[19]

Trial courts were upheld also where, after numerous postponements requested by retained counsel, the court had refused to grant further delay and had appointed counsel;[20] again, where one of several counsel for a defendant withdrew immediately before a motion for a new trial, and in arrest of judgment, without any postponement being granted, but where an exception to the court's ruling was saved by the remaining counsel;[21] and, finally, where the unsuccessful defendant alleged that his counsel had been suffering from a mental disorder, and produced evidence to support this statement, but where the record showed a spirited trial.[22]

In a number of cases the federal courts had reacted favorably where the appellant claimed some denial of the right to counsel. One interesting problem which was solved involved an "outside" counsel who injected himself into a criminal proceeding. Bernard Ades, a twenty-eight-year-old attorney of the International Labor Defense, an organization with recognized Communist tendencies, became involved in three Maryland cases in which the defendants were Negroes. Each situation was confused by the presence of counsel appointed by the court. A long tale of wrangling between trial judges, appointed counsel, and important people in the local communities was climaxed by disbarment proceedings directed against Ades in the Maryland district court. There was no rule against volunteering, the court held, and while certain actions of Ades were in doubtful taste,

17 *United States* v. *Philadelphia and Reading Ry. Co.*, 268 F. 697 (1916).
18 *Paschen* v. *United States*, 70 F. 2d 491 (1934).
19 *Urban* v. *United States*, 46 F. 2d 291 (1931).
20 *Smith* v. *United States*, 288 F. 259 (1923).
21 *Grock* v. *United States*, 289 F. 544 (1923).
22 *Hagen* v. *United States*, 9 F. 2d 562 (1925).

the court admitted that he had won important victories for his clients (changes of venue and inclusion of Negroes on the juries) where the less energetic appointed counsel had failed.[23]

In another case it was declared that a counsel who volunteers to aid an indigent defendant must give sufficient assistance to afford the defendant a fair trial.   Counsel had agreed, during a lunch hour following his offer of assistance, to permit the district attorney to submit important evidence by affidavits.   The technical grounds for reversal were lack of due process and lack of effective assistance of counsel.[24]   Whether this would have been the court's holding if the counsel had been retained, rather than volunteer, is not clear.   The courts have been reluctant to permit any error or indifferent conduct by retained counsel to furnish grounds for reversal, an attitude which has a sound basis in logic and experience.   While it seems ironic that a higher standard of professional conduct should confront an appointed or volunteer counsel, yet it would be difficult to protect the needy defendant in any other way.   The competitive instincts of a retained counsel prevent merely formal service in most cases.

What conclusions can be drawn from this brief review of the law respecting the right to counsel under the Sixth Amendment before 1938, and why was there so little contention concerning this right?   The constitutional provision meant, at a minimum, that defendants in federal courts had the right to retain their own counsel.   Further, it signified that defendants had certain rights concerning counsel which courts must respect, or reversible error would be committed.   Moreover, it seems fair to say that indigent defendants who were accused of capital offenses received their statutory rights in virtually every case.   For indigent defendants who were accused of lesser crimes, and who chose to plead not guilty, it seems probable that counsel were supplied upon request, or counsel volunteered in many, if not in most, districts, depending on the court custom.   There was no feeling before 1938 that defendants who pleaded guilty, or those who failed to request counsel, had a constitutional right to be advised and offered counsel, or that a conviction without counsel was void.   History denied such a meaning to the counsel pro-

[23] *In re Ades*, 6 F. Supp. 467 (1934).
[24] *Dillingham* v. *United States*, 76 F. 2d 36 (1935).

vision of the Sixth Amendment, and no responsible authority, scholarly or judicial, had held it to be within the scope of the Amendment. Yet, as has so often been true with other doctrines, it was possible for a court deeply conscious of the value of individual rights to transform the right to counsel in federal courts into a comprehensive safeguard for all defendants, whether indigent or financially able.

PRECEDENTS FOR JOHNSON v. ZERBST

What precedents did the Court have available as it undertook the task of extending the scope of the right to counsel? How could judges, who commonly regard sudden change as the greatest menace to a mature legal system, agree to expand this modestly defined right into a broad and positive command that defendants must have counsel or waive counsel? As in so many other instances in legal history when the need for change could no longer be ignored, the lawyers and the judges reached back into the past and selected those precedential elements which, when drawn together by a deft hand and combined with the skillfully expressed need for change, yielded a new doctrine capable of compelling respect and allegiance.

One element of precedent was found in the mob-influenced or mob-dominated trial. Holmes's dissent in *Frank* v. *Mangum*,[25] in which he urged that the Supreme Court must look beneath the formal record in cases where a state trial judge and jury had been intimidated, was succeeded by the Court's holding in *Moore* v. *Dempsey* [26] that a trial which was a sham, where counsel, jury, and judge were swept to a conviction by public passion, was not one in which due process had been observed.

Another mob case involved Downer, a Georgia Negro accused of rape who had been convicted at a state trial protected by two hundred national guardsmen. The trial had been preceded by a series of mob attacks on the jail, which were thwarted only by machine-gun fire.[27] The court appointed counsel for Downer, but a brief review of the sequence of events on the day of trial indicates the inadequacy of the defense: at 9:00 A.M., counsel

25 *Frank* v. *Mangum*, 237 U.S. 309, 35 S. Ct. 582, 59 L. Ed. 969 (1914).
26 *Moore* v. *Dempsey*, 261 U.S. 86, 43 S. Ct. 265, 67 L. Ed. 543 (1923).
27 *Downer* v. *Dunaway*, 53 F. 2d 586 (1931).

met the defendant for the first time; at 10:00 A.M., trial began; at 10:00 P.M., a verdict of guilty was returned. Counsel failed to move for a continuance or for a change of venue before the trial, and he omitted the customary motion for a new trial after the judgment. It took no imagination to conclude, as did the federal circuit court, that fear dominated the actions of counsel.[28] In holding that a writ of habeas corpus should issue, the Fifth Circuit Court used very strong language: "It goes without saying that an accused who is unable by reason of poverty to employ counsel is entitled to be defended in all his rights as fully, and to the same extent as is an accused who is able to employ his own counsel to represent him." [29]

Another important precedential element contributing to the new doctrine was the extremely broad and compelling language used in *Powell* v. *Alabama*.[30] The eloquence of Justice Sutherland (whose economic predilections caused American liberals to tag him as a reactionary) in discussing the right of an indigent accused to make his defense by counsel has had an influence far beyond the facts and the holding in the particular trial. Justice Sutherland carefully limited the decision to the facts in the case: "In a capital case where the defendant is unable to employ counsel, and is incapable adequately of making his own defense because of ignorance, feeble-mindedness, illiteracy, or the like, it is the duty of the court whether requested or not, to assign counsel for him as a necessary requisite of due process of law." [31] The standard required of counsel was effective assistance. The Supreme Court would appear to have merely applied to the states through the due-process clause of the Fourteenth Amendment the same requirement which a federal statute had since 1790 imposed on federal courts in capital cases.

Out of his deep concern for the rights of all criminal defendants, Sutherland had gone beyond the narrow decisional ground in his opinion and had so effectively attacked the general indif-

[28] *Ibid.*, p. 589.
[29] *Ibid.* There was a dissent on the ground that the petitioner's remedies under Georgia law had not been exhausted.
[30] *Powell* v. *Alabama*, 287 U.S. 45, 53 S. Ct. 55, 77 L. Ed. 158 (1932). The case, known as one of the Scottsboro cases, will be treated fully in Chap. V, where its implications as a due-process limitation on state trials are dealt with.
[31] 287 U.S. 45 at 71.

ference of the legal system to the right to counsel that future advocates of a broader right were immeasurably strengthened. He disagreed with Lord Coke, who had defended the old English practice of denying the full right of counsel except in treason cases and misdemeanor hearings on the ground that the judge acted as counsel for the prisoner. Sutherland retorted: "But how can a judge, whose functions are purely judicial, effectively discharge the obligations of counsel for the accused? He can and should see to it that in the proceedings before the court the accused shall be dealt with justly and fairly. He cannot investigate the facts, advise and direct the defense, or participate in those necessary conferences between counsel and accused which sometimes partake of the inviolable character of the confessional." [32] It is agreed, said Sutherland, that notice and hearing are part of the requirement of due process. What, then, does a hearing include? "The right to be heard," he continued, "would be, in many cases, of little avail if it did not comprehend the right to be heard by counsel. Even the intelligent and educated layman has small and sometimes no skill in the science of law." [33] After surveying the pitfalls confronting the unaided accused, he concluded: ". . . [the defendant] lacks both the skill and knowledge adequately to prepare his defense, even though he have a perfect one. He requires the guiding hand of counsel at every step in the proceedings against him. Without it, though he be not guilty, he faces the danger of conviction because he does not know how to establish his innocence." [34]

This is a forceful statement, although a dictum. It emphasizes the crucial point that counsel is necessary in order that a proper defense can be presented, and this need exists regardless of the seriousness of the offense charged. It attacks any solution which would attempt to distinguish between laymen who possess adequate legal ability and those who do not, and it destroys the ancient myth that the judge can perform a dual role by acting as both judge and advocate. [35]

[32] 287 U.S. 45 at 61. Cited in Brief for Petitioner, p. 15, *Johnson* v. *Zerbst*, 304 U.S. 458 (1938).

[33] 287 U.S. 45 at 68–69.

[34] 287 U.S. 45 at 69.

[35] Counsel in *Johnson* v. *Zerbst* made liberal use of parts of Sutherland's statement. See Brief for Petitioner, p. 17.

Another element in the chain of cases leading to *Johnson* v. *Zerbst* was a ruling in *Patton* v. *United States*,[36] where the defendant and the government stipulated to waive any objection to trial by a jury of eleven, after one juror became ill part way through the trial. Justice Sutherland, speaking for the Court, held that the accused could waive the right to trial by jury, but that the waiver required the "express and intelligent consent of the defendant." Thus, the argument could later be made that if intelligent consent is needed to waive the right to jury trial, it is a necessary prerequisite if, and when, the accused wishes to waive any other essential right.[37]

Apart from these relatively few cases, there is the influence, although it cannot be assessed with accuracy, arising from the treatment of the counsel question in the Code which the Council of the American Law Institute submitted to its members, and to the legal profession at large, in 1931. The Code placed upon the judge the duty of appointing counsel at the arraignment of one accused of a felony who needed counsel and was without counsel. It was made clear that any defendant might and should procure his own counsel, if that were possible.[38]

These, then, were the slight precedents from which the Supreme Court made a new rule in 1938. When combined with a recognition that in most federal courts the practice of appointing counsel in at least some felony cases less than capital had become well established, and that the standard of a fair judicial procedure had changed since 1789, they made the formulation of a new doctrine a comparatively simple judicial task.

CASE OF JOHNSON V. ZERBST

In November, 1934, two enlisted marines on leave, Bridwell and Johnson, were arrested in South Carolina and charged with feloniously uttering counterfeit notes.[39] At their preliminary hearing before the United States Commissioner they were repre-

---

[36] 281 U.S. 276, 50 S. Ct. 253, 74 L. Ed. 854 (1930).

[37] See *Johnson* v. *Zerbst*, Brief for Petitioner, p. 10.

[38] See *Code of Criminal Procedure* (Official Draft) (Philadelphia: American Law Institute, 1930), § 209. See also §§ 41, 42, pp. 13–14.

[39] The statement of facts is drawn from the opinions of the district, circuit, and Supreme courts, which will be cited where appropriate.

sented by an attorney, but were unable to afford counsel for any subsequent proceedings. After being indicted on January 21, 1935, they were taken to court on January 23, where they first learned of their indictment; there they were arraigned, pleaded "not guilty," were tried and convicted, and were sentenced to four and one-half years in the Atlanta Penitentiary, all on January 23.

Later in 1935 they petitioned for a writ of habeas corpus, which resulted in a hearing before a Georgia federal district court. At the hearing the petitioners claimed that the trial court had failed to offer counsel and had failed to advise them that they could have appointed counsel. The petitioners alleged further that, although they had not asked the court for counsel, they had requested the United States District Attorney to get counsel for them, which he refused to do, stating as his reason the absence of such a practice in South Carolina except in capital cases. The petitioners emphasized their need for counsel by asserting that they had been strangers in the community and were poorly educated and penniless.[40] The government's opposing view was that the petitioners' claims lacked merit because the petitioners had stated, when asked, that they were ready for trial, and because the United States Attorney had not made the alleged remark about South Carolina practice. Moreover, the petitioners had not asked for counsel at any time during the trial. Neither had they sought a new trial at the conclusion of the original proceeding, nor appealed their conviction.[41] The petitioners tried to justify their failure to perfect an appeal by asserting that an attempt to get counsel after conviction had been hindered through a jailer's refusal to permit communication. They verified the fact that an appeal was filed, but too late to be granted.

The district court's decision to discharge the writ was, on its face, a defeat, but in reality it was a great triumph, because in holding that habeas corpus was not the proper remedy for the correction of trial irregularities, which should normally be presented on appeal, and that the judgment was not void because of errors,[42] the court made a finding that petitioners had been "deprived of their constitutional rights." [43] Judge Underwood

[40] *Johnson* v. *Aderhold,* 13 F. Supp. 253 at 254 (1935).
[41] *Ibid.*   [42] *Ibid.,* p. 256.   [43] *Ibid.,* p. 255.

pointed out that the Sixth Amendment provisions for counsel and for obtaining witnesses by compulsory process were contained in the same clauses as the right to jury trial and, disregarding the historical background of the right to counsel, he concluded: "There is no limitation of these rights to cases where the accused is charged with a capital offense, as urged by respondent, and no reason appears in logic, morals, or humanity why an accused, in danger of deprivation of his life or liberty, should in any criminal prosecution, be deprived of these rights by implication." [44]   The obvious answer, of course, is that if the counsel provision when inserted in the Constitution meant only the right to retain counsel in all criminal prosecutions, it is hard to see how the right had been whittled down "by implication."   If Congress in 1790 had chosen to strengthen a weak constitutional requirement by a more generous statute where capital offenses were involved, it had obviously decided against extending this treatment to noncapital cases.

But it is Judge Underwood's argument that concerns us here.   Once having gone so far, it was an easy next step for him to declare it to be a duty of the trial court to appoint counsel, whether requested or not.[45]   He reinforced his conclusion by quoting phrases from *Downer* v. *Dunaway* respecting the necessity of granting equal rights to indigent defendants,[46] and gave substantial space to Sutherland's sweeping language in *Powell* v. *Alabama*.[47]   Apart from the counsel irregularities, the Judge seemed to feel that the trial had been fairly conducted, and that the evidence supported conviction.[48]   He escaped the dilemma of finding and acting upon a denial of constitutional rights in an otherwise satisfactory criminal proceeding by deciding that the petitioners had been lax in failing to perfect an appeal more promptly.   He concluded rather lamely that they could have asked officers at the penitentiary to get counsel and could have attempted to send a message to a judge.[49]

On appeal, the circuit court tried to close some of the legal

[44] *Ibid.*, p. 254.
[45] *Ibid.*, pp. 254–255.
[46] *Downer* v. *Dunaway*, 53 F. 2d 586 at 587 (1931).
[47] *Powell* v. *Alabama*, 287 U.S. 45, 53 S. Ct. 55, 77 L. Ed. 158 (1932).
[48] *Johnson* v. *Aderhold*, 13 F. Supp. 253 at 255 (1935).
[49] *Ibid.*

doors which Judge Underwood had opened. It agreed that
habeas corpus could not be substituted for appeal, and sustained
the lower court's decision on that ground.[50]   Only if the trial
had been a sham could habeas corpus issue,[51] but in this case
there had been an orderly, calm procedure.   Perhaps, said the
court, it would have been better if the judge of his own motion
had appointed counsel, but it quickly added: "We are not advised of any decision of a court of last resort, state or federal,
holding that in a noncapital case he was bound to do so." [52]   The
right to the assistance of counsel, therefore, was not so broad as
the lower court assumed.   Nor had there been any deprivation
of a right guaranteed by due process, continued the court: "Due
process of law does not absolutely require that the defendant in
every criminal case be represented by counsel.   He may ex-
pressly or impliedly waive his right and suffer no wrong.   When
a defendant is without counsel, the judge usually protects his
rights." [53]   Finally, said the court, the evidence supported the
conviction, a matter which was not properly in issue once it
was decided that there was no right to have counsel appointed,
or that a failure to receive counsel was a mere irregularity.

Upon petition for certiorari to the Supreme Court, a curious
situation developed.   The petitioners' counsel cited the Patton
case and the necessity for "express and intelligent consent" or
"waiver" where a constitutional right has not been observed.[54]
And by ignoring historical facts he was able to urge that the
wording of the Sixth Amendment meant nothing less than that
the right to counsel applied "in all criminal prosecutions." [55]
Some state decisions were cited, without any discussion of the
statutory basis for the right in those states,[56] and the language in
Powell v. *Alabama* was quoted extensively.[57]   The due-process
aspect was considered at length and counsel suggested that the

---

[50] *Johnson* v. *Zerbst,* 92 F. 2d 748 (1937).

[51] *Ibid.,* p. 750.

[52] *Ibid.,* p. 751.

[53] *Ibid.*

[54] Petition for Writ, p. 10, *Johnson* v. *Zerbst,* 304 U.S. 458, 58 S. Ct. 1019,
82 L. Ed. 1461 (1938).

[55] Petition for Writ, p. 13.

[56] *Ibid.*

[57] *Ibid.,* p. 14.

familiar phrase from *Hebert* v. *Louisiana* be incorporated into a proposed new rule: "The true test of whether the presence of counsel is essential to the substance of a hearing is whether the denial of the right violates those fundamental principles of liberty and justice which lie at the basis of all our civil and political institutions." [58]   Hopefully, the petitioners' counsel asked the Supreme Court to infer from the fact that this was the first case in which this precise question had been raised a confirmation of the lower-federal-court practice of appointing counsel for indigents, and a "well nigh universal recognition . . . of the fundamental character of the right." [59]

The position of the government was somewhat peculiar. It seemed definitely unhappy with the action of the trial judge, saying: "The parties are agreed that the trial judge might more appropriately have assigned, or offered to assign, counsel even in the absence of a request." [60]   And to an appendix to the Brief in Opposition and to the Brief for the United States there was attached a copy of a circular which Homer Cummings, the Attorney General, had previously sent to all United States attorneys. After noting in this circular that "certain cases had arisen" where district courts had not appointed counsel for indigents who failed to request counsel, in spite of the general custom of appointing in all cases, the Attorney General had indicated that the more generous practice was better, and had stated: "When in any given case such practice is not followed, you are directed to bring the matter to the attention of the court, in order that the defendant may have the assistance of counsel." [61]   Then, after having cited the Powell case in support of the value and necessity of counsel as a part of due process, the Attorney General had expressed this significant view: "While it may be that the right to have the assistance of counsel . . . which is guaranteed by the Sixth Amendment may be waived, and while it may be that the practice followed in most of the jurisdictions is more than a

[58] Brief for Petitioner, p. 17, quoting *Hebert* v. *Louisiana*, 272 U.S. 312, 47 S. Ct. 103, 71 L. Ed. 270 (1929).

[59] Brief for Petitioner, p. 12.

[60] Brief of United States in Opposition, p. 17.

[61] Brief in Opposition, Appendix, p. 18.

compliance with the constitutional requirement, the Department of Justice is under a particular obligation to see that no man who needs counsel is without such assistance." [62]

Yet after having expressed in this strong fashion the sympathy of the Department of Justice for those in the defendants' position, the counsel for the United States was forced in the present case to defend the trial proceedings. First, he said, there was no lack of due process, as in the Powell case. Secondly, in the absence of statute, the state decisions hold generally that the judge need not advise the defendant of his right to counsel.[63] Thirdly, without request, there can be no denial of counsel. Fourthly, the right to counsel may be waived, and a waiver can be inferred in this case, if the testimony of the officials is accepted.[64] Fifthly, the counsel provision of the Sixth Amendment, historically considered, was designed to give only the right to retain counsel.[65]

The United States position was this: Although the custom of appointing counsel in almost all serious federal cases had become firmly established, this practice did not rise to the level of a constitutional requirement.[66] And while the government conceded that the better course, in the absence of an express waiver, was to assign counsel, it was not because of any requirement emanating from the Sixth Amendment.[67] In a final argument *ad horrendum,* the government pictured the practical difficulties which would follow if the petitioners' contentions were accepted. Counsel would then have to be appointed for the host of defendants who wanted to plead guilty, and confessions could not be taken until at least an offer of counsel were made, or, if taken in the absence of counsel, they would become inadmissible.[68] The inevitability of a flood of petitions for habeas corpus, should the petitioners in this case succeed, was not included in the gloomy forecast, although that would be the most certain result of all. One would not have to be unduly acute to conclude from a survey of the government's briefs that the De-

[62] *Ibid.,* pp. 18–19.
[63] Brief in Opposition, pp. 10–11.
[64] *Ibid.,* pp. 12–13.   [65] *Ibid.,* p. 15.
[66] See Brief for the United States, p. 26.
[67] *Ibid.,* p. 27.   [68] *Ibid.,* p. 31.

partment of Justice was quite willing to see the petitioners succeed. The liberal and humanitarian impulses of the Attorney General, Homer Cummings, are a matter of public record. Hardly anyone who surveyed the government's position could help feeling that it made a *pro forma* defense of a federal court and of the United States Attorney in a situation where a departure from the normal judicial action had taken place.

The Supreme Court, speaking through Justice Black, upheld the petitioners' claims and remanded the cause to the district court for a hearing and a finding on the issue of whether there had been an intelligent and competent waiver.[69] The Court was not unanimous, with five justices joining in the opinion of the Court, Justice Reed concurring only in the reversal, Justice McReynolds affirming without statement, and Justice Butler affirming because in his opinion the record showed a waiver. Justice Cardozo did not take part in the consideration or the decision.

Black's opinion is perhaps equally notable for its matter-of-fact tone and for its indifference to the historical aspects of the right to counsel. The probable intentions of the proponents or ratifiers of the Sixth Amendment were ignored. This rather cavalier treatment of the historical phases of a question presented for the first time to the Court suggests that the majority of the justices wished to gain some advantage from the lack of prior decisions which had direct relevance to the interpretation of the Sixth Amendment provision at the time. It was obvious that this particular judicial vacuum could not be filled as the justices wished by recourse to history.

In delivering his opinion Black quoted from a dictum in the Patton case to the effect that the humane policy of modern criminal law now provides counsel for indigent defendants,[70] and from the Powell case he excerpted the eloquent summary by Sutherland of why the layman requires counsel.[71] Then he stated the new rule: "The Sixth Amendment withholds from federal courts, in all criminal proceedings, the power and authority to deprive an accused of his life or liberty *unless he has or waives the assist-*

---

[69] *Johnson* v. *Zerbst,* 304 U.S. 458 at 459, 58 S. Ct. 1019, 82 L. Ed. 1461 (1938).

[70] *Patton* v. *United States,* 281 U.S. 276, 50 S. Ct. 253, 74 L. Ed. 854 (1930).

[71] *Powell* v. *Alabama,* 287 U.S. 45, 53 S. Ct. 55, 77 L. Ed. 158 (1932).

ance of counsel." [72]   And since the district court had not found
that a waiver had been made, the Supreme Court would not
presume one.[73]   Whether or not an intelligent waiver had been
made would depend in each case "upon the particular facts and
circumstances surrounding that case, including the background,
experience, and conduct of the accused." [74]   It was the duty of
the trial judge, said Black, to determine this fact of waiver, and
"it would be fitting and appropriate for that determination to
appear upon the record." [75]   Moreover, he added, the district
court and the circuit court had conceived the scope of habeas
corpus too narrowly.   The district court had the power to inquire into the jurisdiction of the trial court, even if it involved
an examination of facts outside of, but not inconsistent with,
the record,[76] by ascertaining the truth and substance of the cause
of detention.   If it were found that the constitutional requirement of counsel had not been fulfilled, the jurisdictional basis of
the trial-record proceeding should be declared lacking.[77]   As a
warning and aid to the district courts, which might now be
deluged with similar cases, Black cited the well-known rule that
"a judgment carries with it a presumption of regularity," and
is not to be "lightly set aside by collateral attack, even on habeas
corpus," [78] so that the burden of proof was to continue to rest, as
it had in the past, on the petitioner who had been convicted in
a proceeding where he claimed a denial of counsel.[79]

Thus was announced the rule which raised the right to counsel to a level not attained during the previous one hundred and
forty-nine years.   In a technical sense, it was not a "new" rule,
since no precedents were overturned.   It must have been a relief

[72] 304 U.S. 458 at 463, 82 L. Ed. 1461 at 1466 (1938).   Italics mine.
[73] *Ibid.*
[74] *Ibid.*
[75] 304 U.S. 458 at 465, 82 L. Ed. 1461 at 1467.
[76] 304 U.S. 458 at 466, 82 L. Ed. 1461 at 1467.   28 U.S.C.A. [1940], §§ 451,
et seq., provided the statutory basis of this expanded concept of habeas corpus
in Black's view.
[77] 304 U.S. 458 at 467, 82 L. Ed. 1461 at 1468.
[78] 304 U.S. 458 at 468, 82 L. Ed. 1461 at 1468–1469.
[79] *Ibid.*   See also 24 *Corn. L. Rev.* (Feb., 1939), 270; 24 *Iowa L. Rev.* (Nov.,
1938), 190.   The use of habeas corpus whenever a constitutional right has been
infringed is supported by 28 U.S.C.A. (1950), § 2241.   Nevertheless, courts still
use the want-of-jurisdiction concept because that was the traditional approach.

to the Court, which was confronted with so many legislative in-
novations, to be able to express a strong feeling for individual
rights without having to thrust aside a substantial body of case
law. If, in examining the Court's technique, one used the
narrow historical approach to constitutional interpretation, he
would find it difficult to justify this decision. Black, with a
specific goal in view, wisely refrained from the type of historical
reconstruction which the Court so frequently indulges in when
history apparently supports the desired position.[80] He ignored
both the action of the first Congress in passing a law in 1790 which
required the appointment of counsel in capital cases at the very
time that the Sixth Amendment was being proposed and the
generally accepted meaning of the counsel provisions of the
states in 1791, when the Amendment was ratified.

In effect, the Court chose to adopt a more enlightened procedure because modern conditions and attitudes seemed to make
such action desirable. It was certain to be a popular move.
The criminal defendants would appreciate it. The United
States Government, speaking through the Department of Justice,
had indicated its support for a broad and generous rule. The
judges and lawyers in the majority of federal districts would not
oppose it, because their practice and custom had placed them in
most instances under such a rule. A few judges and a few attorneys were the only possible dissidents.

In such ways and for such reasons was a constitutional provision, in a Constitution designed "to endure for ages to come,"
given a new meaning. But problems raised by this newly announced doctrine were destined to plague the federal courts in
the years immediately ahead, and to these problems we now turn.

Right to Counsel in Federal District Courts, 1938 to the Present

The decision in *Johnson* v. *Zerbst* was hardly announced
before attempts to utilize its doctrine and explore its limits
began. Prisoners in federal penitentiaries had ample time in
which to relive the events surrounding their trials and convictions and to conclude that their rights to counsel had been in-

---

[80] The Powell opinion and *Betts* v. *Brady* are good examples.

fringed. Lawyers, after reading the broad rules laid down in *Johnson* v. *Zerbst*, could readily surmise that many trial situations contained defects which, upon appeal, might fail to meet the counsel standard made mandatory by the Supreme Court.[81]

The variety of claims respecting the right to counsel, and the almost infinite ways in which a denial of the right might allegedly occur, make an adequate survey of the law both tedious and difficult. For in addition to the usual problems, there is the almost insuperable task of trying to derive general rules concerning a procedural right from cases which turned largely on the specific facts presented. Moreover, in many of these cases the case reports indicate very little concerning the fact or facts that the judge regarded as decisive. It is, in short, highly dangerous to talk of precedents in this field. Earlier cases are informative, rather than conclusive as precedents. Nevertheless, it seems desirable to consider the aspects of the right to counsel, retained or appointed, in cases involving pleas of not guilty, guilty, and change of plea, on the theory that some useful, though admittedly limited, generalizations may be adduced to aid those who require guidance in this field. Obviously, only the essential facts of most cases can be indicated, and a reading of the full opinions will be necessary for those who desire fuller light on specific problems.

PLEA OF NOT GUILTY WITH ASSISTANCE OF COUNSEL

We will review first those cases where the defendant pleads not guilty and has the assistance of retained or appointed counsel for a part or all of the proceeding. On first thought, difficulties would not seem likely under these circumstances, but six basic situations can be cited where disputes arise: (1) where a defendant receives an unwanted appointed counsel; (2) where the defendant alleges that the judge in some manner limited counsel's ability to serve; (3) where a conflict of interests between defendants is alleged; (4) where a defendant alleges that the court deprived his counsel of sufficient time for adequate preparation;

---

[81] While only twelve cases involving the Sixth Amendment counsel provision had reached circuit courts up to 1939, ninety cases have gone up since 1939. There have been four Supreme Court cases involving the provision since *Johnson* v. *Zerbst*.

(5) where the defendant claims that counsel's assistance was ineffective; (6) where the defendant alleges the absence of the counsel at one or more important stages in the proceeding.

Dissatisfaction with Appointed Counsel.—One can understand the suspicion with which courts will scrutinize claims of dissatisfaction with counsel, since legally qualified counsel appear in each case and all judges know the human tendency to hunt for a scapegoat.   One type of situation is that where a defendant who feels more competent than the counsel appointed by the court shoves the counsel aside in order to conduct his own defense. But then, after his defense is unsuccessful, he is likely to claim that his appointed counsel was not sufficiently active.   The record of the court's appointment and a showing of the reasons why a willing counsel was inactive will result in a denial of habeas corpus.[82]

Sometimes the defendant is more forthright and wants to dismiss his counsel officially.   Thus, in one rather peculiar case involving a twenty-two-year-old Negro convicted of a violation of the Mann Act where his wife was the victim, the defendant asked that his retained counsel, who had served three weeks, be dismissed, which proposal was acceptable to the counsel.[83]   The court, however, not wishing the case to be postponed, then appointed the same attorney to act for the defendant.   Five days later this exchange occurred between the defendant and the judge:

"I would like the dismissal of this attorney.   I'm within my right."
"I've assigned him."
"I refuse to accept him."
"Sit down." [84]

No further objection was made by the defendant.   On appeal the circuit court upheld the conviction, indicating that the danger of a long delay, added to the failure of the defendant to reveal why he was seeking to dismiss his counsel, were reasonable grounds for the trial court's action.   There was a dissent by

[82] *Zahn* v. *Hudspeth*, 102 F. 2d 759 (1939).
[83] *United States* v. *Mitchell*, 137 F. 2d 1006 (1943).
[84] *Ibid.*, p. 1010.

Judge Jerome Frank, who was concerned about the cavalier treatment given by the trial court to the defendant's "ambiguous expression of his intention." He suggested that while the trial court could have denied a request for the appointment of counsel in this case, it should not have denied the defendant's request that he be allowed to defend himself.[85] Whether it would have been a lack of due process to have allowed an ignorant defendant to defend himself was a question not faced by Judge Frank.

One district court had a particularly effective answer to a defendant's claim that the appointed counsel was unsatisfactory: "To confer upon every indigent defendant the power of 'Senatorial courtesy' with respect to the court's appointee would . . . lead only to reluctance on the part of attorneys to accept appointments in unpopular causes, for in effect the appointment would then come by grace of the accused and not that of the court." [86]

It seems clear that the indigent defendant must accept the services of appointed counsel, or at least must give a substantial reason to support his request for dismissal of counsel.[87] If on his request appointed counsel withdraws and he refuses another appointment, he cannot expect the court to protect him from errors.[88] Such a rule appears reasonable, since any other would give to the indigent defendant an advantage not possessed by the great majority of those who do retain counsel but who obviously cannot retain whomever they wish. Further, the tendency of such free choice to delay trials and to create uncertainty in judicial proceedings would be obvious. Finally, free selection would serve as a convenient means of escape for attorneys who find this service distasteful, since it should be rather easy to alienate the typical defendant.

Limitations on Services of Counsel.—The opposite situation occurs when the court takes some action which deprives a defendant of a retained or appointed counsel. Obviously, this is not a common happening, but in one instance a conviction was

---

[85] *Ibid.,* p. 1012.

[86] *United States ex rel. Mitchell* v. *Thompson,* 56 F. Supp. 683 at 689 (1944).

[87] *United States* v. *Gutterman,* 147 F. 2d 540 (1945). Judge Frank dissented in this case, expressing once again his distaste for judicial coercion, and he indicated that it should be reversible error where a defendant was compelled to continue with an undesired appointed counsel.

[88] *Burstein* v. *United States,* 178 F. 2d 665 (1950).

reversed because the trial judge included in a contempt citation an order to retained counsel to refrain completely from serving the defendant in or out of court.[89]   In a dictum, the appellate court indicated that a contempt citation could never go so far as to exclude an attorney from out-of-court activities on behalf of his client, provided that the activities were not contemptuous in themselves.[90]   The basis for this holding is that the court cannot deprive a man of his defense so long as it is properly conducted.   However, if there are two or more active defense counsel, the exclusion of one from further participation, on some discretionary ground, will not result in reversal, since an adequate defense is still available.[91]   It has been held that an order of the trial judge forbidding any consultation between defendant and counsel during an eighteen-hour recess was a denial of the right to effective aid of counsel.[92]   Interference by the authorities with the normal lawyer-client relationship may be termed a denial of effective aid of counsel.[93]

Occasionally the issue is raised as the result of counsel's error. In one odd situation there was an appointed counsel of record and an active retained counsel who had neglected to make an appearance of record, although he had apparently prepared the defense. When the retained counsel failed to appear, the appointed counsel proceeded, with one hour's notice, to defend. On the theory that the defendant should be held responsible for retained counsel's error, the conviction was upheld by the Municipal Court of Appeals, District of Columbia.[94]

In another interesting decision a district-court ruling which had denied permission for counsel from New Jersey to appear in a Pennsylvania district court was reversed on appeal.   A New Jersey judge, who had been specially assigned, excluded the

---

[89] *Meeks* v. *United States,* 163 F. 2d 598, 11 Alaska 378 (1947).

[90] The tolerance of Judge Medina during the 1949 trial of eleven officers of the Communist party was undoubtedly greater than the legally required standard.

[91] *Viereck* v. *United States,* 130 F. 2d 945 (1942).

[92] *United States* v. *Venuto,* 182 F. 2d 519 (1950). See comment, E. P. Miller, 24 *So. Calif. L. Rev.* (Dec., 1950), 105–106.

[93] *Coplon* v. *United States,* 191 F. 2d 749 (1951). The illegal action was the tapping of a telephone line and eavesdropping on defendant's conversation with her lawyer.

[94] *Talbert* v. *United States,* Munic. Ct. of App. D. C., 55 A. 2d 91 (1947).

attorney because he feared the inferences which might be drawn if New Jersey lawyers crossed over the line and injected themselves into his cases in the Pennsylvania court. But the circuit court laid down the broad rule that an attorney in good standing must be allowed to appear.[95] This rule, applying to the federal courts, was reiterated later by the Supreme Court itself.[96] The obvious conclusion is that a court must act with the greatest care if it seeks to deprive a defendant of counsel. While excessively shocking conduct of counsel may permit his exclusion from the court, services outside cannot be forbidden, and other representation in court must be made available.

Conflicts of Interest.—A difficult problem arises in those cases where a conflict between the interests of codefendants is alleged and it is claimed that the trial court failed to consider that fact in appointing counsel. The leading case on this subject is *Glasser* v. *United States.*[97] The defendant Glasser was an attorney who was charged with having conspired to defraud the United States while serving as an Assistant United States Attorney. He had retained an attorney named Stewart as his chief counsel. A codefendant, Kretske, had experienced great difficulty in finding counsel, and told the court of his troubles. The court then asked Stewart if there was any objection to the court's appointing him to represent Kretske. "That would be for your Honor to decide," replied Stewart.[98] Shortly thereafter, when the judge indicated that he would like to appoint Stewart to represent Kretske as well as Glasser, the defendant Glasser spoke up: "I would like to enter my objection. I would like to have my own lawyer representing me."[99] Then, after several inconsequential exchanges, the codefendant Kretske announced that he had just spoken to Mr. Stewart, who was willing to accept appointment. There was no comment from Glasser, and the appointment was made.[100]

[95] *United States* v. *Bergamo,* 154 F. 2d 31 (1946). See comment, 25 *Chi-Kent L. Rev.* (March, 1947), 153.

[96] *Dennis* v. *United States,* 340 U.S. 887, 71 S. Ct. 133, 95 L. Ed. 644 (1950). The eleven Communist leaders sought the admission *pro hac vice* of an English barrister.

[97] 315 U.S. 60, 62 S. Ct. 457, 86 L. Ed. 680 (1942).

[98] *Ibid.,* Transcript of Record, p. 180.

[99] *Ibid.,* p. 181.

[100] *Ibid.,* p. 183.

On appeal the defendant Glasser claimed that he had been deprived of counsel by action of the trial judge, and, with Frankfurter and Stone dissenting, the Supreme Court upheld his claim.[101] Murphy, for the Court, declared that there had been no consent by the defendant Glasser, that Glasser's own professional status had no effect on his constitutional rights, and that a waiver of a right would not be presumed. Since it was clear that the action by the trial court had prejudiced the defense to some degree, the Court would not measure the degree of prejudice.[102]

Frankfurter, expressing his usual interest in technical and procedural issues, called attention to the "belated" character of this ground on appeal. He noted the lack of formal objection by this legally trained defendant during the trial, and underlined the statement of entirely different grounds in support of motions in arrest of judgment and for a new trial on April 23. Even more significant, he said, was the use of twenty other grounds in the notice of appeal on April 26, and he pointed out that it was not until April 27, fifteen weeks after the trial, that the objection concerning counsel had been added in an amendment to the appeal.

It seems true, in any event, that in the later cases in which the Glasser rule had been applied the federal courts have seemed anxious to limit its scope.[103] Nevertheless, where a clear conflict is shown, as it was in one case involving four codefendants, three of whom had signed written statements in which sole responsibility was cast on the fourth, the failure of the trial court to grant a motion for severance made by the appointed counsel was termed error.[104] It also seems apparent that the chances of having such a claim sustained are much less if habeas corpus, rather than appeal, is the procedure used.[105]

[101] *Glasser v. United States*, 315 U.S. 60, 62 S. Ct. 457, 86 L. Ed. 680 (1942). For a view hostile to the decision, see 9 *Univ. of Chic. L. Rev.* (June, 1942), 733. For a more favorable comment, see 41 *Mich. L. Rev.* (Oct., 1942), 321.

[102] 315 U.S. 60 at 75–76.

[103] *Roberts v. Hunter*, 140 F. 2d 38 (1943); *Farris v. Hunter*, 144 F. 2d 63 (1944). An actual conflict must exist, and a prompt protest is essential.

[104] *Wright v. Johnston*, 77 F. Supp. 687 (1948).

[105] *Noble v. Eicher*, 143 F. 2d 1001 (1944). In *Kennedy v. Sanford*, 166 F. 2d 568 (1948), the court had refused to appoint separate counsel for one of several codefendants, and the reviewing court refused habeas corpus, stating that a

The effect of these decisions amounts to this: When a conflict is claimed, a judge must make up his mind whether to appoint separate counsel and avoid the risk of reversal, or to refuse an appointment because no real conflict is apparent. If the latter course is taken, the judge is in an unfortunate position should a real conflict appear later. It is probable that the likelihood of reversal is diminished if the counsel shared by codefendants has been appointed to serve both. In the Glasser situation the trial court seemingly interfered with the long-established right to appear with retained counsel, and the courts had little difficulty placing the presumption against waiver of this right on the defendant's side of the scales.

Since there can be no trial in the true sense unless a defendant has claimed to be innocent, it is only human to expect that a substantial portion of those who are convicted in criminal cases should search through the proceedings in order to find "errors," and a goodly number of these alleged errors pertain to court rulings in respect to the actions of their counsel.

Inadequate Preparation of Counsel.—One ground which gives rise to the claim of error is the fact that counsel was allegedly allowed insufficient time to prepare the case, and his motion for a continuance was denied. Apparently the request for continuance is used excessively by some attorneys, and while judges vary in their generosity in this respect, there comes a time when almost any trial judge must insist that the case proceed, if he is to avoid excessive delays which would disrupt his court calendar. Recognizing this, appellate courts are most reluctant to reverse in such cases, and unless a clear abuse of the trial judge's discretion is shown, his ruling will be upheld.[106]

Forcing a defendant at a court-martial to trial when his appointed civilian counsel had only ten minutes to prepare a defense for murder was held to be a denial of counsel.[107] And in a rather bizarre case involving a young army lieutenant named Shapiro, a federal district court decided that the Army conducted

---

very heavy burden rested on claimants to show a genuine conflict of interests and that the trial judge could best decide whether such a conflict existed.

[106] *United States v. Hartenfield*, 113 F. 2d 359 (1940). Any showing of a lack of diligence on the defendant's part will make the task of the reviewing court easier. See also *Neufield et al. v. United States*, 118 F. 2d 375 (1941).

[107] *Schita v. King*, 133 F. 2d 283 (1943).

its court-martial with more speed than due process allowed. Shapiro, an Army defense counsel, had substituted one Mexican for another who was charged with rape, which caused the chief government witness at the court-martial to identify the pretended defendant as the guilty party. Shapiro revealed the hoax only after the substituted party was convicted. The Army, thrown off stride by this ingenious defense tactic only momentarily, freed the innocent defendant and charged the "original," who was then convicted. There is no need to speculate about the Army's feeling toward Shapiro. It then charged him with delaying a general court-martial, a violation of that military catch-all, the ninety-sixth article of war. Shapiro was arrested at 12:40 P.M., and the trial was set for 2:00 P.M., at a place forty miles away. At that time and place Shapiro's request for continuance was refused. This treatment was held to be a denial of counsel and of due process in what apparently was an enjoyable case for the district court, whose opinion lashed military "justice" thoroughly.[108]

But military courts are not the only offenders. Habeas corpus was granted in a case where counsel, appointed on the day of arraignment and with the trial scheduled for the next day, asked for and was denied a continuance which he required in order to contact two witnesses.[109] In another case, an appointment of counsel one minute before trial began was held to allow an insufficient time for preparation, regardless of counsel's failure to ask for a continuance.[110]

One can conclude that only where a denial of time for preparation is obviously shocking will an appellate court reverse a trial court's denial of a motion for continuance. Appointment, nevertheless, must be made in sufficient time before trial to afford at least a minimum preparation. Apart from these broad limitations, if fairness seems to dominate the remainder of a trial proceedings and if there is no evidence of bias in the judge, his exercise of discretion in denying a continuance will normally be acceptable to the reviewing court, which is more remote in

---

[108] *Shapiro* v. *United States,* 69 F. Supp. 205 (1947). For comment, see 5 *Nat. B. J.* (Sept., 1947), 348.

[109] *Wright* v. *Johnston,* 77 F. Supp. 687 (1948).

[110] *United States* v. *Helwig,* 159 F. 2d 616 (1947).

the judicial hierarchy and hence in a weak position to pass judgment.

Ineffective Counsel.—Convicts find another fertile source of appeal in alleging that they had ineffective counsel. Their attorneys, they claim, were ignorant, incompetent, or indifferent, and for that reason rendered ineffective aid. Since it is obvious that few if any attorneys perform faultlessly, if a criterion of perfection can be devised in so controversial a field as criminal law and procedure, a convicted defendant can almost always find an error by counsel at some stage of the proceedings.

Military defendants have little fortune in this matter. A number of claims on behalf of those convicted by courts-martial have been rejected by the federal courts on the ground that court-martial procedure need not follow civilian-court practice, and for the most part there has been a refusal to pry deeply into the actual facts of military trial,[111] an attitude for which the armed forces must be deeply grateful. With their own procedures, however, the federal courts have been less generous. For instance, where an appointed counsel in a murder trial displayed indifference, failed to examine the transcript of testimony at the coroner's inquest, and did not supply a brief in support of his motion for a new trial, the appellate court reversed.[112] The opinion recognized that while an element of unfairness existed in a system which failed to provide compensation for appointed counsel, it was nevertheless essential that appointed counsel render substantial assistance.[113]

It seems very clear that the errors of retained counsel must be really flagrant before a reversal is possible.[114] A rather extreme example of the unwillingness to upset a conviction is furnished by a habeas corpus application based upon the intoxication of retained counsel which succeeded in the district court but failed in the circuit court.[115] This surprising allega-

---

[111] *Sanford* v. *Robbins*, 115 F. 2d 435 (1940), a conviction for rape; *Ex parte Benton*, 63 F. Supp. 808 (1945), a conviction for murder; *Lewis* v. *Sanford*, 79 F. Supp. 77 (1948), a conviction for sodomy.

[112] *Johnson* v. *United States*, 110 F. 2d 562 (1940).

[113] 110 F. 2d 562 at 563.

[114] *Burton* v. *United States*, 151 F. 2d 17 (1945).

[115] *C. McDonald* v. *Hudspeth*, 41 F. Supp. 182 (1941), and *Hudspeth* v. *C. McDonald*, 120 F. 2d 962 (1941).

tion was supported by evidence that during most of the trial counsel was under the influence of liquor to such a degree that counsel for codefendants, and several newspapermen, were aware of it—in fact, everyone but the trial judge. The circuit court, however, emphasized the lack of timely objection and the failure of the trial judge to detect signs of drunkenness, and concluded rather casually that since the defendant selected his attorney, he should be liable for counsel's unsatisfactory services.

In another interesting, and apparently endless, process of litigation, one Walter McDonald, accused of armed robbery, attacked his conviction on the ground that he and his retained counsel lacked that mutual confidence so necessary in attorney-client relations. Because his counsel had failed to initiate a petition for habeas corpus during the nine months which separated indictment from trial, McDonald filed a complaint with the Michigan Bar Association. He made one attempt at the trial to indicate his lack of satisfaction with counsel, but counsel made no move to withdraw, and the record showed an able and vigorous defense. Two of the four district courts which faced this issue upheld the defendant's claim. Four circuit courts rejected it.[116] Whether the defendant would have fared better had the actions of an appointed counsel been at issue is difficult to say. Certainly the circuit courts in their opinions laid great stress on the fact that the defendant had chosen his counsel and could have dismissed him and selected another if he were dissatisfied.

In these cases where a defect in the service of counsel is asserted the court must necessarily adopt a suspicious attitude toward the claims of unsuccessful defendants. The rule seems clear that the defects of a retained counsel must be brought to the court's attention in a timely manner or else only the most grievous deviations from proper legal conduct and attitude will result in a reversal. A defendant with appointed counsel is in a more favorable position because of the judicial assumption that an indigent defendant will not be so ready to dismiss, or com-

---

[116] McDonald v. Hudspeth, 113 F. 2d 984 (1940); McDonald v. Hudspeth, 129 F. 2d 196 (1942); McDonald v. Johnston, 62 F. Supp. 830 (1945), reversed by Johnston v. McDonald, 157 F. 2d 275 (1946); McDonald v. Swope, 79 F. Supp. 30 (1948), reversed by Swope v. W. McDonald, 173 F. 2d 852 (1949). For a comment, see 39 Mich. L. Rev. (Jan., 1941), 475.

plain of, appointed counsel, and therefore an appointed counsel must render substantial services. This, of course, does not mean that errors in judgment or tactics by counsel will result in an overthrow of a substantially fair trial so long as counsel has made a reasonably professional effort.[117]

Absence of Counsel during Proceedings.—The judges face a difficult choice when counsel is missing at some stage in the trial. If they delay trials, there is added expense, and various problems arise concerning witnesses and the court dockets; they know, moreover, that a common complaint directed against courts is that they move too slowly. Yet in certain situations courts may not be able to act when counsel is absent, since the counsel provision of the Sixth Amendment seemingly guarantees counsel at all stages in the proceedings. Later discipline of the errant counsel is not a complete solution, obviously.

Some courts have solved the problem by holding that prejudice must result from the absence of counsel to constitute reversible error. Thus where a plea of not guilty is entered at the preliminary hearing without the aid of counsel, no prejudice can be shown.[118] Moreover, the circuit courts have rejected their old holding that a plea of guilty at the preliminary hearing was not cured by the later appearance of counsel at the trial.[119] The Canizio case furnished a way out. The Supreme Court held in that instance that the appearance of counsel for the defendant at the trial cured any defects which might have existed as the result of a plea of guilty without aid of counsel because counsel could have moved to withdraw the plea.[120]

It is not necessary that a defendant have counsel continuously from arraignment to conviction. For example, where a retained counsel withdrew and six months elapsed before new counsel was appointed, it was held that there was no lack of counsel because the new counsel was prepared in the succeeding stages of

---

[117] The "presence or absence of judicial character in the proceedings as a whole," is the test of effective aid used in *Soulis* v. *O'Brien,* 94 F. Supp. 764 (1950).

[118] *Thompson* v. *King,* 107 F. 2d 307 (1939).

[119] The old rule, set forth in *Wood* v. *United States,* 128 F. 2d 265 (1942), was changed by *Setser* v. *Welch,* 159 F. 2d 703 (1947).

[120] *Canizio* v. *New York,* 327 U.S. 82, 66 S. Ct. 452, 90 L. Ed. 545 (1946). This case will receive fuller treatment in Chap. V.

the trial.[121]   However, the courts of appeals have increasingly taken a more serious view of the absence of counsel at the verdict and the sentencing.   Courts of appeals remanded two causes where appointed counsel, in one case, and retained counsel, in the other, were absent at these stages.   The inability of the judge to substitute for counsel at these important points was the explanation of the reversal.[122]   In a third case the court held that absence at the sentencing was reversible while absence at the verdict was not.[123]

The practical hardship which results from remanding for judgment and sentence is not great.   But if the verdict stage must be repeated, a new trial is the only workable solution.   Perhaps the view of the appellate courts that counsel must be present is the one feasible view.   It requires trial courts to force their attorneys to live up to proper professional standards.   Absence of counsel at any stage is as serious a reflection on the standards and discipline of the court as it is on the character and attitude of the attorney concerned.

The general conclusion to be drawn from these cases in which defendants pleaded not guilty and had the assistance of counsel is that while courts will attempt to prevent an unfair conviction where a defendant has claimed to be innocent and has counsel, they assume that counsel will do his best, and that some clear showing of harm to the defendant due to counsel's actions or inaction must be demonstrated in order to reverse a conviction. Perhaps it can be said that with retained counsel the defendant's claim must strike deeper into the appellate judge's conscience than in those situations where an appointed counsel is allegedly at fault.   The rather anomalous result is that one who receives a free legal defense may exact a somewhat higher standard of

[121] *Scott* v. *United States,* 115 F. 2d 137 (1940).   Similarly, if one of two defense counsel is forced to withdraw and the less-prepared lawyer is forced to continue, there is no denial of counsel.   See *United States ex rel. Skinner* v. *Robinson,* 105 F. Supp. 153 (1952).

[122] *Thomas* v. *Hunter,* 153 F. 2d 834 (1946), and *Wilfong* v. *Johnston,* 156 F. 2d 507 (1946), overruled the doctrine set forth in *Lovvorn* v. *Johnston,* 118 F. 2d 704 (1941), and *Kent* v. *Sanford,* 121 F. 2d 216 (1941).

[123] *Martin* v. *United States,* 182 F. 2d 225 (1950).   This holding was based on the unimportance of counsel's action at verdict when compared with his usefulness at sentencing.

service than one who pays. Yet any other solution would diminish the value of the service of appointed counsel or, alternatively, would lead to an excessive number of appeals by unsuccessful defendants who could find some fault with their retained counsel long after the heat of the trial.

PLEA OF NOT GUILTY WITH WAIVER OF COUNSEL

A quite different situation is present where a layman who has pleaded not guilty has attempted to waive counsel and defend himself. In the cases to follow, whatever motives prompted this original decision by the defendant, the petitioner has regretted his choice and, in effect, says that he should not have been allowed to choose. The position of the claimant is a favorable one only if he can show that he was not competent to waive counsel, since the *Johnson* v. *Zerbst* decision had held that only where the right to counsel had been waived by a competent defendant could a federal criminal proceeding take place without counsel. However, in one case where the defendant was a practicing lawyer who proceeded to defend himself and his codefendants a waiver of counsel was implied from his action.[124] In another case, where a defendant was shown to have been ignorant, the failure of the judge to inquire at the arraignment whether defendant had counsel, and the failure of a federal marshal to call an attorney, as requested, overcame the presumption of a competent waiver of counsel.[125] Interestingly enough, the court inferred ignorance in this case because the defendant was a sailor who had been twenty years at sea. It gave no weight to the fact that he had had one previous court experience when he had been represented by counsel.

The Supreme Court reversed a decision in which a lower court had held that a layman, even one who had studied law, could not waive a jury trial without the aid of counsel.[126] Speaking through Justice Frankfurter, the Supreme Court stressed the illogic of permitting a defendant to waive counsel and plead

---

[124] *Walker* v. *Chitty*, 112 F. 2d 79 (1940).

[125] *Walleck* v. *Hudspeth*, 128 F. 2d 343 (1942).

[126] *United States ex rel. McCann* v. *Adams*, 126 F. 2d 774 (1942), reversed by *Adams* v. *United States ex rel. McCann*, 317 U.S. 269, 63 S. Ct. 236, 87 L. Ed. 268 (1942).

guilty, and yet of denying him the right to waive a jury trial after a plea of not guilty.[127]   The argument of the petitioner which the circuit court had sustained was that a layman can decide intelligently whether or not to plead guilty, but cannot weigh his chances before a judge or a jury,[128] and that the government's argument for freedom for the defendant to do as he chose was a throwback to the laissez faire doctrines found in discarded classical economics.[129]

The dissent of Douglas, with Black and Murphy concurring, suggested the desirability of a rule requiring the advice of counsel before permitting a layman to waive trial by jury.[130]   These justices analogized the right of the defendant to waive a jury trial without counsel to the old liberty-of-contract right, as one of form but of little substance.[131]   Murphy, in a separate dissenting opinion, advocated a rule which would prohibit the waiver of jury trial, but he agreed that, if he were overruled, it would be desirable to set up rigorous standards to guide trial courts when waiver was attempted.[132]

The minority position is defensible only if one accepts the ultimate conclusion and requires a trial with counsel in every criminal prosecution, regardless of the desires of the defendant. Once a competent waiver of counsel is permitted, it seems absurd to restrict the defendant's waiving of other rights pertaining to trial.   Certainly an intelligent layman who felt that he could defend himself might act most wisely in deciding that a trial by the court, rather than a trial by jury, would enhance his chances, since courtroom experience and forensic skill count for much less with a wise and experienced judge than with a jury.   The majority position is clearly preferable.   In any event, not all waivers are competent, for if a defendant who waives counsel can show that he was insane at, or near, the time that the waiver was made, his conviction will be reversed.[133]

---

[127] 317 U.S. 269 at 275, 87 L. Ed. 268 at 272.
[128] Brief for Respondent, p. 29.
[129] *Ibid.*
[130] 317 U.S. 269 at 284, 87 L. Ed. 268 at 276.
[131] 317 U.S. 269 at 285–286, 87 L. Ed. 268 at 278.
[132] 317 U.S. 269 at 287, 87 L. Ed. 268 at 278–279.
[133] *Honaker* v. *Cox,* 51 F. Supp. 829 (1943).

Presumably the occasions are rare when a defendant will plead not guilty and then waive counsel. The paucity of cases where a defendant has done so suggests that since the case of *Johnson* v. *Zerbst* defendants will accept the appointment of counsel. Only if incompetence of a very grave nature is clearly shown will an appellate court reverse a conviction after a plea of not guilty and a waiver of counsel.

Having examined federal cases in which defendants have pleaded not guilty, we now turn to those where defendants have pleaded guilty. At first thought it would seem incredible for a petitioner to assert that he pleaded guilty although he was in reality innocent. A moment's reflection suggests, however, that one can be guilty of a wrongful act, but not be guilty of the specific act charged, and, again, that one may have done something which harms another, but that a legally acceptable defense can be interposed. After a brief examination of the relatively few cases in which petitioners have challenged the validity of pleas of guilty entered with the assistance of counsel, we shall turn to the more difficult body of case law involving pleas of guilty challenged as invalid because they were entered without the aid and advice of counsel. First, however, we must ascertain the attitude of the courts toward pleas of guilty entered with the advice of either retained or appointed counsel.

PLEA OF GUILTY WITH ASSISTANCE OF COUNSEL

It seems well established that a plea of guilty entered with the advice of counsel will be conclusive unless there is some clear evidence that fraud or coercion was present in the case, and this is true even though counsel was appointed as little as four hours before the defendant's plea was entered.[134] In an instance where appointment of counsel was made on the same day as the plea and where this circumstance was reinforced by an allegation that F.B.I. men had induced a confession through fraud, these facts were sufficient to gain a reversal.[135] Frequently the claim is made after trial that counsel was indifferent or inefficient in advising the defendant to plead guilty, but this claim

[134] *Thornburg* v. *United States*, 164 F. 2d 37 (1947).
[135] *Maye* v. *Pescor*, 162 F. 2d 641 (1947).

is usually rejected.[136]   As one court has phrased it, the defendant's dissatisfaction with results is not enough.[137]

This court attitude reflects a natural skepticism toward the afterthoughts of those who plead guilty.   While it might be suggested by the cynical observer that an appointed counsel may have a strong motive for encouraging a plea of guilty, it probably is true in the great majority of situations that an attorney would have the greatest difficulty in convincing an innocent person of normal intelligence that a plea of guilty was wise.   It is most improbable that an attorney would suggest such a course if he had reasonable doubt of the defendant's guilt.   And unless there is some logical justification for requiring a trial in every situation, and eliminating the possibility of a plea of guilty, the courts must accept the defendant's plea as final when it is made with advice.   In one respect courts treat these defendants differently, because a plea of guilty if made with the advice of counsel renders unnecessary the presence of counsel at later stages.[138]

Nor does the attitude of the appellate courts change if it can be shown that the defendant pleaded not guilty at a preliminary hearing and then changed his plea to guilty at arraignment, or during trial, when counsel advised him.   The significant fact is that at the more crucial stage the defendant pleaded guilty.[139] Obviously the same result would follow if counsel assisted the defendant at the preliminary hearing, as well as at arraignment, and the final plea was guilty.   Courts place little emphasis on the plea at a preliminary hearing because of the well-known fact that magistrates, or others who conduct preliminary examinations, usually enter "not guilty" as the defendant's plea, especially if the defendant is faced with a serious charge, and is without counsel.

---

[136] *Shepherd* v. *Hunter,* 163 F. 2d 872 (1947); *Moss* v. *Hunter,* 167 F. 2d 683 (1948); *Merritt* v. *Hunter,* 170 F. 2d 739 (1948). Even where appointed counsel advised a defendant to plead guilty after a consultation lasting fifteen minutes, the appointment and advice were held effective because the attorney was wise and experienced. See *United States* v. *Wight,* 176 F. 2d 376 (1949).

[137] *Kinney* v. *United States,* 177 F. 2d 895 (1950). The defendant had hoped to get a light sentence.

[138] *Farnsworth* v. *Sanford,* 115 F. 2d 375 (1940); *Willis* v. *Hunter,* 166 F. 2d 721 (1948).

[139] *Beckett* v. *Hudspeth,* 131 F. 2d 195 (1942); *Bugg* v. *Hudspeth,* 113 F. 2d 260 (1940); *Saylor* v. *Sanford,* 99 F. 2d 605 (1938).

It is readily seen, then, that a plea of guilty with the assistance of counsel almost completely forecloses any possibility of later raising the claim that there was a denial of the effective assistance of counsel.

CHANGE OF PLEA TO GUILTY WITHOUT COUNSEL

One type of case which remains unsurveyed is that involving the defendant's change of plea from not guilty to guilty, with the allegation of a lack of proper counsel. If the record shows a waiver, that fact is usually conclusive of such cases.[140] Where the defendant's appointed counsel withdrew and the defendant then decided to plead guilty and stated that he waived counsel, before the judge had fulfilled his promise to appoint a new counsel, the waiver was held valid.[141] Commonly, the defendants in change-of-plea cases urge that they were coerced, but such pleas are usually fruitless, since the presumption which the courts use is that officials perform their duties properly.[142]

The interesting and widely reported case involving Countess von Moltke, and others, furnishes a good example of a confused and confusing record. The defendant, charged with conspiracy against the United States under the Espionage Act, claimed that she was intimidated into changing her plea to guilty.[143] At her arraignment on September 21, 1943, the judge appointed temporarily a lawyer who was present in the courtroom, and a plea of not guilty was entered.[144] The judge promised to appoint permanent counsel for her, but this had not been done by October 7, 1943, when she signed a waiver of counsel and pleaded guilty.[145] It was later alleged on her behalf that a complex of factors, including her German background and her difficulty with the English language, conflicting advice given by F.B.I. agents, inadequate assistance at arraignment, failure of

140 *Jackson v. United States,* 131 F. 2d 606 (1942).

141 *Powell v. Sanford,* 136 F. 2d 58 (1943). This is true whether or not the trial court had any reason to suspect insanity. See *Hallowell v. United States,* 197 F. 2d 926 (1952).

142 *Dorsey v. Gill,* 148 F. 2d 857 (1945).

143 *Von Moltke v. Gillies,* 72 F. Supp. 994; 161 F. 2d 113; 332 U.S. 708, 68 S. Ct. 316, 92 L. Ed. 309 (1948). See 22 *Temp. L. Q.* (July, 1948), 140, for comment.

144 Transcript of Record, p. 51, *Von Moltke v. Gillies,* 332 U.S. 708.

145 *Ibid.,* p. 62.

the promised counsel to appear, and coercion and intimidation by the F.B.I. agents, caused her to change her plea.[146]   In portraying her mental state more specifically, she claimed she had been falsely advised that other defendants would plead guilty and that the question of trial was one for the district attorney. She said she feared that her husband, who had been discharged as an instructor at Wayne University, Detroit, might be implicated if a trial occurred.   She also maintained that she was not properly advised concerning the waiver of counsel which she signed, and that the waiver form was illegible.[147]

The United States, in opposition, said that the only issue was whether her waiver of counsel and plea of guilty were knowingly made.[148]   Its brief depicted a wholly different defendant, one who was "shrewd" and mentally acute and who would have received counsel if she had not decided to plead guilty and waive counsel.[149]   In essence, there was only the defendant's word against that of the F.B.I. agents, and the fact that the agents could not explicitly contradict her version of events in all particulars was natural, since they were being quite honest about their inability to recollect.[150]   The critical issue involved what one F.B.I. agent, Collard, told her concerning the nature of a conspiracy and the acts which constituted participation in a conspiracy.   She claimed that Collard cited as an example of a criminal conspiracy a "rumrunner" scheme, in which one who was present when the conspiracy was planned was guilty, regardless of any direct knowledge or aid.   He allegedly said, and did not deny saying, that the defendant's position was analogous.[151]

The Supreme Court in a six-to-three decision remanded the case to the district court for a factual determination of whether there had been a knowing, competent waiver of counsel.   Justice Black, with Douglas, Rutledge, and Murphy concurring, was willing to hold that no competent waiver had been made

---

[146] Brief for Petitioner, p. 13, *Von Moltke* v. *Gillies*, 332 U.S. 708.
[147] *Ibid.*, pp. 13–15.
[148] Brief for Respondent, p. 30, *Von Moltke* v. *Gillies*, 332 U.S. 708.
[149] *Ibid.*, p. 32.
[150] *Ibid.*, pp. 57–58.
[151] Transcript of Record, pp. 55, 142–143, *Von Moltke* v. *Gillies*, 332 U.S. 708.

and would have granted a new trial on the theory that the judge had failed to make an appointment which was necessary under all the circumstances.[152]   But Justice Frankfurter, with Justice Jackson, wanted a hearing on the question of misleading advice concerning the nature of a conspiracy.[153]   Justices Vinson, Reed, and Burton would have permitted the factual findings of the lower court to stand.[154]

In a later case there is a strong attack on the proposition that a court should either act as counsel and protect the defendant where the defendant waives counsel or should appoint counsel to advise the defendant whether to waive counsel.[155]   A trial court must undertake a more thorough examination of a defendant than has been customary, it seems clear, before accepting a waiver, and where there is doubt concerning the competence of the defendant, appointment of counsel should follow. If the waiver is to hold against attacks, it must be made by a defendant with full knowledge of his rights.[156]   Must the judge give a short course in constitutional law and judicial procedure, or should he appoint counsel to advise the defendant of his rights?   The first alternative is a possible, though perhaps not feasible, solution.   The second presents a difficult situation because no attorney wants to be held responsible for influencing a defendant to waive counsel, and to plead guilty, when his advice will in many cases be the occasion for a later attack on his own "effectiveness" and "interest."

If the courts must go behind a written waiver and attempt to ascertain the competency of the defendant at the time the waiver was made, the possibilities of litigation are endless.   It would seem that compliance with the new Federal Rules of Criminal Procedure [157] and the use of a standard form of instruction and interrogation of defendants which any judge can devise should make it possible for a judge to accept a written

---

[152] *Von Moltke* v. *Gillies,* 332 U.S. 708, 68 S. Ct. 316, 92 L. Ed. 309 (1948).
[153] *Ibid.*
[154] *Ibid.*
[155] *United States* v. *Christakos,* 83 F. Supp. 521 (1949).
[156] In *United States* v. *Wantland,* 199 F. 2d 237 (1952), it was held that merely telling a defendant in general terms of his right to counsel is insufficient. The right to receive appointed counsel must be spelled out.
[157] Discussed *infra,* this chapter.

waiver of counsel and a plea of guilty. After applying this standard form he should be able to appoint counsel, where he feels it necessary, regardless of the defendant's wishes, at least for the purpose of giving full advice. When all this has been done, a plea of guilty should be allowed to stand, unless there is overwhelming evidence that coercion or force was used, or that the procedure was a sham or clearly unfair. Appellate courts must show more confidence in the fairness of trial courts. One suspects that the lack of trial experience of many members of the Supreme Court has made it possible for them to view the claims of felons through rose-colored glasses.

PLEA OF GUILTY AS WAIVER OF COUNSEL

We now turn to the cases where a plea of guilty was entered without advice of counsel. After *Johnson* v. *Zerbst* in 1938 the federal courts were confronted with numerous claims in which defendants asserted that they had not been advised of their right to have counsel appointed and in ignorance of that right had pleaded guilty, adding, usually, that they were not guilty. In self-defense the lower courts evolved a practical formula with which to defeat these claims, though as a logical principle it leaves much to be desired. The elements of this formula were that a defendant who appeared without counsel, who failed to request counsel, and who pleaded guilty was deemed as a matter of law to have waived counsel. This rule applied in a number of instances.[158] In all these and similar cases a heavy burden was placed upon the defendant to show that this waiver, which the court implied as a matter of law, was not made intelligently or competently. In effect, the federal courts were rejecting the admonition contained in Black's opinion in *Johnson* v. *Zerbst* that it would be appropriate to insert the facts surrounding a waiver in the record itself, for in all these cases the record was silent concerning the question of counsel.

However, where the trial court had been careless of a defendant's rights, as in *Zeff* v. *Sanford,* by failing to advise him of the consequences of a plea of guilty, and by conducting a

---

[158] *Sedorko* v. *Hudspeth,* 109 F. 2d 475 (1940); *Moore* v. *Hudspeth,* 110 F. 2d 386 (1940); *Kelly* v. *Aderhold,* 112 F. 2d 118 (1940); *Leonard* v. *Hudspeth,* 112 F. 2d 121 (1940).

private meeting in chambers with the government attorney and a probation officer, the reviewing court held that the silent waiver was not competent.[159] Logically, in *Zeff* v. *Sanford* the court should have rested its decision on due-process grounds, since the validity of the waiver of counsel and what happened to the defendant after the waiver was made were distinct issues. Such judicial confusion, needless to say, hardly clarifies the scope of the right to counsel. Another court, more hostile to the "implied-waiver" doctrine but unwilling to reject it, refused to find a waiver in a case where the defendant was eighteen and ignorant of the charges, and where the record failed to indicate any advice, on the ground that his silent waiver was not "competent." [160]

For the most part, however, reviewing courts have scrutinized the whole factual picture in an effort to find one or more objective details which could be interpreted as an implied waiver. If, for example, the defendant had been in court previously, he was presumed to have learned of his right to counsel and to have waived it by his failure to request appointment.[161] Other petitioners were defeated when it was shown that they had either discussed their cases with lawyers, whom they failed to retain,[162] or had shown a shrewd knowledge of the realities by "bargaining" with the district attorney in an attempt to gain a light sentence.[163] And if similar information were not available, the reviewing courts could emphasize the usual presumption in habeas corpus proceedings that the judgment below was regular, and that a waiver was presumptively competent, and thus overcome a petitioner's proof that he had been ignorant and lacked friends,[164] or had been insane,[165] when the waiver had been entered.

Other courts have rested their decisions on the nature of

[159] *Zeff* v. *Sanford,* 31 F. Supp. 736 (1940).

[160] *United States ex rel. Nortner* v. *Hiatt,* 33 F. Supp. 545 (1940).

[161] *Buckner* v. *Hudspeth,* 105 F. 2d 396 (1939); *United States ex rel. Coate* v. *Hill,* 29 F. Supp. 890 (1939); *Cooke* v. *Swope,* 28 F. Supp. 492 (1939); *Cundiff* v. *Nicholson,* 107 F. 2d 162 (1939).

[162] *Parker* v. *Johnston,* 29 F. Supp. 829 (1939); *Ex parte Rose,* 33 F. Supp. 941 (1940).

[163] *Logan* v. *Johnston,* 28 F. Supp. 98 (1939).

[164] *Blood* v. *Hudspeth,* 113 F. 2d 470 (1940).

[165] *Collins* v. *Johnston,* 29 F. Supp. 208 (1939).

the guilty plea, holding that it was an admission that no defense existed and that counsel would be useless.[166] The plea itself operated as a waiver of counsel, declared other judges.[167] That there was nothing in the opinion in *Johnson* v. *Zerbst* which required the appointment of counsel where a waiver, either express or implied, could be found was the implicit assumption behind all these decisions; this explains the search for every possible technical reason for refusing to grant habeas corpus.[168] One ground for denial that could be used in some cases was the existence of a valid sentence on a proper earlier conviction, which rendered the demand hearing "premature," according to several rulings.[169]

In short, the effect of *Johnson* v. *Zerbst* was severely limited, in the years immediately following the decision, by the federal courts' evolution of the doctrine of implied waiver of counsel, the foundation of which was the double assumption that defendants knew of their right to counsel, so that their silence or failure to request appointment signified a waiver, and that a voluntary plea of guilty was a confession that no defense existed and counsel could serve no useful purpose. *Johnson* v. *Zerbst* seemed to mean much more in theory than the practice of the federal courts would indicate. Unless the Supreme Court were to implement its decision in *Johnson* v. *Zerbst,* the position of the indigent defendant who was ignorant of his rights would not be improved materially. It was almost inevitable that the opportunity to do so should be presented to the Supreme Court before long.

A NEW DOCTRINE OF WAIVER—WALKER V. JOHNSTON

In 1941 an armed-robbery case was brought up on certiorari to the Supreme Court, in which the petitioner, Walker, who had pleaded guilty, alleged that he had not been advised of his right to counsel, that he was ignorant of his right, and that he had failed

---

[166] *Franzeen* v. *Johnston,* 111 F. 2d 817 (1940).
[167] *Erwin* v. *Sanford,* 27 F. Supp. 892 (1939).
[168] *Cooke* v. *Swope,* 109 F. 2d 955 (1940).
[169] *Macomber* v. *Hudspeth,* 115 F. 2d 114 (1940); *Odom* v. *Aderhold,* 115 F. 2d 202 (1940).

to request counsel solely for that reason. He claimed further that the district attorney had refused to give him time to contact relatives from whom he could have obtained enough money to hire counsel, and, finally, that the lower court had improperly refused to grant a hearing on his habeas corpus application in which these allegations were set forth.[170] The appellant argued in his petition that Justice Black in *Johnson* v. *Zerbst* had laid down a rule that the waiver of counsel had to be intelligently made, and that the facts in each case were to be decisive.[171] The facts here were favorable, as the illiteracy of the petitioner was obvious, and other evidence in the record indicated a frightened, coerced defendant.[172] The record was completely silent concerning counsel, and the trial judge had remained mute on the question of whether he had offered counsel.[173] One obstacle to the plea of ignorance was the record of a previous court appearance, but counsel urged that if the defendant had been ignorant of his rights on his previous appearance, it would have taught him nothing.[174] Counsel pointed out correctly in the brief that the Supreme Court in *Johnson* v. *Zerbst* had been careful to draw no distinction between cases where the defendant might decide to plead guilty and those where he decided to plead not guilty.[175] After urging that the facts were more favorable to this defendant than they had been in *Johnson* v. *Zerbst,* counsel reviewed the history of the Sixth Amendment provision,[176] and closed his argument by asserting what turned out to be the crucial legal point in the case, namely, that the practice of the Ninth Circuit Court in disposing of habeas corpus applications on affidavits and other written evidence, even where a conflict of facts was present, was an improper procedure.[177]

The government, while admitting that the petitioner would be entitled to a hearing if an issue of fact were determinative of his right to the writ,[178] urged that the facts in this case, even when construed most favorably to the petitioner, constituted

---

[170] *Walker* v. *Johnston,* 312 U.S. 275, 61 S. Ct. 574, 85 L. Ed. 830 (1941).
[171] Petition for Certiorari, p. 10.
[172] *Ibid.,* p. 11.
[173] *Ibid.,* pp. 14–15.
[174] Brief for Petitioner, p. 17.
[175] *Ibid.,* p. 18.
[176] *Ibid.,* pp. 21–27.
[177] *Ibid.,* p. 33.
[178] Brief for Respondent, pp. 21–22.

a waiver.   Its brief noted that the defendant had escaped from
a New Mexico state penitentiary while serving a life sentence,
and that he was well versed in legal procedure.[179]   Waiver
could consequently be implied in this case as it had been implied in so many others.[180]   Moreover, the defendant had sent
a letter thanking the United States District Attorney for his
treatment and expressing his satisfaction with the sentence.[181]
There was no showing, said the government, of a need for counsel here.[182]   With substantial success the government brief proceeded to destroy the historical argument which the appellant
had produced,[183] and then countered by citing the established
court custom which required a request, or a showing of need,
before the judge would offer counsel to a defendant who intended to plead guilty.   Finally, the government protested that
the tremendous number of guilty pleas entered in federal courts
would present a hopeless situation if counsel had to be appointed
in all cases.[184]

The Supreme Court, in an opinion by Justice Roberts, expressed disapproval of the procedure used by the Ninth Circuit
Court in determining habeas corpus applications, and asserted
that the existence of a factual issue required a hearing.[185]   But,
in order to decide that a factual issue existed in this case, the
Court had to hold that Walker's allegations, if true, would have
indicated that a competent waiver had not been made.   Said
the Court: "If the facts alleged were established to the satisfaction of the judge, they would support a conclusion that the
petitioner desired the aid of counsel, and so informed the District Attorney, was ignorant of his right to such aid, *was not
interrogated as to his desire or informed of his right, and did not
knowingly waive that right* . . . .   He was deceived and coerced into pleading guilty when his real desire was to plead not

179 *Ibid.,* p. 22.   182 *Ibid.,* p. 30.
180 *Ibid.,* p. 15.   183 *Ibid.,* pp. 34–37.
181 *Ibid.*

184 There were 38,000 pleas of guilty entered in the year ending June 30,
1940.

185 Anything less than a full hearing would fail to satisfy the statutory
requirement contained in 28 U.S.C.A. (1940), § 461, now 28 U.S.C.A. (1950),
§ 2243.

guilty or at least *to be advised by counsel as to his course.*" [186]
The effect of this holding was that where a defendant, regardless of whether or not he intended to plead guilty, had not
been advised of this right to have counsel or had not waived the
right in a knowing fashion the consequent judgment was void.
In federal courts, after this decision, a silent record would be
of assistance to one claiming a denial of counsel, even though
at the hearing he would have the burden of proof, for it was no
longer possible for the trial courts to put together a silent record,
a lack of request, and a plea of guilty, and get a "waiver."

APPLICATION OF WALKER V. JOHNSTON

One result of the decision, as might be expected, was that the
flood of applications for habeas corpus increased. In danger
of being engulfed, the courts tried desperately to find a waiver
in most cases, or to rest their decision whenever possible on an
unwillingness to believe the petitioner's story. The reaction of
some courts, it is true, was more generous, but all seemed determined to avoid upsetting a conviction unless some substantial
deviation from fair procedure had occurred, or an unmistakable
departure had been made from the principles of *Johnson* v.
Zerbst and *Walker* v. *Johnston.*

More than a fanciful story was necessary to establish the lack
of a competent waiver. While it was conceded that an unadvised thirty-nine-year-old Negro defendant with a fourth-
grade education was presumably ignorant of his right to counsel,
so that his failure to request counsel and his plea of guilty did
not constitute a waiver,[187] there was no need, the court held, to
advise a defendant who had several previous convictions, and
who had corresponded with an attorney. His plea of guilty
constituted a waiver.[188] Where the failure of a trial judge to
advise a defendant was held to make an intelligent waiver impossible, even though a lawyer representing a codefendant asked
the defendant if he wanted counsel, the court rested its decision

---

[186] 312 U.S. 275 at 286, 85 L. Ed. 830 at 836. Italics mine.
[187] *Evans* v. *Rives,* 126 F. 2d 633 (1942).
[188] *O'Keith* v. *Johnston,* 129 F. 2d 889 (1942).

partly on the background, inexperience, and conduct of the accused.[189]   And in another case where a young defendant had the advice and comfort of an intoxicated father and a hysterical mother, but no advice from the trial court, the reviewing court found that no intelligent waiver had been made; it was aided in this instance by a record of insanity in the accused's history.[190] Again, it was held that where a district attorney undertakes the duty of informing the accused of his rights, he must do so correctly, because if the judge then fails to advise the defendant, his waiver is not made with correct knowledge.[191]   But if the defendant's knowledge of his right to have counsel can be shown from other facts in the case, the failure of the record to show advice and an offer of counsel by the judge is not a fatal error,[192] so that where there had been previous convictions, and where there was some evidence of an offer of counsel though nothing appeared on the record, the court found a competent waiver.[193] On the other hand, if no one can contradict the claims of a defendant, a silent record may work in his favor.[194]

There had been a number of earlier cases where evidence of a court custom of advising all defendants of their right to counsel was held sufficient to overcome the silent record.[195]   But the attempt to prove the general custom after *Walker* v. *Johnston* was apparently thought to be useless, because in the majority of cases the government produced specific evidence of the actual knowledge of the accused where the record was insufficient.   Yet even where a waiver is shown in the record, it may be held in-

[189] *Bayless* v. *Johnston,* 48 F. Supp. 758 (1943).

[190] *Robinson* v. *Johnston,* 50 F. Supp. 774 (1943).

[191] *Michener* v. *Johnston,* 141 F. 2d 171 (1944).

[192] *United States* v. *Steese,* 144 F. 2d 439 (1944).   The same conclusion was reached in *De Jordan* v. *Hunter,* 145 F. 2d 287 (1944), where the defendant had pleaded guilty to murder.

[193] *Widmer* v. *Johnston,* 136 F. 2d 416 (1943); *Pinfold* v. *Hunter,* 140 F. 2d 564 (1944); *Scott* v. *Johnston,* 71 F. Supp. 117 (1947).

[194] In *Allen* v. *United States,* 102 F. Supp. 866 (1952), a conviction obtained in 1933 was reversed.   The court granted that the silent record was not significant at the trial held before *Johnson* v. *Zerbst* (1938). But because all other trial participants were not available, the defendant's unsupported word was sufficient to overcome the presumption of regularity of a judgment.   This seems to be an extreme interpretation.

[195] *Harpin* v. *Johnston,* 109 F. 2d 434 (1940); *Towne* v. *Hudspeth,* 108 F. 2d 676 (1939); *Warden* v. *Johnston,* 29 F. Supp. 217 (1939).

competent.   In one case the fact that the defendant was seventeen upset the presumption of a valid waiver.[196]   But another
seventeen-year-old defendant failed in his effort to show the
incompetence of his waiver when everyone concerned with the
case testified that he had been told by several officials of his
right to counsel.[197]   If, however, the evidence is conflicting concerning advice and offer, and the record is silent, the assumption is that there was no advice and that no competent waiver was
made.[198]   If the record shows insufficient advice before the
waiver and the plea of guilty were accepted, neither is valid.[199]

Where the court appoints counsel whom the defendant dis-
misses before his plea of guilty, the record of offer, acceptance,
and later waiver will overcome the defendant's allegation of a
denial of counsel.[200]   Yet if there has been undue haste, even a
written waiver by a defendant not fully informed may be inconclusive.[201]   It is, moreover, the duty of the judge to ascertain
the limits or fullness of the defendant's understanding by thorough questioning before accepting a waiver of counsel.[202]   The
usual rule, however, is that the written waiver and the recitals
in the record will be held conclusive.[203]   It should be noted,
moreover, that the successful attack on a written waiver in *Snell*
v. *United States* was made on appeal, whereas the unsuccessful
one was made on a habeas corpus application.   Insanity clearly
makes a competent waiver impossible.[204]

Finally, the courts follow the Canizio doctrine and hold that
if counsel appears for the defendant after the plea of guilty, any
previous error is subject to correction by motion to change the

[196] *Williams* v. *Huff*, 146 F. 2d 867 (1945).

[197] *United States* v. *Dunbar*, 55 F. Supp. 678 (1944).

[198] *Richardson* v. *Shuttleworth*, 75 F. Supp. 631 (1948).

[199] *Cherrie* v. *United States*, 179 F. 2d 94 (1949).   The record contained this
question by the trial judge: "Are you ready to plead to this information . . .
without the assistance of counsel to which you are entitled?"   The defendant
answered, "Yes."   On remand the district court found that other facts not appearing on the record indicated a competent waiver, and this finding was upheld
on appeal, *Cherrie* v. *United States*, 184 F. 2d 384 (1950).

[200] *Owens* v. *Hunter*, 169 F. 2d 971 (1948).

[201] *Snell* v. *United States*, 174 F. 2d 580 (1949).

[202] *Ibid.*, p. 582.

[203] *Bankey* v. *Sanford*, 74 F. Supp. 756 (1947); *Caldwell* v. *Hunter*, 163 F. 2d
181 (1947).

[204] *Kuczynski* v. *United States*, 149 F. 2d 478 (1945).

plea. The lack of counsel or of advice as to counsel before, or at the time of, plea is not error in such cases.[205]

RIGHT TO COUNSEL ON APPEAL

It is desirable to survey briefly the claim that the right to counsel extends to appeals and, finally, to enumerate the methods by which denials of the right to counsel can be challenged, although this last subject has not proved to be the source of confusion and debate in the federal courts that it has in state proceedings. In the succeeding chapter, "Right to Counsel as Interpreted by State Courts," the fuller discussion of postconviction remedies made necessary by the manifold problems in the state courts obviates the need of more than a summary here.

The general rule has been that an appeal is not necessary for due process, and that counsel appointed to serve at the trial has no duty to proceed after sentence.[206]

Some courts have been puzzled as to which court, trial or appellate, should appoint counsel if counsel is to be given to an appellant.[207] It is clear that the trial court can replace the original appointed counsel by other counsel if it so desires,[208] but it is also true that counsel can be denied if the trial court thinks that the appeal lacks merit.[209] Yet once an appeal is granted, it has been held error for the trial court to fail to appoint counsel, on the theory that another stage of proceeding requires the presence of counsel;[210] and if the lower court has failed to appoint counsel, the appellate court may appoint one in order to make effective the appeal procedure.[211] The confusion is height-

---

[205] *Gann* v. *Pescor,* 164 F. 2d 113 (1947); *Hiatt* v. *Gann,* 170 F. 2d 473 (1948), reversing *Gann* v. *Gough,* 79 F. Supp. 912 (1948).

[206] *De Maurez* v. *Swope,* 104 F. 2d 758 (1939). It has also been held that the right to counsel does not exist after conviction on a motion to vacate sentence. See *Crowe* v. *United States,* 175 F. 2d 799 (1949), and *Richardson* v. *United States,* 199 F. 2d 333 (1952). On the other hand, where a defendant tried to withdraw his plea of guilty after receiving a four-year sentence, and asked that counsel be appointed, it was held erroneous for the judge to resentence him to five years' imprisonment without appointing counsel. See *United States ex rel. Stidham* v. *Swope,* 96 F. Supp. 773 (1951).

[207] *Garrison* v. *Johnston,* 104 F. 2d 128 (1939).

[208] *Edwards* v. *United States,* 139 F. 2d 365 (1944).

[209] *Gargano* v. *United States,* 140 F. 2d 118 (1944).

[210] *Reid* v. *Sanford,* 42 F. Supp. 300 (1941).

[211] *Holmes* v. *United States,* 126 F. 2d 431 (1942).

ened by a recent two-to-one decision in which the circuit court upheld a refusal of the trial court to appoint counsel for appeal, declaring that no right to counsel exists at this stage, though the strength of this decision was weakened by a finding that there was no likelihood of success in the appellant's claim.[212]

Here again is a problem which admits of no easy solution. So long as courts make mistakes which deprive men of life or liberty there must be a method by which appeal is possible. To say that due process of law in its historic meaning has not required this final step is to fail to keep abreast of the changing temper of legal thought.

If appeals are available to those who can afford to retain lawyers, the opportunity to make an appeal should also be available to indigents with meritorious cases. It cannot be seriously suggested that errors are made only where defendants have costly, retained counsel, for the reverse would seem to be closer to the truth. So long as American courts are generous in permitting appeals, and so long as appellate courts insist on re-examining the recorded facts of cases in order to substitute for the trial judge's firsthand impressions their own second insights, it will be difficult in principle to deny counsel to indigents for appeal purposes. Yet the present practice of the trial and appellate courts, which is to refuse to appoint counsel for frivolous appeals, must be maintained. Reform will have arrived when the number of appeals in all American courts is diminished by the general adoption of the discretionary writ of review.

PROCEDURAL IMPROVEMENTS

Before surveying briefly the possible techniques of raising the issue of a denial of counsel, we should recall the suggestion in *Johnson* v. *Zerbst* that a waiver of counsel, if made, should appear on the record. The Federal Rules of Criminal Procedure, adopted in 1945, which required the United States Commissioners to inform the defendant of his right to retain counsel and, in addition, instructed the trial judge to advise the defendant of his right to counsel [213] and to assign counsel to rep-

---

212 *Thompson* v. *Johnston*, 160 F. 2d 374 (1947).
213 *Federal Rules of Criminal Procedure for the United States District Courts* (Washington, D.C.: Government Printing Office, 1945), Rule 5 (b).

resent the defendant at every stage, unless counsel were waived,[214] tended to make these duties of the trial judge a regular part of the recorded proceeding.   The adoption of the cited provisions of this act was the Supreme Court's answer to the tremendous difficulties which the counsel cases had created.   Another very helpful step was the passage, in 1944, of an act which provided for salaried court reporters in the federal district courts.[215]   A full record was thus made possible for the first time.   These measures which aid the court in recording its proceedings tend to avoid the frustrating situations which had come up in many cases and which ultimately raised the question, What did happen at the arraignment and trial?

POSTCONVICTION REMEDIES

The possible methods of asserting a denial of counsel in the federal courts are:

1. A motion for a new trial.   This motion must be made within five days after a verdict, or a finding of guilty.[216]   Thus it is not available to most defendants convicted without counsel.

2. A motion in arrest of judgment on the ground that the trial court had lost jurisdiction because the defendant had not been granted a basic constitutional right.[217]   Here, again, few defendants are prepared to raise the issue in time.

3. A motion in the nature of a writ of *coram nobis,* an original writ directed to the trial judge for the purpose of asking a trial court to correct its own judgment, after the time for appeal has passed, when material facts become known which were not previously available.[218]   This remedy is generally useless if the facts alleged were known to the trial judge, as is true in most cases involving the right to counsel.

4. A new statutory motion combining features of the traditional habeas corpus and the motions to vacate judgment.   As the result of excessive use of the writ of habeas corpus, with the

[214] *Ibid.,* Rule 44.
[215] Pub. Law No. 222, 78th Congress, 2d Session (1944).
[216] *Federal Rules of Criminal Procedure,* Rule 33.
[217] *Ibid.,* Rule 34.
[218] For an excellent discussion of this writ, see *United States* v. *Steese,* 144 F. 2d 439 at 442–447 (1944).

consequent heavy burden placed on those federal judges whose districts contained a federal penitentiary, Congress in 1949 adopted a new motion to vacate a judgment and sentence which is similar to *coram nobis*.[219] Titled a "motion to vacate, set aside or correct sentence," it is addressed by the movant to the trial court. The motion sets forth alleged violations of law or constitutional rights and may be made at any time after conviction. Its denial may be appealed to a court of appeal. Limiting abuse of the remedy are the requirements that it must precede recourse to habeas corpus, that the prisoner need not be produced at the hearing, and that successive motions need not be entertained. The obvious advantage of this procedural innovation is the initiation of the claim before a judge who knows what happened at the original trial. If appeal follows, or habeas corpus is sought later, an amplified record is available to guide the appellate judges, so that the claims of convicts who have nothing to lose by literary invention will be viewed in a more accurate perspective. Already it is evident that if a real issue is presented by the new motion, a hearing is required.[220]

5. An appeal which may be taken within ten days after the entry of judgment, or after entry of an order denying a motion for a new trial or a motion in arrest of judgment.[221]

It is also provided that "when a court after trial imposes sentence upon a defendant not represented by counsel, the defendant shall be advised of his right to appeal, and if he so requests, the court shall prepare and file forthwith a notice of appeal on his behalf." [222] The time limit once again is the deterrent to the use of this normal remedy.

6. A petition for a writ of habeas corpus. The great bulk of those claiming a denial of counsel have used habeas corpus. The time limit on the other motions on which the claim of a denial of counsel might have been raised makes them unavail-

---

[219] 28 U.S.C.A. (1950), § 2255.

[220] See *Wheatley* v. *United States*, 198 F. 2d 325 (1952), where a convict alleged that counsel appointed at his arraignment had said that he had not practiced criminal law for fifteen years, and therefore a plea of guilty would be wise. In the absence of the convict, the trial judge scoffed at the assertion, and allowed the prisoner's former lawyer to deny this assertion in a very general way. It was held that a hearing was required.

[221] *Federal Rules of Criminal Procedure*, Rule 37(a)(2).

[222] *Ibid.*

able to prisoners who are not aware that they have been denied a right, or who learn of this denial too late. In addition, the writ of *coram nobis* has not enjoyed any great use within the legal profession, and courts have generally construed its scope in the most narrow fashion possible. There is little question but that the writ of habeas corpus has been abused.[223] The essence of the writ, of course, is that one who feels himself unjustly detained must allege facts which show that he is detained, where, by whom, and under what authority, and all the circumstances that support his contention that the restraint is illegal; and he must attach exhibits or portions of the record which will aid the court in reaching a judgment.[224] After service of the writ on the jailer an answer must be made, and if a factual issue is raised a hearing must be held with the prisoner present.[225]

The scope of the review of a trial available on habeas corpus is limited to an examination of the trial court's jurisdiction. It must be shown either that the trial court never had jurisdiction or, having had it originally, lost jurisdiction in the course of its procedure.[226] If an accused has been deprived of a constitutional right, such as the right to counsel, the trial court then loses jurisdiction because it has failed to complete the court.[227] Thus it can be seen that in the past the writ of habeas corpus has been the only remedy available to the great majority of defendants who have been deprived of their right to counsel.

Conclusions

It is obvious why there has been widespread confusion concerning the right to counsel even in the federal courts. And those who like to conceive of the law as a vast number of neatly labeled bundles will be less than satisfied by an explanation which can be little more than a classification of the elements included in the Sixth Amendment provision, but unfortunately

[223] See *Dorsey v. Gill*, 148 F. 2d 857 (1945), for a detailed account of the use and misuse of the writ.

[224] 28 U.S.C.A. (1950), §§ 2242, 2243.

[225] *Ibid.* See also, *Walker v. Johnston*, 312 U.S. 275 (1941).

[226] See cases cited in *Dorsey v. Gill*, 148 F. 2d 857 at 872, n. 91.

[227] See *Johnson v. Zerbst*, 304 U.S. 458 at 466–468 (1938).

decisions of the Supreme Court and the lower federal courts permit no other answer.

For a long period, as has been seen, there was a doctrine of what the "right to have the assistance of counsel" included, but there was no Supreme Court case which spread its meaning on the law books. It is clear that the federal courts never thought they were required by the Sixth Amendment to appoint counsel for indigent defendants at any time before *Johnson* v. *Zerbst,* in 1938. In that case the Supreme Court reversed a constitutional doctrine without overruling any of its own precedents. It proceeded to enunciate a doctrine which was new only in that the proposers of the counsel provision of the Sixth Amendment obviously intended nothing so broad, and in that a long-standing, though informally held, interpretation of the counsel provision was thrust aside. By judicial pronouncement the Supreme Court made the law conform to a practice or custom which had grown up in many of the federal district courts, and then enlarged its scope.

Once the new doctrine was laid down in *Johnson* v. *Zerbst,* the courts moved on to the application and exploration of the new rule. The most intense battle centered on the issue of what constituted a waiver of counsel. The answer to this apparently simple problem was bound to have tremendous consequences because thousands of federal defendants had pleaded guilty without benefit of counsel. If the Supreme Court had said that a formal waiver was essential in order for a conviction on a plea of guilty to stand, the federal district courts would have been overwhelmed with petitions for habeas corpus.

As it was, in *Walker* v. *Johnston* the Supreme Court laid down the requirement that an "intelligent and competent" waiver must be found, even where the plea was one of guilty. But this meant only that courts subjected to the new wave of petitions had to exercise some ingenuity to find an implied waiver in the older trial situations. With the rigid requirement laid down in 1945 in the Federal Rules of Criminal Procedure the chance of a trial proving defective because of a denial of counsel was materially lessened.

Another important problem involves the quality of representation.   It seems clear that where counsel is appointed by the court a lack of vigor, or a serious deviation from proper professional standards, in defending the accused may result in a reversal.   But with retained counsel it appears obvious that only the most shocking deficiencies will ever give rise to reversal. Again, when a conflict of interests is alleged as grounds for reversal where codefendants shared counsel, the courts are less generous than the Supreme Court decision in the Glasser case might indicate.

It can be concluded that defendants who plead not guilty and allege some defect in counsel have a better chance to convince a reviewing court of the truth of their story than defendants who plead guilty.   Although courts deny, in theory, that guilt or innocence is an influencing factor in deciding whether a defendant has been deprived of a constitutional right, in practice the contrary seems true.

Finally, two general weaknesses have been apparent, although there are signs that the one is substantially corrected. First, there has been evidence in the past of a lack of proper administrative supervision in the federal court system.   The new Rules and the addition of court stenographers show that a strong effort is under way to remedy this weakness.   Very few counsel cases should, therefore, arise in the future.   The inconclusive records and the lack of unified policy in the federal trial courts were until very recent times a shocking example of judicial ineptness in self-administration.   Secondly, there is a noticeable tendency of the lower courts, concerned directly with the trial cases, to whittle down the seemingly ironbound rules which the Supreme Court has set forth.

It is true that the Supreme Court opinions, and especially the statements of the minority in certain cases, have exhibited a rather perfectionist attitude toward procedure which is quite remote from what busy lower courts believe they can adhere to in practice.   No trial record ever appears in a perfect light when reviewed by men who are predisposed to think that justice probably was not done below and that every defendant, no matter how vicious his record, is in all likelihood a victim of social injustice.   But while the law must have the leavening quality of mercy, it seems a destructive and costly method of asserting that quality to overturn constantly the informed judgments of those who attempt to apply the law in the lower courts. The citizens at large will have more confidence in the federal court system when the members of the Supreme Court exhibit trust in the intelligence and the integrity of those who serve below.

CHAPTER IV

RIGHT TO COUNSEL AS INTERPRETED BY STATE COURTS

OBVIOUS difficulties face one who attempts to analyze any legal doctrine as applied in American state courts. State constitutions, statutes, and customs must be pressed into workable classifications without excessively distorting their individual meanings. The very bulk of the material and the richness of detail make brevity a goal more easily sought than achieved. To treat the state doctrines regarding the right to counsel one by one would prove excessively wearying and would draw out the narrative unduly. At the sacrifice, then, of comparing state with state, I shall try to depict the similarities and the differences in the state doctrines respecting this right under a number of arbitrarily selected headings.

The decisions of the highest state courts in applying state statutes and constitutional provisions, influenced recently to some extent by the due-process clause of the Fourteenth Amendment, have supplied the material for this study. Since in Chapter V, "Right to Counsel, Due Process, and the Federal Courts," an attempt will be made to analyze the decisions of the United States Supreme Court in reviewing certain state decisions, discussion of those state cases has been omitted here. It is hoped that this examination of state-court interpretations of state laws will give a reasonably accurate picture of the right to counsel as enjoyed in the states today and will furnish an adequate background for the treatment of the cases under the due-process clause of the Fourteenth Amendment in the chapter to follow.

STATE CONSTITUTIONAL PROVISIONS

All state constitutions save that of Virginia contain a provision of long standing respecting counsel for the accused in

criminal cases. In the wording of these clauses seven states follow the federal provision, and declare that the accused shall
have the assistance of counsel.[1] Nineteen use a form employed
in some of the early state constitutions, those of Massachusetts
and Pennsylvania in particular, to the effect that the accused
shall have a right to be heard by himself or by counsel, or
both. Eighteen adhere to an alternative form used in other
early state constitutions, such as those of New York and Delaware, and provide that an accused shall have the right to appear
and defend himself in person or by counsel, or both. North
Carolina, which grants the "right to the aid of counsel," Georgia,
which grants the "privilege and benefit of counsel," and Maryland, which grants the "right to be allowed counsel," are unique
in their phraseology. As will appear, an examination of the
decisions of the highest state courts tends to prove that variations in the phrasing of the constitutional provisions are of no
significance. What, then, is the scope of the state constitutional
right to counsel?

This simple question requires, unfortunately, a rather complex answer. The main difficulty arises from the existence of
statutes in all states treating certain aspects of the subject; hence
most state courts have not been forced to interpret an isolated
state constitutional provision. However, a number of states
have no statutes requiring the appointment of counsel in less-
than-capital cases, and a few state courts have boldly asserted
what the state constitutional right itself means.

Generally, the constitutional provisions have been construed
narrowly as giving to a defendant the right to appear in court
and defend himself with retained counsel, and this is true
whether the state guarantees the "right to be fully heard . . .
by himself or his counsel," as in Massachusetts,[2] or the right "to
appear and defend in person and by counsel," as in Illinois,[3]
or, in the third popular form, the right to the "assistance of
counsel," as in West Virginia.[4] Similarly, in Maryland, where

---

[1] See Appendix I for a listing of states in the various classifications.

[2] *Const.*, Pt. First, Art. XII; see *Commonwealth* v. *Millen*, 289 Mass. 441, 194
N.E. 463 (1935); *Allen* v. *Commonwealth*, 324 Mass. 558, 87 N.E. 2d 192 (1949).

[3] *Const.*, Art. II, § 9; see *People* v. *Cohen*, 402 Ill. 574, 85 N.E. 2d 19 (1949).

[4] *Const.*, Art. III, § 14; see *State* v. *Kellison*, 56 W. Va. 690, 47 S.E. 166
(1904).

the "right to be allowed counsel" is granted,[5] and in North Carolina, where the accused has the right "to have counsel for his defense," [6] the courts have described the state constitutional right as that of retaining and appearing with counsel in court.

The general acceptance of this narrow interpretation becomes apparent when one examines the court attitudes in each of the seven states in which the constitutional provision has been given a broad construction. The New York provision, "In any trial, in any court whatever the party accused shall be allowed to appear and defend in person and with counsel as in civil actions . . . ," [7] has been held to require that a defendant be advised of his right to have counsel appointed, and that the court appoint counsel for all indigents, apart from any statutory provision concerning counsel.[8] The broad sweep of the constitutional language, however, makes this conclusion almost inevitable. The California court has been even more decisive, for it has declared that the right to "appear and defend in person and with counsel" means that the accused must have counsel in every case unless he competently waives counsel.[9] Georgia courts have construed their provision extending the "privilege and benefit of counsel" to mean that every accused must have counsel unless he knowingly waives his right.[10] Indiana is the most outspoken of all states in reading into the right "to be heard by himself and counsel" a duty upon trial courts to advise the accused and to offer counsel in all cases [11] including appeals.[12]

[5] *Const.*, Art. 21, Decl. of Rights; see *Raymond v. State ex rel. Szydlowski* (Md.), 65 A. 2d 285 (1949).

[6] *Const.*, Art. I, § 11; see *State v. Hedgebeth*, 228 N.C. 259, 45 S.E. 2d 563 (1947).

[7] *Const.*, Art. I, Bill of Rights, § 6.

[8] *People ex rel. Moore v. Hunt*, 258 App. Div. 24, 16 N.Y.S. 2d 19 (1939); *People v. McLaughlin*, 291 N.Y. 480, 53 N.E. 2d 356 (1941); *People v. McAllister*, 87 N.Y.S. 2d 643, 194 Misc. 674 (1949).

[9] *Const.*, Art. I, Decl. of Rights, § 13; see *People v. Avilez*, 86 C.A. 2d 289, 194 P. 2d 829 (1948); *In re Jingles*, 27 C. 2d 496, 165 P. 2d 12 (1946). Bertram Edises has an excellent note on the early California situation in 21 *Calif. L. Rev.* (July, 1933), 484.

[10] *Const.*, Art. I, §§ 2-105; see *Jones v. State*, 57 Ga. App. 344, 195 S.E. 316 (1938); *Cook v. State*, 48 Ga. 224, 172 S.E. 471 (1933).

[11] *Const.*, Art. I, § 13; see *Batchelor v. State*, 189 Ind. 69, 125 N.E. 773 (1920); *Bielich v. State*, 189 Ind. 127, 126 N.E. 220 (1920).

[12] *State ex rel. White v. Hilgemann*, 218 Ind. 572, 34 N.E. 2d 129 (1941).

This has now been held applicable to misdemeanors.[13] The Nevada right to "appear and defend in person and with counsel" appears, at least in dicta, to be a broad though waivable right,[14] and New Mexico, with a similar provision, seems to have reached the same conclusion.[15] Nebraska, with the "right to appear and defend in person or by counsel," uses it as the basis of a broad right to counsel, but one which can be waived by a plea of guilty.[16]

With the exception, however, of these seven states in which the highest court has rested the right to counsel on a broad interpretation of the state constitutional provision, of the six states in which there are no decisions in which the issue is squarely raised,[17] and of Virginia, which has no constitutional guarantee,[18] it can be said that the constitutional provisions have either been construed narrowly as the right to appear with retained counsel, or have been ignored because of the existence of statutes concerning the subject. In the final analysis either of these situations reflects the courts' feeling that the constitutional right was designed to do one thing, to make it possible for an accused to retain legal assistance in a criminal prosecution where a felony is charged.[19] Or, expressed differently, there is evidence that in only seven states[20] has the state constitutional provision been given an interpretation comparable to that which

---

[13] *Bolkovac* v. *State*, 229 Ind. 294, 98 N.E. 2d 250 (1951).

[14] *Const.*, Art. I, § 8; see *State* v. *Crosby*, 24 Nev. 115, 50 P. 127 (1897); *State* v. *MacKinnon*, 41 Nev. 182, 168 P. 330 (1917).

[15] *Const.*, Art. II, § 14; see *State* v. *Garcia*, 47 N.M. 319, 142 P. 2d 552 (1943).

[16] *Const.*, Art. I, § 11; see *Alexander* v. *O'Grady*, 137 Neb. 645, 290 N.W. 718 (1940).

[17] Colorado, Connecticut, Delaware, Maine, New Hampshire, and New Jersey.

[18] Virginia has interpreted the due-process clause to include the right to retain counsel. See *Stonebreaker* v. *Smyth*, 187 Va. 250, 46 S.E. 2d 406 (1948). See also Chap. II, *supra*.

[19] Cases clearly illustrating this conception are: *Johnson* v. *Mayo*, 158 Fla. 264, 28 So. 2d 585 (1946); *People* v. *Cohen*, 402 Ill. 574, 85 N.E. 2d 19 (1949); *Luntz* v. *Commonwealth*, 287 Ky. 517, 154 S.W. 2d 548 (1941); *People* v. *Haddad*, 306 Mich. 556, 11 N.W. 2d 240 (1943); *In re Elliott*, 315 Mich. 662, 24 N.W. 2d 528 (1946); *Odom* v. *Mississippi*, 205 Miss. 572, 37 So. 2d 300 (1948); *Tenpenny* v. *State*, 151 Tenn. 669, 270 S.W. 989 (1924); *Ford* v. *State*, 114 Tex. Cr. 77, 24 S.W. 2d 55 (1930); *Smith* v. *State*, 51 Wis. 615, 8 N.W. 410 (1881).

[20] California, New York, Indiana, Georgia, Nevada, New Mexico, Nebraska.

the United States Supreme Court gave to the Sixth Amendment provision in *Johnson* v. *Zerbst*.[21]   It thus appears that Justice Roberts was clearly right when he stated in *Betts* v. *Brady* that the original state constitutional provisions were designed primarily to abrogate the old English rule which in effect denied the right to appear with counsel on felony charges, and not to create the broad duty of furnishing counsel in every state criminal trial.[22]

STATUTORY PROVISIONS [23]

It should be apparent already that most states have tried to solve the counsel problem by statute, rather than by constitutional interpretation.   Nothing more than certain crude groupings can be made of these statutory attempts to meet the question of counsel for indigent defendants.   There are eight states which have statutes requiring the trial court to appoint counsel for indigents in capital cases only.[24]   This is the least generous appointment provision.   Almost equally narrow is that of three states which have statutes requiring an appointment in capital cases and in cases where the possible punishment is imprisonment either for life or for a specified term of years.[25]   In the remaining thirty-seven states, however, there is some statutory basis for an appointment of counsel for indigent defendants in cases less than capital, although in three of these states the

[21] *Johnson* v. *Zerbst,* 304 U.S. 458, 58 S. Ct. 1019, 82 L. Ed. 1461 (1938).

[22] *Betts* v. *Brady,* 316 U.S. 455, 62 S. Ct. 1252, 86 L. Ed. 1595 at 1603 (1942).

[23] State statutory provisions relating to the office of public defender are treated later in this chapter.

[24] Pennsylvania: *Purdon's Pa. Stat. Ann.,* 1930, Tit. 19, § 783, is identical with the statute of 1718, 3 *Stats. at Large of Pa.* (Busch, 1896), 199.   Other statutes are found in Alabama: *Ala. Code,* 1940, Tit. 15, § 318; Florida: *Fla. Stat.,* 1941, § 909.21; Massachusetts: *Ann. Laws of Mass.,* 1933, c. 276, § 37A; Mississippi: *Miss. Code of 1942,* Tit. 11, § 2505; North Carolina: *Gen. Stat. of N. C.,* 1943, § 15–5; South Carolina: *Code of Laws,* 1942, § 980; Texas: *Vernon's Texas Stat.,* 1936, Code Crim. Proc., Tit. 7, c. 4, Arts. 491, 494.   Texas does require the appointment of counsel for indigents before they are permitted to waive a jury trial: *Vernon's Texas Stat.,* 1936, Code Crim. Proc., Tit. 7, c. 4, Art. 10a.   See *Wilson* v. *State* (Tex. Cr.), 252 S.W. 2d 197 (1952).   See Appendix II for a classification of state statutory provisions regarding counsel.

[25] Maine: *Rev. Stat. Me.,* 1944, c. 135, § 11, life imprisonment; Nebraska: *Rev. Stat.,* 1943, § 29–1803, life imprisonment; New Hampshire: *Rev. Laws,* 1942, c. 428, § 2, three years' imprisonment.

statute declares that the decision to appoint shall rest in the court's discretion.[26]

Thirty-four states, then, have statutes which seemingly place a duty on the trial court to appoint counsel for indigents in ordinary felony cases, but even this statement needs qualification. A threefold division can be made of the statutory provisions where an obligation to appoint counsel in felonies is set forth. First, there are those statutes which create a duty either to advise the accused of his right to have counsel appointed if he is indigent or to appoint counsel in every case unless the defendant objects. Twelve states have such provisions.[27] Second, there are those statutes which enjoin the trial court to appoint counsel upon a request by the accused or upon submission of an affidavit, but do not require that the accused be advised or informed of this right. Nine states have such provisions compelling the defendant to take the initiative.[28] Third, there are those statutes which do not in specific terms call either for advice concerning counsel, or for the appointment of counsel upon a request from the accused. The import is that counsel shall be appointed for all who need counsel, but more than one interpretation is possible. Thirteen states have such provisions [29]

[26] Rhode Island: *Gen. Laws R. I.*, 1938, c. 625, § 62, "may appoint whenever occasion may require"; Michigan: *Stat. Ann.*, 1938, Code Crim. Proc., § 28.1253, "when the president judge shall appoint"—this was interpreted as a discretionary power in *People* v. *Harris*, 226 Mich. 317, 253 N.W. 312 (1923); Maryland: *Md. Code*, 1939, Art. 26, § 7, "may appoint."

[27] Arizona: *Ariz. Code Ann.*, 1939, § 44–904; California: *Pen. Code of Cal.*, 1941, Pt. 2, Tit. 6, c. 1, § 987; Iowa: *Code of Iowa*, 1950, §§ 775.4–775.6; Kansas: *Kan. Gen. Stat.*, 1935, 1947 Supp., Art. 13, § 62–1304; Montana: *Rev. Code of Mont.*, 1935, c. 73, § 11886; Nevada: *Nev. Comp. Laws*, 1929, §§ 10883, 11357, 11358; New York: *McKinney's Consolidated Laws of N. Y.*, 1942, Code Crim. Proc., § 308; North Dakota: *N. D. Rev. Code*, 1943, § 29–1303; Oklahoma: *Okla. Stat.*, 1941, Tit. 22, § 464; Oregon: *Ore. Code*, 1943, § 26–803; Utah: *Utah Code Ann.*, 1943, Tit. 105, c. 22, § 12; Virginia: *Va. Code of 1950*, § 19–214.1.

[28] Arkansas: *Ark. Stat.*, 1947, § 43–1203; Illinois: *Smith-Hurd's Ill. Ann. Stat.*, 1935, c. 38, § 730; Indiana: *Burns' Ann. Ind. Stat.*, 1933, § 2–211; Kentucky: *Ky. Rev. Stat.*, 1946, § 455.010; Louisiana: *La. Code Crim. Laws & Proc.*, 1943, Tit. XIII, Art. 143; Minnesota: *Minn. Stai. Ann.*, 1949, § 611.07; Missouri: *Mo. Rev. Stat.*, 1939, c. 30, § 4003; Washington: *Rem. Rev. Stat.*, 1932, Tit. 14, § 2305; Wyoming: *Wyo. Comp. Stat.*, 1945, § 10–805.

[29] Colorado: *Colo. Stat. Ann.*, 1935, c. 48, § 471; Connecticut: *Gen. Stat. of Conn.*, 1949, Tit. 65, § 8796; Delaware: *Del. Rev. Code*, 1935, chaps. 114, 4306; Georgia: *Code of Ga. Ann.*, 1935, § 27–704; Idaho: *Idaho Code*, 1932, § 19–1513; New Mexico: *N. M. Stat.*, 1941, § 42–1102; Ohio: *Page's Gen. Code Ann.*, 1939,

creating an ambiguous position for the accused and the court.

It should be noted that in many states there is also some statutory provision which requires an examining magistrate or judge at the preliminary examination to advise the accused of his rights, and among these rights is the right to hire counsel, with the additional proviso that a message to any designated attorney must be delivered by a police officer.[30]   Such a statutory command does nothing more than insure that the accused is aware of his right to retain counsel, a right probably known by the great majority of individuals.   It indicates in a crude way the stage at which counsel can enter proceedings, but adds nothing to the solution of the problem of how far the state must go in protecting all accused, regardless of financial ability, by extending counsel for their defense.

This brief review indicates that there is no dominant pattern of state legislation on this subject.   All states have provisions guaranteeing counsel in capital cases, and the majority have statutes which make possible an appointment in noncapital cases, either upon request or affidavit or where the accused appears unable to procure his own counsel.   Unfortunately, only twelve states take the reasonable precaution of requiring that the accused be advised of his legal right to have counsel appointed, a measure which would prevent his loss of this important right through ignorance.   Finally, none of the statutory schemes is so clear and complete that all, or even most, of the counsel

---

Crim. Proc., § 13439–2; South Dakota: *S. D. Code*, 1939, Jud. Proc. Crim., §§ 34.1401, 34.1901; Tennessee: *Williams' Tenn. Code*, 1934, Tit. IV, § 11733; Vermont: *Vt. Stat. Rev.*, 1947, Tit. 9, § 2397; West Virginia: *Code*, 1943, c. 62, § 6190; Wisconsin: *Wis. Stat.*, 1947, § 357.26; New Jersey: *N. J. Rev. Stat.*, 1937, §§ 190–2, 190–3.

[30] California: *Const.*, Art. 1, Decl. of Rights, § 8; Florida: *Fla. Stat.*, 1941, § 902.03; Idaho: *Idaho Code*, 1932, § 19–802; Iowa: *Code of Iowa*, 1946, § 761.1; Kansas: *Kan. Gen. Stat.*, 1935, 1947 Supp., Art. 13, § 62–1304; Kentucky: *Ky. Rev. Stat.*, 1948, § 455.010; Minnesota: *Minn. Stat. Ann.*, 1947, § 630.10; Missouri: *Mo. Rev. Stat.*, 1939, c. 30, § 3867; Nevada: *Nev. Comp. Laws*, 1929, §§ 10883, 11357, 11358; New Hampshire: *Rev. Laws*, 1942, c. 423, § 7; New Mexico: *N. M. Stat.*, 1941, § 42–301; New York: *McKinney's Consolidated Laws of N. Y.*, 1942, Code Crim. Proc., § 188; North Carolina: *Gen. Stat. of N. C.*, 1943, §15–4; North Dakota: *N. D. Rev. Code*, 1943, §§ 29–0701, 29–0704; Ohio: *Page's Ohio Gen. Code Ann.*, 1939, § 13422–16; Oklahoma: *Okla. Stat.*, 1941, Tit. 22, § 251; South Dakota: *S. D. Code*, 1939, Jud. Proc. Crim., § 34.1401; Tennessee: *Williams' Tenn. Code*, 1934, Tit. IV, §§ 11547, 11548; Texas: *Vernon's Texas Stat.*, 1936, Tit. 5, c. 3, Art. 245; Utah: *Utah Code Ann.*, 1943, Tit. 105, c. 15, §§ 1, 2.

problems can be resolved from a reading of a statute. It will be seen later how courts dealing with essentially similar statutes have reached strikingly opposed conclusions.

COURT RULES

It would be virtually impossible to survey American court rules in their infinite variety. What can be pointed out, however, is that the rule-making power of the courts has been utilized in some instances to fill in the gaps in the statutes, or to clarify statutory rules. Moreover, there has been a trend toward the wider use of the rule-making power by those states whose highest-court decisions have been criticized by the United States Supreme Court.

Examples of court rules on the local, or trial, level are to be found in certain circuits in Michigan, dealing with such subjects as:

1. The power in the judge to appoint other counsel when counsel for the defense is not present; [31]
2. The scale of payment for attorneys who serve by appointment; [32]
3. The investigation by the prosecuting attorney of applications based on poverty; [33]
4. A list of attorneys willing to accept appointment.[34]

These and similar provisions were found in a minority of Michigan circuit courts; they were designed to clarify certain vague features of the old Michigan statute which allowed judges to appoint counsel as a matter of discretion upon a request.

As a result of the rebuke received in the De Meerleer case [35] in 1946, the Michigan Supreme Court adopted a new rule. In essence, it altered the Michigan procedure by directing the trial court upon arraignment of the accused to take positive steps, i.e., "to advise the accused that he is entitled . . . to have counsel, and that in case he is financially unable to provide counsel

---

[31] Recorder's Court, Detroit, 1939, Rule 1.
[32] *Ibid.*, Rule 31; Third Circuit Court (Wayne), Rule 26.
[33] Twenty-second Circuit Court Rule (unnumbered).
[34] Sixteenth Circuit Court, Rule 5, § 1.
[35] *People* v. *De Meerleer*, 313 Mich. 548, 21 N.W. 2d 849 (1946); *De Meerleer* v. *Michigan*, 329 U.S. 663, 67 S. Ct. 596, 91 L. Ed. 584 (1947).

the court will, if accused so requests, appoint counsel for him." [36]
In addition, the new rule requires that the defendant who wishes
to retain counsel be given sufficient time to do so; it urges
caution on the court when accepting a plea of guilty, and orders
trial courts to make a full record of all the proceedings regarding counsel.[37]

The Illinois Supreme Court, after receiving severe criticism
from three members of the United States Supreme Court in the
Marino case,[38] decided to end the uncertainty which had surrounded attempts to assert the right to counsel in that state,
whose statute provided for appointment on request.   In 1948
it promulgated a rule that the trial court before receiving a
plea must "advise the accused he has a right to be defended by
counsel.   If he desires counsel and states under oath he is unable
to employ such counsel, the court shall appoint competent counsel to represent him." [39]   The rule also forbids a waiver of
counsel by an accused under eighteen or by one who, in the
opinion of the court, is incapable of understanding his position
and the consequences of his decision.[40]

Other states which have used the rule-making power are
Missouri, which reaffirmed its statutory provision that trial
courts should appoint counsel upon request and a showing of
inability to employ counsel,[41] and West Virginia, which strengthened the right to counsel through a rule promulgated in 1938
by its Supreme Court to the effect that, "if the defendant has
no counsel, nor means to employ one, the court shall assign
counsel . . . ." [42]   This is a great improvement over the in-
explicit West Virginia statutory provision which had declared
that "the accused shall be allowed counsel if he desire it, to assist him in his defense." [43]   Finally, the New Jersey Supreme
Court utilized its extensive rule-making power to adopt a meas-

[36] Michigan Court Rules, Rule 35-A, § 1.
[37] *Ibid.*, §§ 2, 3.
[38] *Marino* v. *Ragen*, 332 U.S. 561 at 563, 68 S. Ct. 240, 92 L. Ed. 170 (1947).
[39] Ill. Sup. Ct. Rules of Prac. and Proc., Rule 27-A, 400 Ill. (1948).
[40] *Ibid.*
[41] Mo. Sup. Ct. Rules, 1945, 352 Mo. XXV, Rule 5, 5.07.
[42] Rules of Proc. for Tr. Cts., App., *W. Va. Code,* 1949, p. 2591, Rule IV(a).
[43] *W. Va. Code,* 1943, c. 62, § 6190.

ure comparable to Federal Rule 44: "If the defendant appears in court without counsel, the court shall advise him of his right to counsel and assign counsel to represent him at the trial unless he elects to proceed without counsel or is able to obtain counsel." [44]

An additional factor, although one of undetermined importance, is a rule found in the code of ethics of several of the state bar associations to the effect that "a lawyer assigned as counsel for an indigent prisoner ought not to be excused for any trivial reason, and should always exert his best efforts in his behalf." [45] Those states which do not have this specific canon have, by a general rule, adopted all of the American Bar Association canons.[46]

While it is obvious that the rule-making power of the courts has not been utilized to the extent possible or desirable, it can be predicted that this medium will be used more frequently as its advantages become apparent. It is increasingly recognized that judicial procedure can be best regulated by means of rules promulgated by the courts. It is an efficient and flexible technique, far superior to the slow, haphazard, and rigid statutory attack on the problems of administration. As the volume of litigation increases, more states will undoubtedly resort to this modern way of solving counsel and other procedural difficulties.

RIGHT TO RETAIN COUNSEL AND RIGHT TO DEFEND IN PERSON

Perhaps the most certain conclusion which can be drawn is that under the constitutional provision regarding counsel in forty-seven states and the due-process clause of the Virginia constitution, one has the right to retain counsel and to appear in court with him. If the Virginia interpretation of due process had been followed, other states might have reached the same conclusion. With specific constitutional provisions available,

---

[44] N. J. Sup. Ct. Rules, Super. and Co. Cts. (1948), Rule 2:12–1. This has been replaced by the more detailed Rule 1:2–31, adopted Jan. 1, 1953. The import is unchanged.

[45] 164 Kan. xii, which follows the 1908 American Bar Association rule.

[46] E.g., Sup. Ct. Wyo. Rules, Rule 19.

however, there was no occasion to apply the test of due process to the right to counsel.[47]

It is fair to suggest from the paucity of cases alleging ignorance of this right that defendants know they are legally entitled to retain and appear with counsel if they are able to pay for such service.[48] Nevertheless, problems inevitably emerge, and a brief discussion of the situations in which the defendant claims he was deprived of the right to retain counsel is not unwarranted.

Perhaps the chief source of difficulty appears in cases where the defendant who allegedly is able to hire counsel claims that he was not given fair opportunity to find and retain it. Obviously, the search for counsel must have limits, and there is no right to endless continuances while the defendant shops around for an attorney who will charge him little or nothing.[49] But it has been held error if a retained counsel shows good cause for his inability to appear and the court, in spite of such a showing, appoints counsel.[50] Similarly, a peremptory assignment of counsel by an impatient judge is a denial of the right to retain one's own counsel.[51]

[47] Representative cases are: *Walker* v. *State,* 194 Ga. 727, 22 S.E. 2d 462 (1942); *People* v. *Cohen,* 402 Ill. 574, 85 N.E. 2d 19 (1949); *People* v. *McLaughlin,* 291 N.Y. 480, 53 N.E. 2d 356 (1941); *Addyston* v. *Liddle,* 54 Ohio App. 323, 6 N.E. 2d 877 (1935); *Ford* v. *State,* 114 Tex. Cr. 77, 24 S.W. 2d 55 (1930). Varying statutory schemes are in effect in these jurisdictions. The Virginia right is outlined in *Stonebreaker* v. *Smyth,* 187 Va. 250, 46 S.E. 2d 406 (1948).

[48] Wide newspaper publicity given to the trials of wealthy murderers has stressed the skill of the lawyers retained at great cost. One of the folk beliefs is the notion that if you have sufficient means to hire a brilliant lawyer, no jury will convict. The charitable endeavors of the bar, however, have never struck public consciousness with such force as have those of the medical profession.

[49] See *People* v. *Adamson,* 34 C. 2d 320, 210 P. 2d 13 (1949), where defendant had "rejected" an appointed counsel.

[50] See *People* v. *Gordon,* 262 App. Div. 534, 30 N.Y.S. 2d 625 (1941), where the lack of good sense in the trial judge is strongly condemned.

[51] When a full record exists, the trial judge's state of mind becomes rather clear. At 12:30 P.M., in one case, the defendant said that he was forced to get a new lawyer. At 2:00 P.M. he had not yet succeeded, whereupon the judge said, "You are going to get a lawyer," and appointed one over the defendant's protests. See *People* v. *McLaughlin,* 291 N.Y. 480 at 482, 53 N.E. 2d 356 (1941). In a Pennsylvania case, *Commonwealth* v. *Strada,* 171 Pa. Super. 358, 90 A. 2d 335 (1952), a conviction was reversed where the trial judge permitted retained counsel to withdraw in the absence of the defendant, and then refused to grant a continuance so that the defendant could find new counsel. His offer to appoint counsel was held immaterial.

Although it is difficult to generalize about continuances, it can be said that the refusal to grant the first request for a continuance in order to get counsel is probably error, but that each request after the first can be turned down in the discretion of the judge.[52] Moreover, if counsel has been retained, he must indicate by compliance with the requisite forms that he is going to appear, and a failure to show his relationship to the defendant in the customary way will defeat his client's claim to counsel.[53] Yet even where retained counsel admitted his fault in not appearing upon the return of the indictment, it was held error for the trial court to deny a motion for continuance.[54]

Courts have rightly insisted that the defendant must aid his own cause, and any lack of interest or diligence by the defendant will justify the court in assuming that he is not going to retain counsel.[55] It is noteworthy that defendants who obviously know of their right to hire counsel, who gain continuances from the court in order to do so, and who probably have the means to pay for counsel, frequently receive the benefit of appointed counsel. Perhaps this results from the jogging of the judicial mind by so much talk about the problem. Or is it due to the fear that a higher court might reverse if a further continuance were denied and no counsel appointed?

One complaint sometimes made is that the proceeding involving the defendant was carried out with such dispatch that there was no opportunity to hire counsel.[56] But if retained counsel has notice, and the time allowed him is not unreasonably short, his failure to appear is his own fault.[57] Similarly, if the defendant has the unquestioned ability to hire counsel, his neg-

---

[52] *Addyston* v. *Liddle,* 54 Ohio App. 323, 6 N.E. 2d 877 (1935). If the defendant has been in jail with little opportunity to retain counsel, his request for a continuance is more reasonable. See *Zasada* v. *State,* 19 N. J. Super. 589, 89 A. 2d 45 (1952).

[53] See *Commonwealth* v. *Portner,* 92 Pa. Super. 48 (1927), where the attorney failed to file an appearance or a retainer, and did not communicate with his client.

[54] *Chenault* v. *Commonwealth,* 282 Ky. 453, 138 S.W. 2d 969 (1940).

[55] See *State* v. *Williams,* 162 La. 590, 110 So. 766 (1926), where a patient court appointed three attorneys for a vacillating defendant.

[56] See *People* v. *Avilez,* 86 C.A. 2d 289, 194 P. 2d 829 (1948), where a police inspector misinformed the attorney, who appeared when the case was concluded; see also *People* v. *Napthaly,* 105 C. 641, 39 P. 29 (1895).

[57] *Ford* v. *State,* 114 Tex. Cr. 77, 24 S.W. 2d 55 (1930).

lect either to request a continuance or to take any action which shows an intention to hire counsel absolves the court from any duty to inquire.[58]   Perhaps an extreme example of how far courts will go in insisting that a man who can pay for counsel must do so is a Texas case where an appointed attorney, after being adjudged in contempt by the appointing court for his refusal to serve, was vindicated by the highest court on the theory that the appointment was void since the defendant had the wherewithal to pay for counsel.[59]

Occasionally a court shows little interest in affording a defendant an opportunity to hire counsel.   In one instance a Negro charged with the murder of a white officer had an attorney who was ready to serve if a one-week continuance were granted. The judge denied the request after he and the prosecutor agreed that delay would not be feasible because "the people" would be incensed and would never in the future allow other Negroes to come to trial if the request were granted.[60]   If the state, on the other hand, restricts the freedom of communication of the defendant so that he is unable to contact counsel or to tell his family to retain counsel, such action is error and the conviction is reversible.[61]   A conviction was also reversed in a case where the trial court, without any explanation, refused to permit the appearance of retained counsel after the court had appointed the public defender.[62]

A different problem may arise where the defendant wishes to retain an out-of-state attorney.   Normally such a request is granted and the "foreign" attorney is admitted *pro hac vice.* Nevertheless, like the attorneys of the home state, he is subject to

[58] *McGhee* v. *State,* 71 Ga. App. 52, 30 S.E. 2d 54 (1944); *Sweet* v. *State,* 226 Ind. 556, 81 N.E. 2d 679 (1948); *Holland* v. *Commonwealth,* 241 Ky. 813, 45 S.W. 2d 476 (1932); *State* v. *Weston* (Mo.), 202 S.W. 2d 50 (1947); *State* v. *Gomez,* 89 Vt. 490, 96 A. 190 (1915); *Watkins* v. *Commonwealth,* 174 Va. 518, 6 S.E. 2d 670 (1940).

[59] *Ex parte Mays,* 152 Tex. Cr. 172, 212 S.W. 2d 164 (1948).

[60] *Ball* v. *State,* 252 Ala. 686, 42 So. 2d 626 (1949). The attorney's request does not seem unreasonable, since one week added to the thirty days which had elapsed between arrest and trial would hardly have mattered except for the community attitude. It is an excellent illustration of the influence of community feeling on judicial administration, even when that feeling is not expressed in overt action.

[61] *Walker* v. *State,* 194 Ga. 727, 22 S.E. 2d 462 (1942).

[62] *People* v. *Cohen,* 402 Ill. 574, 85 N.E. 2d 19 (1949).

the control and discipline of the local court.   A federal decision, though not conclusive, intimates that an out-of-state attorney should not be excluded from a state trial except after hearing and for sufficient cause.[63]   This, it may be remarked, is no greater protection for the accused than he would receive if a native attorney were retained.   It does suggest that one may select widely, and then demand a "reasonable" attitude by the court toward one's counsel.

Finally there are a few cases where defendants have chosen to defend themselves and have later claimed that counsel should have been imposed on them, or that errors occurred during trial to which no objection was made because the defendant was unfamiliar with the law.   Such belated modesty is of no avail unless the defendants are mentally incompetent or not *sui juris*. Reasonably enough, courts have asserted that they are under no duty to force counsel on defendants, that the state constitution guarantees the right to defend in person, and that once a defendant chooses to defend himself he is responsible for his defense.[64]   This is so even in a capital case.[65]

In substance, then, one has a right to retain counsel which courts are usually alert to protect.   The number of cases involving alleged limitations on the right is small because almost all defendants with the ability to pay know that they may retain counsel.   Most cases on this subject result from hasty action by the courts in forcing appointed counsel on the defendant or in failing to give him sufficient time to obtain counsel.   It is rather ironic that with so many courts reluctant to appoint counsel for indigents, others impose counsel prematurely, but surely this is one of the less serious defects which emerges from a study of the right to counsel.

[63] *Cooper* v. *Hutchinson*, 184 F. 2d 119 (1950). This was one incident in the prolonged "Trenton Six" case. The trial judge became incensed with the out-of-court speeches made by O. John Rogge, of New York, and two of his colleagues.

[64] *Dietz* v. *State*, 149 Wis. 462, 136 N.W. 166 (1912); *Woods* v. *State*, 152 Tex. Cr. 525, 215 S.W. 2d 334 (1948). In Georgia a defendant has a right to participate with appointed or retained counsel. See *Loomis* v. *State*, 78 Ga. App. 153, 51 S.E. 2d 13 (1948).

[65] In *People* v. *Chessman* (Cal.), 238 P. 2d 1001 (1952), the defendant had dismissed two private counsel and the public defender before assuming his own defense.

Right to Appointed Counsel in the Absence of Statutory or Constitutional Requirement

Although all states provide for the appointment of counsel where necessary in capital cases, eight states, Pennsylvania, Massachusetts, Alabama, Florida, North Carolina, Mississippi, South Carolina, and Texas, have no statute which applies to noncapital cases,[66] and their courts do not interpret the constitutional provision to include the right to appoint counsel in less-than-capital cases. Maryland has a statute allowing appointment at the judge's discretion. In these states the trial courts are thus under no duty to appoint, whether on request or without request, and a trial may proceed with an undefended accused.[67]

Since the question of whether this treatment of the accused conforms to the due-process requirements of the Fourteenth Amendment will be examined in Chapter V, "Right to Counsel, Due Process, and the Federal Courts," all that need be said here is that the Fourteenth Amendment does place a limitation on state action in many instances, that the number of petitions to the Supreme Court based on alleged denial of the right to counsel has increased, and that a generally unsatisfactory situation exists where no state constitutional or statutory provision applies to noncapital cases.

Duty to Advise Defendants of Their Right to Counsel

WHERE STATUTES DO NOT REQUIRE ADVICE AS TO COUNSEL

If a state specifies by statute or constitutional provision that a defendant can "appear by counsel," and further stipulates that an indigent shall have counsel appointed by the court or, in a different phraseology, appointed at his request, the question remains whether or not the trial court should, or must, as a matter of law, advise the accused of this right, or offer to appoint counsel of its own volition.

The answer to the question would seemingly rest on the answer to a more fundamental question, Should a court presume that every defendant is familiar with his rights? Since

[66] See p. 84 *supra*, n. 24.

[67] *Commonwealth ex rel. Berry* v. *Ashe,* 167 Pa. Super. 171, 74 A. 2d 727 (1950); *State ex rel. Loane* v. *Warden* (Md.), 75 A. 2d 772 (1950).

one of the axioms of Anglo-American jurisprudence is that ignorance of the law is no defense, there is a plausible note in the attitude which has been expressed in the past by the Illinois Supreme Court, and implied by other state courts, that the accused is presumed to know of his rights in respect to counsel and therefore it is not necessary for the court to advise him. The accused, under this view, must request appointment or state on oath his inability to retain counsel as required by statute.[68] In a similar vein, the Florida Supreme Court in interpreting a statutory provision that the trial court should allow counsel "if he [accused] desires it" also concluded that the defendant must speak up and express his desire for counsel, and that no duty to advise him existed under the statute.[69]

In sharp contrast to the old Illinois and the present Florida views is that of the Louisiana court, which, without a statute requiring advice, has held that it is the duty of a trial court to find out why an accused appears without counsel in a felony case and to appoint one if the defendant desires counsel and is indigent.[70]   Of the same import are the decisions of the Indiana Supreme Court, which, in the absence of a statute requiring advice, has declared that a part of the broad constitutional right to counsel is the right to be advised, and that courts cannot waive the right to counsel for indigent defendants, but rather must ascertain the defendant's wishes in all cases where a defendant charged with any criminal offense appears without counsel.[71]   Both courts emphasize that the purpose of the statutory enactment is to extend practical assistance to defendants.

A state court which has changed its view on the necessity of advising defendants is that of Kentucky.   Until 1948 it had held that the statute which required an appointment upon request permitted the trial court to remain silent.[72]   But the Kentucky Supreme Court, apparently impressed with the difficulties which state proceedings were experiencing upon review by the United States Supreme Court, decided in 1948 that henceforth the ac-

---

[68] *People* v. *Bernovich,* 391 Ill. 141, 62 N.E. 2d 691 (1945).
[69] *Weatherford* v. *State,* 76 Fla. 219, 79 So. 680 (1918).
[70] *State* v. *Youchunas,* 187 La. 281, 174 So. 356 (1937).
[71] *Bielich* v. *State,* 189 Ind. 127, 126 N.E. 220 (1920); *Cassidy* v. *State,* 201 Ind. 311, 168 N.E. 18 (1929); *Harris* v. *State,* 203 Ind. 505, 181 N.E. 33 (1932).
[72] *Moore* v. *Commonwealth,* 298 Ky. 14, 181 S.W. 2d 413 (1944).

cused must be informed of his right to counsel as part of a fair trial.[73]

Thus in states which have no statutory provision explicitly calling for advice a division of opinion exists concerning the necessity for advice. There is little doubt that many judges have told defendants of their rights concerning counsel, even though such advice was not required by law. One suspects that in small communities and rural areas there has been, and is, a tendency to insure representation for all defendants. But the volume of city criminal business, the prevalence of "deals" between prosecutor and accused, and the persistent interest of the prosecution in obtaining "guilty" pleas, all tend to diminish concern for defendants' representation in urban areas.

The question still remains, Which practice is correct? Should advice be given even though not required by statute, or should the typical statute which demands appointment upon request or if the defendant is indigent be construed as imposing a duty on the defendant to take the initiative by asking for the aid of appointed counsel? The theory of the Louisiana, Kentucky, and Indiana courts that advice should be given is obviously more desirable in logic, in fairness, and in practical efficiency. Let us consider these three aspects in turn.

It is not logical to assume that defendants know their procedural rights as they are presumed to know the substantive law in general. Actions which are *mala in se* are recognized by virtually all normal persons, and actions which are *mala prohibita* become known to most of those strongly affected by the pertinent statutes.[74] Certainly, the first offender, suffering under the shock of finding himself afoul of the law and awed by the strange and rather forbidding atmosphere of the typical courtroom, feels little inquisitiveness when confronting the court. To the rejoinder that anyone knows that a lawyer should be retained as soon as one is in legal trouble, the counter can be made that if one is indigent the prospect of a lawyer's fee eliminates such a thought quickly.

It can be argued persuasively that matters of procedure and

---

[73] *Gholson* v. *Commonwealth*, 308 Ky. 82, 212 S.W. 2d 537 (1948).

[74] Businessmen, for example, through special "services" and retained lawyers keep abreast of the numerous tax- and administrative-law changes.

of the rights which an individual may claim at the hands of the judicial system can and should be treated differently from matters of substantive law. A legal system in which the state would have to prove that the accused was aware of the substantive rule which he had supposedly broken, and had willfully transgressed it, would either be a miserable failure or would require state-sponsored compulsory legal education for all of its citizens in order that none could claim ignorance. The security of the state and the vital interests which its legal system is designed to protect demand that each citizen be treated as though he were cognizant of the substantive legal rules applicable to his conduct. But the rights of individuals within the maze of legal procedure need not rest on such an assumption. Of what danger to the efficient functioning of our legal system is the presumption that most men do not know of their rights within the courtroom? The defendant with retained counsel will have his rights protected regardless of his personal ignorance, but the defendant without counsel can learn of his rights only by means of brief but accurate instructions from the court.

Inconclusive as this sort of speculation may be, it seems reasonable to assume that the intention in the legislative mind when statutes were enacted providing for the appointment of counsel for indigents was not to make possible a cat-and-mouse game between court and accused, but to extend the right to have counsel to all defendants who needed and were without counsel. The right should create a rough equality among defendants, so that a conviction in any case would result from the state's success in bearing the burden of proof after the competent presentation of the defense, rather than from a default of the defense due to the defendant's ignorance of his right. The final logical difficulty inherent in the assumption that all know the law in respect to counsel is the contradiction afforded by the great number of defendants who allege that they did not know it. Even assuming that a great many claims are unsubstantial, it is still rather difficult to see why in so many cases men would fail to ask for counsel if they knew that counsel would be appointed to serve without cost.

In the matter of fairness, it is hard to defend the silence of a trial court when a defendant appears without counsel. To paraphrase a deservedly famous phrase of George Orwell, "All defendants are equal, but some defendants are more equal than others." [75]   The defendant who is ignorant of his rights is not treated like the more fortunate defendant who "knows" his rights or like the even more fortunate defendant who simply hires a competent lawyer.   If this difference is deemed proper, it suggests that lawyers, legal scholars, and wealthy citizens enjoy rights at law not shared by other citizens.

As a practical matter, state courts which refuse to advise defendants are acting unwisely in view of the holding of the United States Supreme Court that even in a state which requires a request there are some defendants who have characteristics which make the appointment of counsel without request essential.[76] It seems almost certain that a youthful or ignorant defendant who has not been advised can successfully seek a reversal of his conviction because he is able to rebut the presumption that he knew his rights.   Undoubtedly there is confusion today.   Missouri, which has a statute requiring a request before appointment, apparently advises and offers counsel.[77]   Pennsylvania, with no statute stipulating appointment in less-than-capital cases, has developed a practice, at least in some counties, of appointing upon request in less-than-capital cases, and, in other counties, of advising and offering counsel.[78]   Wherever there is a right to appointed counsel today, trial courts should take the next step and advise defendants of the right.   It requires of judge and state nothing which the legislature has not sanctioned; it means everything to the indigent defendant.

WHERE STATUTES REQUIRE ADVICE AS TO COUNSEL OR OFFER OF COUNSEL

Seemingly, there would be little chance for error if a statute required advice or an offer to appoint counsel; yet errors do occur.   Failure to comply with a court rule requiring advice is error.[79]   Frequently the error consists in neglecting to place the

[75] It was of certain pigs on a communistic animal farm that the original remark was made.

[76] See Chap. V, *infra.*

[77] *State* v. *Medley,* 353 Mo. 925, 185 S.W. 2d 633 (1945).

[78] *Commonwealth* v. *Valerio,* 118 Pa. Super. 34, 178 A. 509 (1935).

[79] *State* v. *Griffith,* 14 N. J. Super. 77, 81 A. 2d 382 (1951).

fact of offer or advice in the trial record. If the record does not show an offer, several alternatives are available. Some courts have solved the matter, to their own satisfaction at least, by allowing the state to present evidence outside the record concerning events which should have been narrated in the record. In order to show advice or an offer of counsel, testimony of judges, court attachés, detectives, chiefs of police, policemen, county attorneys, and, on occasion, spectators has been introduced.[80] But if the state fails in its proof of facts outside the record where the record is silent, that failure will result in a remand and a new trial.[81]

New York's statute requiring advice on arraignment has generally been interpreted strictly against the state, and silence on the record is construed as a denial in most instances.[82] But in one case where a defendant who had been found guilty as an offender for the fourth time sought to reverse two of the previous convictions (obtained after pleas of guilty six and thirteen years earlier) on the ground that he had not been advised, the court held that the silent record was not enough, even when coupled with the defendant's testimony, because of laches—his excessive delay in seeking the remedy.[83] In the jurisdictions which do not construe the defective record against the state, if the defendant's story of what occurred is contradicted by other witnesses the court will usually declare that the claimant has not overcome the presumption of regularity which attaches to a court judgment, since the court has presumably advised as the statute required.[84]

An even heavier burden rests on a claimant where the trial record contains a notation that defendant was advised and he alleges improper or insufficient advice. In one case in which

---

[80] *Fairce* v. *Amrine*, 154 Kan. 618, 121 P. 2d 256 (1942); *Crisp* v. *Hudspeth*, 162 Kan. 567, 178 P. 2d 228 (1947).

[81] *Brandt* v. *Hudspeth*, 162 Kan. 601, 178 P. 2d 224 (1947).

[82] See *People* v. *Sedlak*, 53 N.Y.S. 2d 51 (1944); *People ex rel. Moore* v. *Hunt*, 258 App. Div. 24, 16 N.Y.S. 2d 19 (1939); *People* v. *Koch*, 299 N.Y. 378, 87 N.E. 2d 417 (1949). The same result has been reached in Indiana: *Campbell* v. *State* 229 Ind. 198, 96 N.E. 2d 876 (1951).

[83] *People* v. *Crispell*, 60 N.Y.S. 2d 85, 185 Misc. 800 (1945). This lower-court decision seems to run counter to the prevailing New York attitude.

[84] *Ex parte Smith*, 85 Okla. Cr. 299, 187 P. 2d 1003 (1947); *Ex parte Story*, 88 Okla. Cr. 358, 203 P. 2d 474 (1949).

the judge said to the defendant, "You have the right to have counsel to aid you. If you haven't counsel, we will appoint counsel for you," and the defendant refused and later asserted that the judge failed to tell him that the promised appointment would cost him nothing, his claim was denied as unreasonable.[85]

Presumably, if the record contains a reference that the defendant "waived counsel" a reviewing court may conclude safely that the defendant was advised.[86] But there have been situations where the record noted a waiver and yet on appeal the reviewing court found that the defendant had not been adequately informed; although it is probable that if these cases had been brought up on habeas corpus, rather than appeal, the result would have been different.[87] From these examples it follows that the court, upon arraignment, and the magistrate, at the preliminary examination, are wise if they place the full details of their advice to the defendant in the record. In fact, the more completely detailed the report about the counsel discussion, the less likelihood there is that the defendant's later claims will be believed.[88]

What should be the result when a statute requires that advice be given and yet the record fails to show compliance? First, courts can prevent the problem's arising by adopting a rule that the judge-defendant discussion must appear in the record of each case.[89] After a given date set by court rule or statute, the failure of a record to show essential facts should in itself result in a reversal and a new trial, whether the matter is raised by appeal, habeas corpus, *coram nobis,* or arrest of judgment, or on motion for a new trial, or by any other means. Only in this way will courts learn to comply with the legislative assertion

[85] *State* v. *Cowan,* 25 Wash. 2d 341, 170 P. 2d 653 (1946).

[86] *State* v. *Scofield,* 129 Wash. 295, 224 P. 941 (1924); *State* v. *Fowler,* 59 Mont. 346, 197 P. 847 (1921); *State* v. *Mewhinney,* 43 Utah 135, 134 P. 632 (1913).

[87] *State* v. *Tennyson,* 73 N.D. 262, 14 N.W. 2d 168 (1944); *State* v. *Sewell,* 69 S.D. 494, 12 N.W. 2d 198 (1943). See also *State* v. *Lawrence,* 70 Idaho 422, 220 P. 2d 380 (1950), where four drunken Indians were allowed to plead guilty to grand larceny involving one sheep.

[88] See *State* v. *Calkins,* 63 Idaho 314, 120 P. 2d 253 (1941), and *State* v. *Butchek,* 121 Ore. 141, 253 P. 367 (1927), for illustrations of the value of a complete narrative.

[89] Fed. Rule 44, Ill. Rule 27–A, Mich. Rule 35–A, N.J. Rule 2:12–1 are examples of proper rules.

that indigents have a right to counsel. Such action will have the obvious and desirable effect of diminishing what is at present an avalanche of proceedings based on the alleged earlier failure to advise defendants. Courts which have never been reluctant to enforce formal requirements against litigants should learn from their own teaching.

With the older case situations, there is no good expedient but to follow the present practice of scrutinizing all the allegations and evidence in each case, and to attempt to do justice when a meritorious claim is pressed. The alternative, a remand for a new trial in every case in which the record does not show full advice, would force society to pay a rather high price for the carelessness, or the poor administrative technique, of our courts. And since the doctrines relating to the expanded right to appointed counsel are relatively modern, there is something to be said in defense of the courts' failures to act more efficiently in the past. But there is no excuse for the highest state courts not to act now so as to avoid future difficulties.

Failure to Request Counsel Where Statute Requires

If the trial record fails to show a request by the defendant that the court appoint counsel and the statute calls for appointment on request, it is most difficult for the petitioner to urge successfully a denial of counsel. The simple theory upon which the state courts proceed is that if a defendant fails to request counsel, it must of necessity mean that he does not wish the aid of counsel, and since the statute requires a request, the lack of compliance indicates that the defendant does not want to claim his privilege. These courts act on the assumption that there is no implied duty upon the courts to inform the accused of his rights so that he may request or not as he chooses.[90] In other

[90] *James* v. *State,* 27 Wyo. 378, 196 P. 1045 (1921); *State* v. *Kellison,* 56 W. Va. 690, 47 S.E. 166 (1904); *Commonwealth ex rel. Geisel* v. *Ashe,* 165 Pa. Super. 41, 68 A. 2d 360 (1949); *Alexander* v. *O'Grady,* 137 Neb. 645, 290 N.W. 718 (1940); *Skiba* v. *Kaiser,* 352 Mo. 424, 178 S.W. 2d 373 (1944); *Quicksall* v. *Michigan,* 322 Mich. 351, 33 N.W. 2d 904 (1948), a case in which Michigan Court Rule 35-A was not applicable; *State* v. *Lyons,* 180 La. 158, 156 So. 207 (1934), but a custom of appointing on court's own motion existed; *Jones* v. *Amrine,* 154 Kan. 630, 121 P. 2d 263 (1942); *Korf* v. *Jasper County,* 132 Iowa 682, 108 N.W. 1031 (1906); *People* v. *Bindrin,* 404 Ill. 532, 89 N.E. 2d 530 (1949), a case in which Illinois

words, the defendant presumably knows of his rights or is under a duty to learn of them, and, therefore, a lack of a request is a judicial waiver. More difficult questions arise where a defendant attempts in a fumbling way to request that counsel be appointed.

The inquiry, "Could I see a lawyer?" from a person accused of murder could be interpreted as a request that counsel be appointed. To one court, at least, this was too general a request, and the decision implied that a particular attorney should have been designated.[91] A more liberal court would, without doubt, not have expected such a high degree of technical proficiency from the defendant, and any demonstrated desire to have counsel coupled with a failure to appoint would result in a reversal and remand.[92]

Difficulties exist, however, even where the defendant's request is as precise and clear as the English language permits, for if the judge fails to appoint, and the defendant fails to "except" to the judge's decision, or if the whole process is omitted from the record, the defendant cannot perfect an appeal, since appeal is confined to errors appearing in the record. On habeas corpus, the usual alternative procedure for challenging a conviction, the petitioner will have the rather weighty burden of proving by his testimony alone facts which will usually be denied by the judge and the other officials. It is generally recognized that allegations of a request, if not supported by the record, are usually rejected by appellate courts.[93] It is not suggested that a large percentage of these claims are meritorious. Clearly, however, even when a defendant attempts to comply with a statute construed restrictively, as are many of the "request" statutes, he has

Supreme Court Rule 27–A was not applicable; *Scott* v. *State,* 71 Ga. App. 794, 32 S.E. 2d 549 (1944); *Patterson* v. *State,* 157 Fla. 304, 25 So. 2d 713 (1946); *Newell* v. *State,* 209 Miss. 653, 48 So. 2d 332 (1950).

[91] *Patterson* v. *State,* 157 Fla. 304, 25 So. 2d 713 (1946), certiorari denied 329 U.S. 789, 67 S. Ct. 352, 91 L. Ed. 676 (1948).

[92] *People* v. *McGarry,* 61 C.A. 2d 557, 142 P. 2d 92 (1943); *Ex parte McCoy,* 32 C. 2d 73, 194 P. 2d 531 (1948); *Cook* v. *State,* 48 Ga. 224, 172 S.E. 471 (1933); *State* v. *Blankenship,* 186 La. 238, 172 So. 4 (1937).

[93] *Cutts* v. *State,* 54 Fla. 21, 45 So. 491 (1907), held that it was not usual for the record to show the practice of appointing on request; *In re Taylor,* 229 N.C. 297, 49 S.E. 2d 749 (1948); *People* v. *Barrigar,* 401 Ill. 471, 82 N.E. 2d 433 (1948); *People* v. *Easter,* 398 Ill. 430, 75 N.E. 2d 688 (1947).

little chance to raise the issue successfully later unless he is sufficiently versed in legal lore to cry out "Exception!" or to take an even more fantastic action and ask that "all of this be placed in the record." Thus states such as Illinois which use the brief common-law record completely frustrate the defendant who fails to "except" and to present a bill of exceptions on appeal.[94]

This does not mean that courts are engaged in a vicious scheme to deprive defendants of their legal rights, and it is true that a large number of those convicted are quite willing to sign affidavits asserting any facts which may conceivably effect their release. Moreover, several years may have elapsed since a trial, and judges, court attachés, and other officials in busy judicial districts cannot be expected to remember all the details. Of necessity, these officials rely on their knowledge of the customary procedure. If the judge habitually appoints on request, as required by statute, he is not prone to recall a "mistake." Other officials who have been familiar with the judge's custom will certainly not contradict his "recollection," and their combined stories will inevitably support the conclusion that the man in the penitentiary is a liar. It is all very reasonable and very natural. The defect here, as was true in the issue of advice concerning counsel, is the failure of many courts to make adequate records. For if adequate records are made of the events surrounding a request for counsel, the occasional mistakes by judges can be detected and a new trial given.[95]

The decisions of the United States Supreme Court under the due-process clause have influenced a few state courts recently, with the result that the courts have termed a denial of a request, when coupled with other factors, to be a denial of a fair trial.[96] But, on the whole, if the defendant is convicted on a plea of guilty and if he is not young, ignorant, a stranger in the community, or the like, a claim that counsel was requested, if it is

[94] Gerald Chapman, "Right of Counsel Today," 39 *J. Crim. L. and Crim.* (Sept.–Oct., 1948), 342, gives a clear picture of the old Illinois procedure.

[95] *Commonwealth ex rel. Hice* v. *Ashe,* 166 Pa. Super. 35, 70 A. 2d 479 (1950); *Commonwealth ex rel. Piccerelli* v. *Smith,* 150 Pa. Super. 105, 27 A. 2d 484 (1942), based on custom, rather than statute.

[96] *Raymond* v. *State ex rel. Szydlowski* (Md.), 65 A. 2d 285 (1949); *Stonebreaker* v. *Smyth,* 187 Va. 250, 46 S.E. 2d 406 (1948).

based on the absence of notations as to counsel in the record, is easily refuted.[97]

In summary, it can be seen that the problems surrounding requests for counsel in state courts are not the most difficult ones. If a request is required by statute and the defendant fails to request, or if the record fails to show a request, the prisoner has only the slightest chance of obtaining a new trial. Fortunately, there are relatively few cases where the defendant claims that the trial court denied his clearly expressed request for counsel. This suggests that if a defendant is aware of his rights he will receive the assistance of appointed counsel upon request in those states which permit an appointment in less-than-capital cases.

WAIVER OF COUNSEL

WAIVER IMPLIED FROM FAILURE TO REQUEST

Three options face a defendant who wishes to plead "not guilty" in most state courts. First, he can hire a lawyer; second, he may by means of appropriate words or actions have counsel appointed to defend him; third, he can choose to defend himself. We are concerned here with that rather substantial group of unsuccessful defendants who, having once waived counsel, later decide or ascertain that they did not intend to waive their right to have counsel appointed, or, if we look at their claim from the state's point of view, that group of discontented prisoners who claim, usually falsely, that they wanted counsel and were deprived of counsel through the wrongful action of the court or of other public officials.

The difficulties of one group of complainants arise from their failure to request counsel, for a failure to request is termed a waiver by some courts.[98] A "waiver" to most people and to most courts means a knowing relinquishment of a legally pro-

[97] *Tesar* v. *Bowley*, 144 Neb. 623, 14 N.W. 2d 225 (1944); *Davis* v. *O'Grady*, 137 Neb. 708, 291 N.W. 82 (1940).

[98] *People* v. *Bassinger*, 403 Ill. 108, 85 N.E. 2d 758 (1949); *Oller* v. *Amrine*, 155 Kan. 703, 127 P. 2d 475 (1942); *Weatherford* v. *State*, 76 Fla. 219, 79 So. 680 (1918); *Skiba* v. *Kaiser*, 352 Mo. 424, 178 S.W. 2d 373 (1944); *Alexander* v. *O'Grady*, 137 Neb. 645, 290 N.W. 718 (1940); *James* v. *State*, 27 Wyo. 378, 196 P. 1045 (1921); *People* v. *Ross*, 400 Ill. 237, 79 N.E. 2d 495 (1948), and numerous other Illinois decisions.

tected right.   Under this view, a defendant would have to know that he had a right to counsel before he could waive counsel. In Illinois, which has followed the implied-waiver rule, there is a duty to appoint counsel in capital cases unless appointment is competently waived, and the waiver is deemed competent only after the defendant has been questioned concerning his financial ability and has been told that the court will appoint counsel.[99] Yet the same Illinois court when interpreting its statute requiring a request in noncapital cases has held firmly to the rule that failure to request is a waiver.[100]

The language of the Illinois capital-charge statute, "Whenever it shall appear to the court that a defendant . . . is . . . indigent and unable to pay counsel for his or her defense, it shall be the duty of the court to appoint," does not seem sufficiently different from the language of the noncapital-case statute, "Every person charged with crime shall be allowed counsel and when he shall state upon oath that he is unable to procure counsel the court shall assign him competent counsel . . ." to make two different rules concerning waiver either logical or inevitable. Certainly the result in Illinois has been strongly criticized by thoughtful observers.[101]   If the more serious nature of the capital crime is claimed to justify the more generous provision, one might argue that a person charged with a greater crime would have been more careful to learn of his rights.   And in terms of actual punishment, a life sentence for murder usually results in practice in no greater deprivation of liberty than does a fifty-year sentence.

Some courts, unwilling to proceed on such slight logic, have attempted to discover in the actions or the background of the accused one or more characteristics indicating that the defendant probably knew of his rights, so that his failure to request could be termed a knowing or competent waiver.[102]   In a large

---

[99] *People* v. *Williams,* 399 Ill. 452, 78 N.E. 2d 512 (1948).

[100] As in *People* v. *Ross,* 400 Ill. 237, 79 N.E. 2d 495 (1948) and *People* v. *Burnett,* 407 Ill. 269, 95 N.E. 2d 319 (1950). Illinois Supreme Court Rule 27–A, which became effective in 1948, naturally has no influence on trial procedure before that time; the claims being raised antedate the new rule.

[101] For an attack on the Illinois court's logic, see Gerald Chapman, "Right of Counsel Today," 39 *J. Crim. L. and Crim.* (Sept.—Oct., 1948), 342.

[102] See *Simpson* v. *State,* 141 Tex. Cr. 324, 148 S.W. 2d 852 (1941), where an educated Negro failed to request.

number of cases the court satisfied itself that the waiver was competent because the defendant had been on trial before.[103] In the absence of previous courtroom experience by the defendant, courts have been able to find other evidence that the accused intended to waive counsel. Such evidence might be the defendant's dismissal of the public defender; [104] the statement, after being advised, that he would hire counsel; [105] the dismissal of two attorneys and the announcement that he would represent himself; [106] the expression of dissatisfaction with each of four attorneys appointed successively by the court; [107] the fact of being a businessman, who "knows his way around"; [108] simple neglect or procrastination in hiring counsel; [109] and the presence of parents who had consulted attorneys on the defendant's behalf.[110]

One doubt that lingers after reading some of the cases where previous court experience has been cited is whether or not the defendant actually learned of his rights on his earlier visits. While allegations of ignorance should be more difficult to sustain in the future, since prisoners are apparently busy with research in this area of law today, still it seems somewhat illogical to assume that prisoners in the past must have known what so many courts did not learn until recent years, that a waiver had to be competent in order to be acceptable.

WAIVER IMPLIED FROM PLEA OF GUILTY

Another well-established principle which has been followed by many courts is that a voluntary plea of guilty serves as a waiver of the right to have counsel appointed, as well as a waiver

[103] *Commonwealth ex rel. McGlinn v. Smith,* 344 Pa. 41, 24 A. 2d 1 (1942); *Berry v. State,* 61 Ga. App. 315, 6 S.E. 2d 148 (1939); *State ex rel. Wenzlaff v. Burke,* 250 Wis. 525, 27 N.W. 2d 475 (1947); *Commonwealth ex rel. Quinn v. Smith,* 144 Pa. Super. 160, 19 A. 2d 504 (1941).

[104] *People v. O'Neill,* 78 C.A. 2d 888, 179 P. 2d 10 (1947).

[105] See *People v. Rose,* 42 C.A. 540, 183 P. 874 (1919), in which the defendant was a court reporter.

[106] *People v. Jewett,* 84 C.A. 2d 276, 190 P. 330 (1948).

[107] *People v. Walker,* 93 C.A. 2d 54, 208 P. 2d 724 (1949).

[108] *State v. Martin,* 223 Minn. 414, 27 N.W. 2d 158 (1947).

[109] *State v. Longo,* 132 N.J.L. 515, 41 A. 2d 317 (1945); *Stanfield v. State,* 152 Tex. Cr. 324, 212 S.W. 2d 516 (1948).

[110] *Ex parte Ray,* 87 Okla. Cr. 436, 198 P. 2d 756 (1948).

of other constitutional rights.[111]   The courts of New York, however, have clearly stated that a plea of guilty is not to be construed as a waiver of counsel,[112] and Indiana and Oklahoma courts have reached the same result.[113]   Other states are rejecting the older view in favor of the New York, Indiana, and Oklahoma rule as a result of the broadened concept of due process applied by the United States Supreme Court, a concept which permits the acceptance of a plea of guilty without counsel being present only if the defendant is mature, reasonably intelligent, and knows of his right to counsel or reveals that he does not need counsel.[114]

On first thought, it seems justifiable that a plea of guilty which serves as a waiver of jury trial should be considered a waiver of counsel, on the theory that it is a confession that no legal defense exists.   Common sense suggests that a man must know if he is guilty or not.   On the other hand, defendants who are financially unable to retain counsel and who are ignorant of their rights regarding appointed counsel may well be ignorant about many other legal principles.   A man may have killed another man without knowing the various degrees

111 See *In re Jingles,* 27 C. 2d 496, 165 P. 2d 12 (1946), where the defendant was advised, but claimed he was "incompetent"; *Brewer v. Amrine,* 155 Kan. 525, 127 P. 2d 447 (1942), where the defendant had consulted an attorney; *Jones v. Amrine,* 154 Kan. 630, 121 P. 2d 263 (1942), where the defendant had "bargained" with the county attorney; *Wilson v. Hudspeth,* 166 Kan. 214, 199 P. 2d 776 (1948), where the presumption of regularity was emphasized; *Tesar v. Bowley,* 144 Neb. 623, 14 N.W. 2d 225 (1944), where the defendant was an old offender; *State v. Garcia,* 47 N.M. 319, 142 P. 2d 552 (1943), where the defendant had discharged an attorney who had been retained; *In re Burson,* 152 Ohio St. 375, 89 N.E. 2d 651 (1949), where the defendant's mental age was 12 plus; *Commonwealth ex rel. Billings v. Ashe,* 144 Pa. Super. 209, 19 A. 2d 749 (1941), where the court made the flat assertion that the constitutional provision does not apply to one who pleads guilty; *State v. Young,* 361 Mo. 529, 235 S.W. 2d 369 (1950), where the right to counsel is said to be waived by a voluntary plea of guilty on the part of the defendant.

112 *People ex rel. Moore v. Hunt,* 258 App. Div. 24, 16 N.Y.S. 2d 19 (1939).

113 *Batchelor v. State,* 189 Ind. 69, 125 N.E. 773 (1920); *Parker v. State,* 189 Ind. 85, 125 N.E. 772 (1920).   A recent Oklahoma decision holds that in a capital case a plea of guilty cannot be accepted unless there has been advice by counsel. See *Hampton v. Burford* (Okla. Cr.), 232 P. 2d 407 (1951).

114 *Gholson v. Commonwealth,* 308 Ky. 82, 212 S.W. 2d 537 (1948); *Stonebreaker v. Smyth,* 187 Va. 250, 46 S.E. 2d 406 (1948).   In both cases the court made clear that its holding was dictated by the Fourteenth Amendment and not by any state requirement.

of homicide and their elements.[115]   A person filled with re-
morse may plead guilty to murder although the facts may prove
accidental killing, self-defense, or manslaughter, or it may be
that the only evidence in the case was illegally seized.[116]   Experience shows, too, that there are sources of unfair pleas of
guilty apart from the ignorance of defendants, such as the overzealous activities of the police in producing "confessions" and
the "deals" often made between a prosecutor who wants to gain
a conviction and an accused who thinks that a strong case, which
cannot be defended, has been made against him.   This situation is fairly common with young defendants who would rather
accept a shorter term of imprisonment than risk a longer term,
or, in some cases, the death penalty.[117]

The truth is that, in spite of popular feeling to the contrary,
one must have legal advice in many cases to know whether a
plea of guilty is warranted.   Even if a defendant has been guilty
of a criminal act there may be extenuating factors which, when
produced at the trial, would make a very light sentence probable.
This possibility alone might appear to demand that before a
plea of guilty could be accepted the court should appoint counsel, regardless of the state statutory requirements.   At the least,
before a court permits a defendant to waive counsel, and to
plead guilty, he should be carefully informed of his right to
counsel and the consequences of his plea.

In those jurisdictions which do not advise defendants concerning counsel it would seem necessary, however, for courts to
assume some of the functions of a counsel if the present unsatisfactory situation is to be avoided.   A series of questions designed
to reveal the defendant's age, education, parental background,
and occupation, the nature of his offense, and his claims might

[115] The facts in a California case revealed that an ignorant, illiterate farm
hand who had been involved in a gambling fracas over fifty-five cents, in which
a man had been killed, was allowed to plead guilty to first-degree murder.   At the
most, the evidence proved manslaughter.   The conviction was reversed, in *Ex
parte James,* 240 P. 2d 596 (1952).

[116] As it was in *Gholson v. Commonwealth,* 308 Ky. 82, 212 S.W. 2d 537 (1948);
or the plea of guilty may have followed a coerced confession, as in *Stonebreaker
v. Smyth,* 187 Va. 250, 46 S.E. 2d 406 (1948).   See *State v. Seward,* 163 Kan. 136, 181
P. 2d 478 (1947), where a confession was obtained from a seventeen-year-old whose
parents were not notified of his arrest.

[117] See *Dunfee v. Hudspeth,* 162 Kan. 524, 178 P. 2d 1009 (1947).

well precede an acceptance of his plea of guilty. If the judge still had any doubt, he could then defer acceptance of the plea and appoint counsel. Unfortunately, courts as well as prosecuting officials have too frequently looked upon the plea of guilty as the easy and swift method of disposing of criminal cases. The judge who would never think of hurrying a legal proceeding if he suspected that an injustice were being committed frequently accepts the plea of guilty with hardly a second thought of its possible defects.

EXPRESS WAIVER

Frequently the aftermath of a criminal trial reveals that the defendant and the state have decidedly different views as to what actually happened at the trial. From the state's point of view any clear expression by the defendant before or at arraignment that he does not want or need counsel is a sufficient waiver. The defendant, on the other hand, is prone to rationalize the language purported to embody his waiver and to emphasize his ignorance of court procedure and of his rights, the atmosphere of confusion at the trial, and any other element which would serve to indicate that he did not intend to waive counsel.

In analyzing these claims some courts assert that whether or not a waiver was made and made competently will be determined from the totality of facts in each situation,[118] and this is so, irrespective of what appears on the record.[119] Other courts approach the problem by declaring that a recital either of a waiver or of a refusal of counsel is presumptively correct, and they thus place a heavy burden on any defendant who denies such recitals.[120] For example, if the defendant expresses a desire to represent himself, this alone acts as a waiver of counsel.[121]

[118] *State* v. *Jameson* (S.D.), 38 N.W. 2d 441 (1949).

[119] *Garrison* v. *Amrine,* 155 Kan. 509, 126 P. 2d 228 (1942).

[120] *State* v. *Mewhinney,* 43 Utah 135, 134 P. 632 (1913); *Elam* v. *Rowland,* 194 Ga. 58, 20 S.E. 2d 572 (1942); *People* v. *Shapiro,* 85 C.A. 2d 253, 194 P. 2d 731 (1948); *Ex parte Gault,* 78 Okla. Cr. 172, 146 P. 2d 133 (1944); *In re Hazel,* 80 Okla. Cr. 66, 157 P. 2d 225 (1945); *State ex rel. Johnson* v. *Broderick,* 75 N.D. 340, 27 N.W. 2d 849 (1947); *Nelson* v. *Burford,* 92 Okla. Cr. 224, 222 P. 2d 382 (1950).

[121] *Todd* v. *State,* 226 Ind. 496, 81 N.E. 2d 530 (1948); *State* v. *Duncan,* 233 Iowa 1259, 11 N.W. 2d 484 (1943).

Or if the defendant shows indecision, or procrastinates, he may find that his whole manner of conduct will be considered a waiver and that a last-minute desire for counsel, after an earlier refusal, will be rejected by the court.[122]

On the other hand, if statute or practice requires a written waiver by the defendant, such a waiver will be treated as conclusive,[123] unless a state official coerced the defendant to sign the waiver.[124]   With consistency the same courts have held that the failure to have the defendant sign the waiver is a fatal error.[125]   Moreover, if a defendant can show the existence of certain facts which tend to cast doubt on the validity of an express waiver, such a waiver will be held ineffective.[126]   In one situation, where the waiver was recorded after the plea of guilty, when the judge finally remembered to do his duty, the Indiana court followed the Canizio rule and held that since the defendant could have asked to have counsel and could have withdrawn his plea, or could have obtained counsel and moved for a new trial on the ground of lack of advice and an improperly received plea, the trial court's error was not fatal.[127]

The tendency today is toward a more complete recording of the facts of waiver, and in many jurisdictions a rule requiring written waivers is in effect.   While such practices will not wholly eliminate the issue of whether a competent waiver has occurred, they will go far toward minimizing disputes subsequent to conviction.

ATTEMPTED WAIVER BY INCOMPETENT DEFENDANT

The most frequently and successfully urged ground on which a purported waiver is claimed to be incompetent is the ignorance of the defendant, either as a general attribute or as a quality

---

[122] *State* v. *Fowler,* 59 Mont. 346, 197 P. 847 (1921); *State* v. *MacKinnon,* 41 Nev. 182, 168 P. 330 (1917).

[123] *Downs* v. *Hudspeth,* 162 Kan. 575, 178 P. 2d 219 (1947).

[124] *State* v. *Perkins,* 156 Kan. 323, 133 P. 2d 160 (1943).

[125] *Davis* v. *Hudspeth,* 161 Kan. 354, 167 P. 2d 293 (1946); *Brandt* v. *Hudspeth,* 162 Kan. 601, 178 P. 2d 224 (1947).

[126] See *People* v. *Pisoni,* 233 Mich. 462, 206 N.E. 986 (1926), where the evidence had been seized illegally and an attorney had been denied permission to see his client; *State* v. *Sewell,* 69 S.D. 494, 12 N.W. 2d 198 (1943), where, on a murder charge, the defendant had been informed in casual fashion of his right to counsel.

[127] *Chandler* v. *State,* 226 Ind. 648, 83 N.E. 2d 189 (1949).

present at the time of trial.[128]   This ground is available mainly where the state courts do not presume that defendants know their constitutional rights, but, rather, presume that a defendant would not want to waive rights known by him.[129]

Often the claim of ignorance is combined with allegations of other defects in procedure, which makes it difficult to determine the relative weight given to each of the factors by the reviewing court.   However, it is clear that the ignorance of the defendant is important, because an intelligent defendant would presumably protect himself against some of the errors allegedly committed.   For example, where there was a speedy proceeding coupled with the threat of mob violence against an ignorant Negro, a purported waiver was held incompetent.[130]   Similarly, a waiver by an ignorant thirty-seven-year-old Negro, wounded when seized, was held incompetent as late as fourteen years after a first-degree murder conviction, because of an open doubt expressed at the time of sentencing by the trial judge as to whether premeditation had existed.[131]   It seems, further, that a purported waiver of counsel in a serious case is more easily attacked than one in a less serious case, because the presumption is less favorable to the state.[132]

[128] A Negro youth of eighteen with moron-level intelligence was allowed to sign a waiver of counsel by a New Jersey court. He received five sentences totaling thirty-five years, although he thought he was charged with only one offense. The conviction was reversed as a denial of due process. See *Ex parte Carter,* 82 A. 2d 652 (1951). A defendant's confused state of mind may yield the same result. See *People* v. *Lewis,* 413 Ill. 116, 108 N.E. 2d 473 (1953), where a middle-aged woman charged with shoplifting pleaded guilty without being advised of her right to counsel, and was sentenced twenty-four hours after arrest. She successfully attacked her conviction. It should be noted that this is a sharp break with the previous Illinois decisions wherein pleas of guilty were held to be waivers of counsel.

[129] Compare the presumptions in *State* v. *Haas,* 69 S.D. 204, 8 N.W. 2d 569 (1943), where the necessity of a voluntary and intelligent waiver is stressed, with those in *Ex parte Grayson,* 153 Tex. Cr. 91, 217 S.W. 2d 1007 (1949), where a boy of fifteen, assisted by a confused father, was allowed to waive counsel. A New York court has stated flatly that the presumption is against the waiver of the right to counsel. See *Miller* v. *People,* 114 N.Y.S. 2d 838 (1953).

[130] *Ex parte Hollins,* 54 Okla. Cr. 70, 14 P. 2d 243 (1932). It was the lack of a fair trial which caused the reversal. Without haste and mob pressure, the waiver would probably have been held good.

[131] *Jones* v. *Heinze,* 88 C.A. 2d 167, 198 P. 2d 520 (1948).

[132] See *People* v. *Chesser,* 29 C. 2d 815, 178 P. 2d 761 (1947), where on a first-degree murder charge the trial court had expressed doubt about the lack of counsel.

Sometimes the ignorance of the defendant and the indifference of the judge appear vividly on the record, as the following excerpt from a Georgia larceny case shows:

Court: "George, have you got a lawyer?"

Defendant: "No, Sir."

Court: "Have you tried to get one?"

Defendant: "No, Sir, I ain't. . . . I was just caught up yesterday."

Court: "Call the first 12 jurors to the box. —George, does that jury look all right to you?"

Defendant: "Yes, Sir, I guess they will do."

Court (at the close of the evidence) : "George, do you want to argue the case?"

Defendant: "If I had a lawyer I would like to argue it."

The state supreme court found no waiver here.[133] In another case a waiver of counsel and a plea of guilty by a defendant who was a stranger and thus ignorant of the law applicable to the jurisdiction of the court were held incompetent.[134]

In basically the same position as the ignorant defendant is the youthful defendant who attempts to waive counsel. Seemingly, physical age would be a rather inefficient guide to a defendant's mental capacity, but since the legal system must deal with readily applied standards, the arbitrary age of twenty-one is meaningful in this specific area, as it is in so many other phases of law. That is not to say that a minor is incapable of waiving counsel, but his minority is significant and, when coupled with one or more additional factors, such as his ignorance of legal procedure, the speed of the proceedings, the seriousness of the crime, and the lack of evidence, may render a waiver incompetent.[135] That the defendant's age alone is not the decisive ele-

---

[133] *Cook* v. *State,* 48 Ga. 224, 172 S.E. 471 (1933).

[134] *State* v. *Tennyson,* 73 N.D. 262, 14 N.W. 2d 168 (1944).

[135] See *Ex parte Cornell,* 89 Okla. Cr. 2, 193 P. 2d 904 (1948), where a plea of guilty and a waiver of counsel were accepted from a seventeen-year-old defendant with no previous courtroom experience; *Willey* v. *Hudspeth,* 162 Kan. 516, 178 P. 2d 246 (1947), where the reviewing court asserted that a seventeen-year-old did not know enough about constitutional rights to waive them intelligently, and the presence of the boy's father made no difference; *State* v. *Oberst,* 127 Kan. 412, 273 P. 490 (1928), where a seventeen-year-old defendant pleaded guilty to seven murders after saying, "I don't care," when asked if he wanted an attorney. In

ment is demonstrated by cases in which the waiver by a minor is allowed to stand, chiefly on the ground that the particular defendant knew what he was doing or was advised by a person of sufficient maturity and competence.[136]

Some idea of the relative importance of age and other factors can be seen from a situation where a defendant of seventeen and one of twenty-three were jointly charged with burglary. Each waived counsel and pleaded guilty. The difference in age and one previous conviction of the older defendant permitted the state supreme court to distinguish the two cases and to decide that only the younger man's waiver was not competent.[137] A unique claim arose where a defendant waived counsel, pleaded guilty, and two or three minutes later fell over in a dead faint. The reviewing court allowed the waiver of counsel and the plea to be withdrawn.[138] A similar result followed a claim that the defendant waived counsel when intoxicated, police officers substantiating the defendant's story concerning his "shaking" and lack of self-control.[139] Thus it is not enough for a court to obtain a spoken or written waiver of counsel. It is necessary that a sufficiently persistent inquiry be made of each defendant to ascertain whether he is of adequate maturity, intelligence, and experience to make a waiver acceptable, and to insure that he has been free from coercive or other unwarranted actions by public officials which would tend to show that his waiver was not freely given.

---

the last case no corpus delicti was shown on the record; three of the seven judges dissented, asserting that this defendant was mature for seventeen. And compare the result of the De Meerleer case involving a seventeen-year-old defendant with that of another almost factually identical Michigan case involving a twenty-seven-year-old defendant, *People* v. *Mahler,* 329 Mich. 115, 45 N.W. 2d 14 (1950).

[136] See *Frazee* v. *State,* 79 Okla. Cr. 224, 153 P. 2d 637 (1944), where a father who had the ability to hire a lawyer was present; *Haughey* v. *Smyth,* 187 Va. 320, 46 S.E. 2d 419 (1948), where a nineteen-and-a-half-year-old sailor had "traveled"; *Ex parte Grayson,* 153 Tex. Cr. 91, 217 S.W. 2d 1007 (1949), where the father of a fifteen-year-old was present but did not ask for counsel or claim indigence. In *People* v. *Adomaitis,* 112 N.Y.S. 2d 38, 201 Misc. 707 (1952), the age of the defendant, sixteen, was decisive.

[137] *Ex parte Cook,* 84 Okla. Cr. 404, 183 P. 2d 595 (1947), the seventeen-year-old; *Ex parte Cobb,* 89 Okla. Cr. 82, 205 P. 2d 518 (1949), the twenty-three-year-old.

[138] *People* v. *Stachowitz,* 88 N.Y.S. 2d 528, 194 Misc. 1031 (1949).

[139] *Vanderschmidt* v. *State,* 226 Ind. 439, 81 N.E. 2d 782 (1948).

Defendants Who Must Receive Appointed Counsel

It is well established that if a defendant has certain characteristics, a court is under a duty to appoint counsel whether or not the defendant is aware of his rights and regardless of the actions or lack of action by the accused. This is true whatever the state law may be, and it rests on the assumption that such defendants cannot receive a fair trial, or due process in the case at hand, without the aid of counsel.[140]

A defendant must have normal mental capacity, for example, to be allowed to defend himself in a criminal proceeding,[141] and if counsel is appointed for a deficient defendant he must serve to the end of the trial and cannot waive the defense of the accused.[142] Age is also an important factor, and the Kansas Supreme Court has declared flatly that a sixteen-year-old boy cannot defend himself.[143] In an even more generous mood, this court has stated that a twenty-year-old defendant should have had counsel because of his inexperience.[144] At the least, it can be said that a court must proceed with extreme caution when the defendant appears to be young, ignorant, or illiterate; a silent record in such circumstances will be construed against the state.[145] Any evidence of past mental incapacity necessitates an appointment,[146] and a frightened, ignorant youth is in similar need.[147] Thus an illiterate defendant of Polish extraction who continually repeated, "I no mean to kill," required counsel to

---

[140] In the cases discussed previously a waiver was attempted, but held incompetent. Here there is no attempt at waiver.

[141] *Burgunder* v. *Arizona,* 55 Ariz. 411, 103 P. 2d 256 (1940), where the defendant had declared his inability to continue at the trial after his appointed counsel withdrew.

[142] See *Garner* v. *State,* 97 Ark. 63, 132 S.W. 1010 (1910), where an emotional white attorney bade "farewell" to a fourteen-year-old Negro accused of murder.

[143] *McCarty* v. *Hudspeth,* 166 Kan. 476, 201 P. 2d 658 (1949). *Ex parte Cornell,* 87 Okla. Cr. 1, 193 P. 2d 904 (1948), reaches a different conclusion, however. Kansas courts have said the same thing about seventeen-year-old defendants, so apparently a person under eighteen is in a favorable position in Kansas, but not in neighboring Oklahoma.

[144] *Dunfee* v. *Hudspeth,* 162 Kan. 524, 178 P. 2d 1009 (1947).

[145] *Ex parte Meadows,* 70 Okla. Cr. 304, 106 P. 2d 139 (1940).

[146] *Ex parte Hicks,* 90 Okla. Cr. 144, 211 P. 2d 539 (1949).

[147] See *McDorman* v. *Smyth,* 188 Va. 474, 50 S.E. 2d 423 (1948), in which the Fourteenth Amendment due-process clause was applied.

assist him.[148]   Furthermore, if the trial court makes promises to the defendant who is without counsel and fails to carry them out, that failure may cause a reviewing court to decide that counsel should have been appointed,[149] which is an alternate way of saying there was a lack of due process.

Thus there are a limited number of situations in which a trial court should appoint counsel on its own motion in order to insure a fair trial to the extremely youthful, the ignorant, the illiterate, the mentally deficient, and the psychologically unfit, to all of whom the law extends more paternal protection than it does to hardier citizens.   That such a task makes difficulties for our trial courts is clear.   No formula will lead to complete success in determining which defendants require counsel in spite of their wishes.   It seems equally clear, however, that with the assistance ordinarily available to any court it should be possible to ascertain far more about defendants than has been attempted in the past.   The present situation in the courts varies, although efforts toward reform have been and are being made. The essential difficulty arises because of the well-established assumptions upon which the legal system has dealt with criminals —that unless shown to be otherwise, they are presumed to be intelligent, competent adults, to be dealt with like so many identical molecules drawn by chance from the mass of society. Courts are reluctant to enlarge the categories or increase the number of those who can claim the protection of a different set of assumptions.

LIMITATIONS ON THE ENJOYMENT OF THE RIGHT TO COUNSEL

A right is not merely an abstract conception; it necessarily involves the means or conditions by which it can be enjoyed in practice.   Consequently, there are many instances when defendants feel that their right to counsel has been infringed because of a substantial interference by the court with retained or appointed counsel, so that the defense effort has been weakened.

---

[148] *State ex rel. Drankovich* v. *Murphy,* 248 Wis. 433, 22 N.W. 2d 540 (1945). For comment see 30 *Marq. L. Rev.* (Dec., 1946), 204.
[149] *Ex parte Robnett,* 69 Okla. Cr. 235, 101 P. 2d 645 (1940).

One type of complaint arises from the denial of the request for continuance or from other time limitations on the preparation for trial, another from time and other limitations on the counsel's argument, and a third from restrictions on the privilege of consultation between counsel and client.

TIME FOR PREPARATION

One of the most common features in criminal proceedings is the inevitable request for a continuance.   There are many causes, some justified and some quite frivolous, which account for this tendency.   The very able attorney is overwhelmed with clients and has the difficult task of coördinating his efforts on their behalf with the operation of a court calendar which is not designed primarily to please him.   There are hesitant lawyers, as there are hesitant practitioners in every profession, who are incapable of feeling fully prepared and who dread a showdown. It is very possible, furthermore, that the practice of criminal law has attracted men of lesser ability in recent decades.   Apart from such speculative factors, it seems true that courts are frequently unaware of the complexity and difficulty of a case, and set it for trial much too soon.   This is most likely to happen when community feelings are outraged by an especially vicious crime and the judge feels bound to respond to that feeling, even though these are in many instances the very cases where more time should be afforded the defense.

Speedy justice is too often injustice, and the great number of needlessly drawn-out posttrial proceedings should not deter trial courts from granting to all defendants a reasonable opportunity to prepare for trial.   This is a principle with which all state courts agree, and such phrases as "the right to effective preparation," "the right to a reasonable time to prepare," "the right to proper preparation," "ample opportunity," are strewn throughout the opinions.[150]   Moreover, it is agreed by the highest state courts that the decision of the trial court to grant or deny a continuance is a matter of discretion.[151]

[150] *Garrett* v. *State*, 248 Ala. 612, 29 So. 2d 8 (1947); *Smith* v. *State* (Md.), 56 A. 2d 818 (1948); *Christie* v. *State*, 94 Fla. 469, 114 So. 450 (1927); *Lowe* v. *State*, 95 Fla. 81, 116 So. 240 (1928); *Johnston* v. *Commonwealth*, 276 Ky. 615, 124 S.W. 2d 1035 (1939).
[151] E.g., *Prescott* v. *State*, 56 Okla. Cr. 259, 37 P. 2d 830 (1934); *State* v. *Bigham*,

The element known as "judicial discretion" is not uncontrolled, however, and the reviewing court, after scrutinizing the record and receiving other evidence properly produced, may decide that the lower court "abused" its discretion, or, to put it bluntly, it says that the trial court reached a decision which the highest court would not have reached. The highest court has the valuable advantage of hindsight, and it is debatable whether all the denials of continuance which it terms erroneous on review would have been decided differently had it been the court of first instance. To explore in detail the law relating to motions for continuance would be fruitless. The facts of each situation present a different problem, and each case must be decided with minimum reference to other cases.[152] In short, there can be no rules except the general vague rules described above.

In applying these rules courts reach decisions seemingly at variance. In one case three days was held to be sufficient time to prepare for trial.[153] Yet in another situation, in which the defendant was moved one hundred miles from where his attorney lived, the court said that the inconvenience and the shortness of time (twelve days) required a continuance.[154] Two or three minutes was declared insufficient for preparation in a rape case, even though no motion for continuance was made.[155] If one can generalize, it is probably error for the court to deny a motion made by an attorney appointed or retained on the day of arraignment, where the plea is not guilty.[156] Even one full day of preparation is probably not sufficient in a serious case.[157]

One suspects that in passing judgment each justice of the

---

119 S.C. 368, 112 S.E. 332 (1921); *Daugherty v. State,* 33 Tex. Cr. 173, 26 S.W. 60 (1894); *People v. Staryak,* 396 Ill. 573, 72 N.E. 2d 815 (1947); *Mixon v. Commonwealth,* 282 Ky. 25, 137 S.W. 2d 710 (1940).

152 *Lowe v. State,* 95 Fla. 81, 116 So. 240 (1928); *Hoy v. State,* 225 Ind. 428, 75 N.E. 2d 915 (1947).

153 *Charlon v. State,* 106 Ga. 400, 32 S.E. 347 (1898).

154 *Christie v. State,* 94 Fla. 469, 114 So. 450 (1927).

155 *Jackson v. State,* 176 Ga. 148, 167 S.E. 109 (1932). But the trial judge's temper made contempt the likely result if such a motion had been made in this case.

156 *Hoy v. State,* 225 Ind. 428, 75 N.E. 2d 915 (1947); *McDaniel v. Commonwealth,* 181 Ky. 766, 205 S.W. 915 (1918).

157 *Shelton v. Commonwealth,* 280 Ky. 733, 134 S.W. 2d 653 (1939). A substantial number of "speedy" proceedings in serious cases have taken place in Kentucky. Negroes are the defendants in many of these cases.

reviewing courts scrutinizes the case, observes the nature of the defense, the number of witnesses, the amount of expert testimony, and other factors, and tries to compute the time he would have required had he been cast in the role of defense counsel. The existence of special or complicating elements in addition to the brief time allowed makes it easier for the reviewing court to reverse.[158] The youth of the appointed or retained lawyer, for example, might make the length of time allowed for preparation appear excessively short.[159] On the other hand, many reviewing courts seem most reluctant to interfere with the trial court's judgment, and offer a variety of reasons for this attitude, such as the lack of diligence demonstrated by counsel,[160] the unlikelihood of any better defense if more time had been allowed,[161] or the failure to make the motion in proper form or to submit an affidavit when required.[162] The most common reasons given for denial are, of course, the simple ones that the time allowed was sufficient and that the defendant has failed to sustain the very heavy burden placed on him in challenging the lower court's exercise of discretion.[163]

It is counsel's duty, obviously, where he believes that not

[158] *Jackson v. State,* 176 Ga. 148, 167 S.E. 109 (1932), defendant of low mentality; *Hoy v. State,* 225 Ind. 428, 75 N.E. 2d 915 (1947), witnesses not obtainable immediately; *Johnston v. Commonwealth,* 276 Ky. 615, 124 S.W. 2d 1035 (1939), and *State v. Simpson,* 38 La. Ann. 23 (1886), scene of crime remote; *Cruthirds v. State,* 190 Miss. 892, 2 So. 2d 145 (1941), out-of-state witnesses; *State v. Farrell,* 223 N.C. 321, 26 S.E. 2d 322 (1943), insanity plea in case; *State v. Speller,* 230 N.C. 345, 53 S.E. 2d 294 (1949), special venire drawn from a neighboring county; *Cartee v. State,* 85 Ga. App. 532, 69 S.E. 2d 827 (1952), a day or two was required to find a defense witness.

[159] *State v. Jackson,* 344 Mo. 1055, 130 S.W. 2d 595 (1939); *State v. Hollingsworth,* 134 La. 554, 64 So. 409 (1914).

[160] *Smith v. State* (Md.), 56 A. 2d 818 (1948); *Neighbors v. State,* 83 Okla. Cr. 331, 177 P. 2d 133 (1947); *Prescott v. State,* 56 Okla. Cr. 259, 37 P. 2d 830 (1934).

[161] *Carter v. Commonwealth,* 258 Ky. 807, 81 S.W. 2d 883 (1935); *Cass v. Commonwealth,* 236 Ky. 462, 33 S.W. 2d 332 (1930); *State v. Gibson,* 229 N.C. 497, 50 S.E. 520 (1948).

[162] *People v. Kowalski,* 332 Ill. 167, 163 N.E. 399 (1928); *Caswell v. Commonwealth,* 285 Ky. 394, 147 S.W. 2d 1045 (1941); *Neighbors v. State,* 83 Okla. Cr. 331, 177 P. 2d 133 (1947).

[163] *Garrett v. State,* 248 Ala. 612, 29 So. 2d 8 (1947); *Sam v. State,* 33 Ariz. 383, 265 P. 609 (1928); *Lowe v. State,* 95 Fla. 81, 116 So. 240 (1928); *People v. Staryak,* 396 Ill. 573, 72 N.E. 2d 815 (1947); *Mixon v. Commonwealth,* 282 Ky. 25, 137 S.W. 2d 710 (1940); *State v. Dubose,* 169 La. 585, 125 So. 626 (1929); *State v. Sauls,* 190 N.C. 810, 130 S.E. 848 (1925); *State v. Bigham,* 119 S.C. 368, 112 S.E. 332 (1921).

enough time is available, to make his motion for continuance in proper form and to see that the record contains all the reasons in support of the motion, so that a reviewing court will have a substantial basis for a possible reversal. It is clear that the right to appear by counsel means the right to have an adequate period for counsel's preparation, but the determination of what a reasonable period is and of when a motion for continuance should be granted is subject to the discretion of the trial court, and this discretion will be upheld except in cases of clear abuse.

PRESENTATION OF CASE

It is commonly held by the courts that counsel has a right to argue the case to the jury as part of the right to be heard by counsel or to appear by counsel,[164] and it is also agreed that the limitation to be placed on counsel's argument is within the discretion of the trial judge.[165] However, the reviewing court may decide that the trial court's action was an abuse of its discretion. For example, an arbitrary refusal to permit any argument to the jury is reversible error,[166] and equally erroneous are instructions to the jury which in effect advise it to ignore the argument of counsel.[167] Beyond these obvious rules, the time limitation which trial courts place upon argument will be judged in the light of the length, complexity, and volume of testimony of the proceeding. As one would expect, the higher courts have little difficulty with cases where the trial court has acted arbitrarily, holding that five minutes is too little,[168] as is

[164] *Crawford v. State*, 112 Ala. 1 (1895); *People v. McMullen*, 300 Ill. 383, 133 N.E. 328 (1921); *Sizemore v. Commonwealth*, 240 Ky. 279, 42 S.W. 2d 328 (1931); *People v. Mayer*, 132 App. Div. 646, 117 N.Y.S. 520 (1909); *State v. Hardy*, 189 N.C. 799, 128 S.E. 152 (1925); *Dille v. State*, 34 Ohio St. 617 (1878); *State v. Rogoway*, 45 Ore. 601, 78 P. 987, 81 P. 234 (1904, 1905); *Commonwealth v. Polichinus*, 229 Pa. 311, 78 A. 382 (1910); *Kinney v. State*, 133 Tex. Cr. 260, 110 S.W. 2d 63 (1937); *State v. Mayo*, 42 Wash. 540, 85 P. 251 (1906).

[165] E.g., *Peagler et al. v. State*, 110 Ala. 11 (1895); *Mills v. Commonwealth*, 240 Ky. 359, 42 S.W. 2d 505 (1931); *Lee v. State*, 51 Miss. 566 (1875).

[166] *Cartright v. Clopton*, 25 Ga. 85 (1858); *State v. Verry*, 36 Kan. 416, 13 P. 838 (1887); *Kinney v. State*, 133 Tex. Cr. 260, 110 S.W. 2d 63 (1937); *Stewart v. Commonwealth*, 117 Pa. 378, 11 A. 370 (1887).

[167] *State v. Hardy*, 189 N.C. 799, 128 S.E. 152 (1925); *Commonwealth v. Polichinus*, 229 Pa. 311, 78 A. 382 (1910); *Commonwealth v. Thacker*, 328 Pa. 402, 194 A. 924 (1938).

[168] *White v. People*, 90 Ill. 117, 32 Am. Rep. 12 (1878); *Cooper v. State*, 106 Fla. 254, 143 So. 217 (1932).

fifteen minutes, in a serious case.[169]   When from thirty minutes to one hour has been allowed, courts vary in their judgment in view of other factors,[170] and yet periods of one, and even of one and one-half hours, may be too short.[171]

Moreover, it is not necessary that the trial court permit all attorneys for the defendants to address the court, and an additional counsel hired after trial has commenced may be denied the right to argue.[172]   As has been said, it is a matter resting within the trial court's discretion.   A limit must be placed on counsel's arguments, or trials would last for excessively long periods because of the mistaken notion of some lawyers that the longer they talk the more the jury will absorb.   Experience shows that any presentation of more than one or one and one-half hours' length is weakened by that fact alone.   Today there is a tendency toward the shorter argument, and it is perhaps notable that the relatively few modern cases on this point arise in rural areas and in the South, where the art of the legal orator is highly prized and apparently zealously guarded.

RIGHT TO CONSULTATION

It is obvious that defense is impossible without opportunities for consultation between client and counsel.   A court must give notice of the trial date to counsel when that is the custom,[173] and must provide facilities for private consultation between defendant and counsel.   This right also includes a right to consult counsel before trial without a public official being present,[174]

[169] *People* v. *Mayer*, 132 App. Div. 646, 117 N.Y.S. 520 (1909).

[170] Convictions after thirty minutes for preparation: upheld in *Lee* v. *State*, 51 Miss. 566 (1875), and in *Mills* v. *Commonwealth*, 240 Ky. 359, 42 S.W. 2d 505 (1931), a murder case, reversed on other grounds, in which the reviewing court suggested that a longer time be allowed in the future; reversed in *People* v. *McMullen*, 300 Ill. 383, 133 N.E. 328 (1921), where the testimony was substantial, and in *Dille* v. *State*, 34 Ohio St. 617 (1878), where the number of witnesses was large. Convictions after one hour for preparation: reversed in *Wingo* v. *State*, 62 Miss. 311 (1884), where a dozen witnesses and extensive circumstantial evidence were decisive factors, and in *State* v. *Rogoway*, 45 Ore. 601, 78 P. 987, 81 P. 234 (1904, 1905), where there were twenty-one witnesses.

[171] *State* v. *Mayo*, 42 Wash. 540, 85 P. 251 (1906).   Contra: *Crawford* v. *State*, 112 Ala. 1 (1895) and *Sizemore* v. *Commonwealth*, 240 Ky. 279, 42 S.W. 2d 328 (1931).

[172] *Spencer* v. *Commonwealth*, 237 Ky, 283, 35 S.W. 2d 319 (1931).

[173] *Commonwealth* v. *Jester*, 256 Pa. 441, 100 A. 993 (1917).

[174] *In re Rider*, 50 C.A. 797, 195 P. 965 (1920).

and the state does not satisfy its obligation to the accused by setting aside for this purpose between 9:00 A.M. and 5:00 P.M. a large room so heavily used by other defendants and counsel that confidential disclosures cannot be made.[175]

After the trial commences, too, the defendant and the counsel must have a chance to consult; thus a protested seating of twenty-two defendants and their counsel so that consultation could take place only at recess was held to be error.[176] And while the constitutional right to due process refers primarily to trial, it has also been held a denial of due process to refuse a prisoner in a penitentiary the right to consult with counsel concerning his appeal.[177]

Finally, if a counsel has a direct interest in attending any trial, he cannot be excluded, as, for example, where an attorney wishes to attend the trial of one accused of the same offense, and by the same accuser, as his client.[178] It is permissible, however, for the trial court to decide that only one of a defendant's eight attorneys should be allowed to get witnesses' depositions.[179] The relative scarcity of cases hinging on the right to full consultation suggests that the right is widely observed.

INEFFECTIVE DEFENSE BY COUNSEL

A common complaint after trial is that the defeated party, though represented by retained or appointed counsel, was not adequately defended. Counsel, it is claimed, was ignorant, lazy, indifferent, or malicious, or exhibited some equally undesirable trait. Another, though less common, allegation is that a conflict of interests existed, so that codefendants should not have had the same counsel. Trial defects sometimes cited are that counsel was absent at some stage of the proceedings and it was error for the court to continue in his absence, or that the court acted improperly when the defendant tried to dismiss counsel or change counsel. Each of these complaints will be discussed briefly.

[175] In re Qualls, 58 C.A. 2d 330, 136 P. 2d 341 (1943).
[176] People v. Zammora, 66 C.A. 2d 166, 152 P. 2d 180 (1944).
[177] Thomas v. Mills, 117 Ohio St. 114, 157 N.E. 488 (1927).
[178] Beauchamp v. Cahill, 297 Ky. 505, 180 S.W. 2d 423 (1944).
[179] Adams v. State, 176 Ark. 916, 5 S.W. 2d 946 (1928).

INEFFICIENCY OF COUNSEL

It is very difficult for a defendant to claim successfully that counsel chosen by him was so inefficient that the trial judgment should be reversed. The general attitude of courts is that the onus for having made a bad choice rests with the defendant,[180] or, stated differently, that a judgment carries a presumption of regularity, and what a counsel might have done when viewed in retrospect should not be allowed to upset the verdict.[181] Obviously there are few, if any, perfectly conducted defenses, and all that a defendant may expect is a fair hearing and substantial justice. Occasionally, however, even with retained counsel, the deficiencies of counsel's presentation are so gross and obvious that the reviewing court will reverse,[182] but the great majority of such claims are denied on the ground that substantial justice was done,[183] or on the more specific ground that incompetence was not proved or was not so gross that it destroyed the fairness of the hearing.[184]

Even where an appointed counsel appears, the presumptions employed by the state courts are the same, namely, that counsel

[180] *People* v. *Pierce,* 387 Ill. 608, 57 N.E. 2d 345 (1944).

[181] *Miller* v. *Hudspeth,* 164 Kan. 688, 192 P. 2d 147 (1948).

[182] See *Wilson* v. *State,* 222 Ind. 63, 51 N.E. 2d 848 (1943), where counsel's appearance was clearly "perfunctory." For brief comments, see 42 *Mich. L. Rev.* (June, 1944), 1125; 19 *Ind. L. J.* (April, 1944), 274. See also *Sanchez* v. *State,* 199 Ind. 235, 157 N.E. 1 (1927), where the counsel, hired by friends of an eighteen-year-old illiterate Mexican, was unaware of forcible process for obtaining witnesses, failed to object to obviously incompetent evidence, failed to tender instructions, and failed to produce character witnesses for the defendant, who had no previous record; and see also *People* v. *Nitti,* 312 Ill. 73, 143 N.E. 448 (1924), where gross incompetence was displayed in the error-filled trial of an ignorant Italian.

[183] *Ingram* v. *State,* 230 Ind. 25, 99 N.E. 2d 410 (1951); see also *Stice* v. *State,* 228 Ind. 144, 89 N.E. 2d 915 (1950), where the defendant, a broken-down prize-fighter, known as "one-round Muldoon," was apparently shocked by the trial court's ruling that his fists were "dangerous weapons" when used on a forty-six-year-old woman.

[184] *People* v. *Barnes,* 270 Ill. 574, 110 N.E. 881 (1915); *People* v. *Pierce,* 387 Ill. 608, 57 N.E. 2d 345 (1944); *Miller* v. *Hudspeth,* 164 Kan. 688, 192 P. 2d 147 (1948); *O'Brien* v. *Commonwealth,* 115 Ky. 608, 74 S.W. 666 (1903); *State* v. *Thompson,* 56 N.D. 716, 219 N.W. 218 (1928); *Ex parte Lovelady,* 151 Tex. Cr. 358, 207 S.W. 2d 396 (1947, 1948); *Penn* v. *Smyth,* 188 Va. 367, 49 S.E. 2d 600 (1948); *State* v. *Lee,* (R.I.), 78 A. 2d 793 (1951).

did his duty.[185]   Efforts made to challenge the quality of the defense after trials in which the defendant received the services of the public defender, on the ground that the public defender was in reality an *amicus curiae,* or a friend of the court, have uniformly failed.[186]   If the court appoints men who are not lawyers, however, their service is deemed inadequate,[187] or if an attempted appointment is merely formal, it may violate due process.[188]   Obviously, courts are reluctant to upset a judgment below, and there seems to be no discernible distinction between the presumptions used where retained counsel served and where appointed counsel served.   A substantially fair trial will be upheld in either case.

ABSENCE OF COUNSEL FROM PROCEEDINGS

There is agreement that counsel can be changed, even though the defendant lacks representation for short periods, so long as representation is substantially continuous and adequate,[189] but there is a division of judicial opinion as to the effect of the absence of counsel at any of the various stages in the trial.   One line of decisions holds that counsel must be present at every stage, and deems it error when the court proceeds without counsel.[190]   Other courts take the view that counsel can be absent,

185 *Delk* v. *State,* 99 Ga. 667, 26 S.E. 752 (1896); *State* v. *Arbuno,* 105 La. 719, 30 So. 163 (1901).

186 *In re Hough,* 24 C. 2d 522, 150 P. 2d 448 (1944); *People* v. *Boreman,* 401 Ill. 566, 82 N.E. 2d 459 (1948); *State* v. *Arbuno,* 105 La. 719, 30 So. 163 (1901).

187 See *Jones* v. *State,* 57 Ga. App. 344, 195 S.E. 316 (1938), where two law students were appointed.

188 *Powell* v. *State* (three cases), 224 Ala. 524, 531, 540, 141 So. 215, 195, 201 (1931); *Powell* v. *Alabama,* 287 U.S. 45, 53 S. Ct. 55, 77 L. Ed. 158 (1932).

189 *Stockholm* v. *State,* 24 Tex. Cr. 598, 7 S.W. 338 (1888); *State* v. *Lofton,* 164 La. 496, 114 So. 109 (1927); *People* v. *Barrow,* 62 C.A. 2d 590, 146 P. 2d 42 (1944); *Commonwealth* v. *Ashe,* 149 Pa. Super. 423, 26 A. 2d 217 (1942). Similarly, one of several counsel may be absent at any time so long as effective representation is given. See *State* v. *Dowdy,* 217 La. 773, 47 So. 2d 496 (1950).

190 *Smith* v. *State,* 51 Wis. 615, 8 N.W. 410 (1881), counsel absent at verdict; *State* v. *Beeny,* 115 Utah 168, 203 P. 2d 397 (1949), judge failed to reinstruct jury because of counsel's absence; *People* v. *Cavanaugh,* 246 Mich, 680, 225 N.W. 501 (1929), attorney excluded just before trial; *State* v. *Davenport,* 33 La. Ann. 231 (1881), judge charged jury in absence of counsel; *State* v. *Moore,* 61 Kan. 732, 60 P. 748 (1900), arraignment without counsel; *People* v. *Fields,* 88 C.A. 2d 30, 198 P. 2d 104 (1948), counsel absent at judgment; *Lee* v. *State,* 244 Ala. 401, 13 So. 2d 590 (1943), counsel absent at verdict.

and that absence acts as a waiver unless it is due to erroneous court action.[191]

There are merits in each position. Those courts which require counsel to be present emphasize the importance of counsel to the defense at every stage of the proceedings; without counsel present, they hold, the court is incomplete. They argue that it is the court's fault if one of its officers, and attorneys are officers of the court, is absent, and they assert that it is the defendant who suffers most from a proceeding without counsel. This is a strong argument (it seems obvious, moreover, that subsequent punishment of counsel by the court means nothing to the defendant). The courts which treat absence of counsel as a waiver emphasize the "fight" theory of the law and stress the umpire role of the court. They urge, and with some justification, that court business must proceed on schedule. With less logic they add that no harm is done in the typical case because there is little that counsel can do at the stages when his absence usually occurs. A fair conclusion is that courts should severely discipline attorneys who are absent, so that absence will occur even less frequently than it now does, that the "fight" theory has little validity on the criminal side of the law, where the strength of the parties is unequal, and that the rule that no proceeding shall occur without counsel present is the wiser.

OBJECTIONS TO COUNSEL

In many situations it is convenient for one attorney to represent codefendants. If a conflict of interests exists when two or more defendants are being jointly tried, however, it is error for the court to force counsel to represent all the defendants. The

---

[191] *Brown* v. *State*, 62 Tex. Cr. 592, 138 S.W. 604 (1911), counsel absent during testimony; *Schwartz* v. *State*, 103 Miss. 711, 60 So. 732 (1912), counsel absent at verdict; *People* v. *Piszczek*, 404 Ill. 465, 89 N.E. 2d 387 (1949), counsel absent at sentencing; *People* v. *Moore*, 405 Ill. 220, 89 N.E. 2d 731 (1950), counsel absent at arraignment; *Presecan* v. *Ashe*, 168 Pa. Super. 267, 77 A. 2d 684 (1951), counsel absent during charge, but no harm shown. A unique situation was presented in *Ex parte Sabongy*, 18 N. J. Super. 334, 87 A. 2d 59 (1952), when a conviction was reversed because the absence of counsel at sentencing was the result of his reliance on the promise by an assistant district attorney to recommend a sentence concurrent with one which the defendant was then serving. The judge was not informed and accepted a nonvult plea and imposed a consecutive sentence.

troublesome situation arises usually where one defendant appears with counsel and the other without, and the error results when the court forces one counsel to represent two men whose interests conflict.[192] For reversal, the courts on appeal require that defendants show objections based on an alleged conflict at the time of appointment, and prove that a substantial deprivation of right resulted from the conflict.[193]

How tolerant a court must be in allowing a defendant to reject the counsel appointed is not clear. It has been declared that there is no right to a specific attorney.[194] At least one court has taken the position that the defendant must take whoever is appointed and that if the defense is unsatisfactory, grounds for appeal exist,[195] but another solution has been advanced, namely, that the defendant be allowed to dismiss appointed counsel and defend himself.[196] That this poses a dilemma is clear, for if the defendant is legally incapable of waiving counsel because of incompetence, how can the court permit the dismissal of the appointed counsel? Perhaps the best solution is to appoint the dismissed counsel *amicus curiae,* and permit the defendant to defend himself.[197] It would be folly to allow the defendant to select and reject counsel at will. Even those able to retain counsel have limitations imposed upon them by their financial resources and the unavailability of desired counsel, which may in some instances restrict them to counsel less competent than those appointed to serve indigents. Moreover, as a source of delay the opportunity for repeated rejection of counsel would have too obvious an attraction for many defendants.

---

[192] *People* v. *Lanigan,* 22 C. 2d 569, 140 P. 2d 24 (1943); *People* v. *Bopp,* 279 Ill. 184, 116 N.E. 679 (1917). A different conclusion is reached in *People* v. *Courtney,* 307 Ill. 441, 138 N.E. 857 (1923), on the specious theory that the same result would have followed if the court had acted correctly.

[193] *People* v. *Meacham,* 84 C.A. 2d 193, 190 P. 2d 262 (1948); *In re Egan,* 24 C. 2d 323, 149 P. 2d 693 (1944); *People* v. *De Lisle,* 374 Ill. 437, 29 N.E. 2d 600 (1940); *People* v. *McKay,* 403 Ill. 417, 86 N.E. 2d 218 (1949).

[194] *Commonwealth* v. *Thompson,* 367 Pa. 102, 79 A. 2d 401 (1951); *State ex rel. Bradford* v. *Dinwiddie,* 361 Mo. 940, 237 S.W. 2d 179 (1951). In *Cogdell* v. *State* (Tenn.), 246 S.W. 2d 5 (1951), the defendant rejected three appointed counsel in turn.

[195] *State ex rel. Brown* v. *Thompson,* 226 Ind. 392, 81 N.E. 2d 533 (1948).

[196] *State* v. *Hillstrom,* 46 Utah 341, 150 P. 935 (1915).

[197] *People* v. *Boyce,* 99 C.A. 2d 439, 221 P. 2d 1011 (1950).

Scope of the Right to Counsel

The previous discussion has revealed the statutory differences concerning the right to counsel which exist in various states and the applications of these provisions which state courts have made in regard to indigents in capital and noncapital cases. The discussion to follow attempts to explain at what proceedings analogous to a criminal proceeding the right may be enjoyed, and at what points in a criminal prosecution the right to counsel begins and ends.

In surveying the proceedings in which there might be a need for counsel, it is obvious that one can retain counsel to appear in civil cases, but that unless a specific statute allows the public defender or other counsel to be appointed for indigents there is no right to receive appointed counsel in civil cases.[198]   Since habeas corpus is regarded by the courts as a civil procedure, there is no right to appointed counsel in this proceeding, although in a meritorious case courts generally will make appointments.[199]   Furthermore, it is generally true that while one can retain counsel, there is no right, except in the state of Indiana, to have counsel appointed for misdemeanor or minor cases.[200]

A few cases indicate that under broadly phrased constitutional provisions there is a right to counsel in courts-martial,[201] but that there is no right to counsel on appearances before legislative bodies or committees.[202]   The "opportunity to be heard," as required in statutes governing the removal of police and other public officers in New York,[203] means that the right to retain and appear by counsel is guaranteed.[204]

[198] In re Rozgall, 147 Neb. 260, 23 N.W. 2d 85 (1946); Rosen v. Seidenberg, 111 Pa. Super. 534, 170 A. 351 (1934).

[199] People ex rel. Ross v. Ragen, 391 Ill. 419, 63 N.E. 2d 874 (1945).

[200] Houk v. Board of Commissioners, 14 Ind. App. 662, 41 N.E. 1068 (1895); State v. Davis, 171 La. 449, 131 So. 295 (1930); Brack v. State, 187 Md. 542, 51 A. 2d 171 (1947); Milliman v. State (Tex. Cr.), 238 S.W. 2d 970 (1951). See note, 27 Neb. L. Rev. (Nov., 1947), 87, on the right as extended in misdemeanor cases. The Indiana decision which holds differently is Bolkovac v. State, 229 Ind. 294, 98 N.E. 2d 250 (1951). See note "Right to Counsel in Indiana," 26 Ind. L. J. (Winter, 1951), 234.

[201] People v. Allen, 55 N.Y. 31 (1873); State v. Crosby, 24 Nev. 115, 50 P. 127 (1897).

[202] People v. Keeler, 99 N.Y. 463, 2 N.E. 615 (1885).

[203] Sess. Laws, 1873, c. 335, § 25.

[204] People v. Nichols, 79 N.Y. 582 (1880).

It is with the elements directly related to the criminal prosecution that we are chiefly concerned, however, and it is most convenient to deal with the right to counsel in such cases at three phases: before, during, and after trial.

Strangely enough, it is impossible to say just when the right to counsel begins. There is no duty on the arresting officer to inform the defendant of his right to counsel.[205] In Indiana it has been held that a jailer must consult with the court when an accused asks for counsel.[206] Apparently, in our state jurisdictions there is no procedure short of obtaining a court order which can compel officials to permit access to the prisoner by retained counsel. The general attitude seems to be that matters antecedent to trial are not essential to the fairness of the subsequent proceeding.[207] One need not have counsel before interrogation takes place.[208] It is increasingly obvious, however, that refusal to allow the defendant to talk to counsel may have substantial weight in determining the question of the validity of a confession made while under arrest.[209]

There is no right to have counsel appointed for a coroner's inquest,[210] nor for the preliminary examination, unless a statute so provides, even in those states which require appointment in all felonies,[211] and it has been held that there is no right to counsel for one summoned by a grand jury, even though his indictment is being considered.[212] As defined by statutes and by decisions already discussed, the right to counsel begins in most states upon arraignment, although a plea of "not guilty" followed by an appointment or retention of counsel obviously

[205] *Commonwealth* v. *Bryant,* 367 Pa. 135, 79 A. 2d 193 (1951).

[206] *Dearing* v. *State,* 229 Ind. 131, 95 N.E. 2d 832 (1951).

[207] *People* v. *Kelly,* 404 Ill. 281, 89 N.E. 2d 27 (1949); *State* v. *Murphy,* 87 N.J.L. 515, 94 A. 640 (1915).

[208] *Lenoir* v. *State* (Md.), 80 A. 2d 3 (1951); *Audler* v. *Kriss* (Md.), 79 A. 2d 391 (1951).

[209] See *Stagemeyer* v. *State,* 133 Neb. 9, 273 N.W. 824 (1937); *People* v. *Stroble,* 36 C. 2d 615, 226 P. 2d 330 (1951), where an attorney waited ten hours and still was not allowed to see the defendant. Later "voluntary" confessions saved the state's case.

[210] *People* v. *Coker,* 104 C.A. 2d 224, 231 P. 2d 81 (1951).

[211] *State* v. *Crank,* 105 Utah 332, 142 P. 2d 178 (1943); *Lyons* v. *State,* 77 Okla. Cr. 197, 138 P. 2d 142 (1943); *Roberts* v. *State,* 145 Neb. 658, 17 N.W. 2d 666 (1945); *People* v. *Coker,* 104 C.A. 2d 224, 231 P. 2d 81 (1951).

[212] *People* v. *Lauder,* 82 Mich. 109 (1890).

is not prejudicial.[213]   And one has the right to counsel in the *voir dire* examination of prospective jurors.[214]

In a contempt proceeding that arises during a trial or in a contempt proceeding stemming from failure or refusal to carry out a court order there is no right to counsel since it is a civil, not a criminal, proceeding.[215]   A judge investigating alleged tampering with the jury need not permit counsel for the witnesses, but the right arises when the judge orders a witness into custody.[216]   Nor is there a duty to appoint counsel at statutory proceedings to determine sanity of a defendant under a death sentence, even though the right existed at the trial.[217]

Upon the right to counsel on appeal there is a divergence of views.   Courts which have interpreted constitutional and statutory provisions broadly extend the right to have counsel appointed to appeal.[218]   There are courts, however, which have decided to limit the right to counsel to the trial.[219]   As a matter of practice, courts will usually appoint counsel where the appeal has some merit, and counsel appointed for trial will customarily appeal in cases where such a course seems desirable.   The great weight of authority supports the position that there is no right to counsel on hearings to determine if probation terms have been violated.[220]

---

[213] In Massachusetts the duty to provide counsel begins only when the defendant appears in court, *Commonwealth* v. *McNeil*, 104 N.E. 2d 153 (1952).

[214] *State* v. *Guidry*, 160 La. 655, 107 So. 479 (1926).

[215] *Guiraud* v. *Canal County*, 79 Colo. 290, 245 P. 485 (1926); *Ex parte Hamilton and Smith*, 51 Ala. 66 (1874); *People* v. *Cochrane*, 307 Ill. 126, 138 N.E. 291 (1923). Contra: *Hunter* v. *State*, 251 Ala. 11, 37 So. 2d 276 (1948).

[216] *Gallagher* v. *Municipal Court of Los Angeles*, 31 C. 2d 784, 192 P. 2d 905 (1948).   This is obviously an exception to the prevailing rule, which gives no right to counsel upon arrest.

[217] *People* v. *Riley* (Cal. App.), 235 P. 2d 38 (1951).

[218] *Vowell* v. *State*, 132 Tenn. 349, 178 S.W. 768 (1915), as part of "due process"; *State* v. *Hudson*, 55 R.I. 141, 179 A. 130 (1935), in order to "conduct the defense," provided in *Gen. Laws R. I.*, 1923, c. 407, § 69; *People* v. *Price*, 262 N.Y. 410, 187 N.E. 298 (1933); *State ex rel. White* v. *Hilgemann*, 218 Ind. 572, 34 N.E. 2d 129 (1941).

[219] *Agnes* v. *People*, 104 Colo. 527, 93 P. 2d 891 (1939).

[220] *Ex parte Swain*, 88 Okla. Cr. 235, 202 P. 2d 223 (1949); *Ex parte Dearo*, 96 C. 2d 141, 214 P. 2d 585 (1950).   A review of the state decisions in the Dearo case reveals that only in Florida, New Mexico, Washington, and Utah is counsel allowed on probation hearings.

Broadly stated, the present scope of the right to have counsel appointed is bounded by arraignment and judgment, although practice in many jurisdictions may afford the protection of counsel at an earlier time and may extend the right through appeal. An unsolved and important problem is at what point subsequent to arrest the right to counsel should arise. The social advantage of obtaining voluntary confessions of guilt before an attorney can advise a prisoner to remain silent is balanced by the injustice in the coerced and unwarranted confessions of those who feel that they are in a hopeless position, with no escape possible. There should be a definite time limit placed on the detention of accused without counsel. It is suggested that counsel, whether retained or appointed, should be furnished as a matter of right no later than forty-eight hours, or some similar period, after arrest or detention. Honestly obtained voluntary confessions should appear in that time, although it would undoubtedly be difficult to convince some American police officials that a method other than confession exists by which the state can convict malefactors.

PROTECTION OF THE RIGHT TO COUNSEL

Denial of the right to counsel, such as by the failure to permit retained counsel to appear, by the failure to appoint counsel in capital cases, or in felonies, depending on the state statutory pattern, or by the failure to appoint regardless of statutes where due process requires appointment, is a fundamental error, proof of which will result in a reversal of conviction when shown in a proper proceeding. Failure to comply with counsel requirements is jurisdictional and indicates a failure to complete the court.[221] But substantial enjoyment of the right is all that is required, and minor deviations where no injury is suffered will not cause a reversal.[222]

[221] *State ex rel. Baker* v. *Utecht*, 221 Minn. 146, 21 N.W. 2d 328 (1946); *Wilcoxon* v. *Aldredge*, 192 Ga. 634, 15 S.E. 2d 873 (1941); *Bissell* v. *Amrine*, 159 Kan. 358, 155 P. 2d 413 (1945). Contra: *Smith* v. *Buchanan*, 291 Ky. 44, 163 S.W. 2d 5 (1942), jurisdiction of person and subject matter was held sufficient.

[222] *Ellis* v. *State*, 149 Tex. Cr. 583, 197 S.W. 2d 351 (1946); *Augustine* v. *State*, 201 Miss. 277, 28 So. 2d 243 (1946).

MOTION FOR A NEW TRIAL [223]

The defendant who has suffered a conviction because of the denial of one or more of the attributes associated with the right to counsel is interested in claiming the right by proving that the denial occurred. There are several remedial routes by which he may do this. Upon a verdict of guilty a defendant who feels he has been denied counsel may by motion ask the trial court to grant a new trial. This must ordinarily be done before judgment, but there are specific time limitations set forth in various states. One general ground upon which the motion can be granted is the phrase "when from any other cause not due to his own fault the defendant has not received a fair and impartial trial." [224] In fourteen states an appeal will lie from a denial of the motion.[225] The weakness of this remedy is that few defendants who have been denied counsel will learn of this procedure in time to take advantage of it, so that it is only where counsel is injected into the picture at the conclusion of a trial that it has any value. In the thirty-four states which do not allow an appeal from denial of the motion, the remedy is virtually worthless.

ARREST OF JUDGMENT

A second possibility is the motion in arrest of judgment, which is of common-law origin and lies only for matters appearing in the record, of which lack of jurisdiction is one ground upon which it will be granted.[226] In those states which hold the lack of counsel to be a jurisdictional defect, the motion in arrest is available. But appeals from a denial can be taken in only

[223] The standard work on criminal appeals is Lester B. Orfield, *Criminal Appeals in America* (Boston: Little, Brown, 1939). The remedies are summarized in the same author's *Criminal Procedure from Arrest to Appeal* (New York: New York Univ. Press, 1947).

[224] American Law Institute, *Code of Criminal Procedure* (Official Draft) (Philadelphia: American Law Institute, 1930), § 365(g).

[225] Orfield, *Criminal Procedure from Arrest to Appeal*, p. 513. See also *Patterson v. State*, 157 Fla. 304, 25 So. 2d 713 (1946); *People v. O'Neill*, 78 C.A. 2d 888, 179 P. 2d 10 (1947).

[226] See Orfield, *Criminal Procedure from Arrest to Appeal*, pp. 516–520.

a handful of states; [227] and the same limitations which restrict the value of the motion for a new trial exist here.

CORAM NOBIS

The third possibility is the writ of, or in the nature of, *coram nobis*. *Coram nobis* is of ancient common-law origin, and, as expanded in this country, allows an application to the trial court for the purpose of presenting facts allegedly unknown to the court at the time judgment was passed. In most of our states, appeals are allowed from a denial of this motion, although the writ in theory is one within the trial court's discretion.[228] It is being used to a greater extent in many jurisdictions on the basis that the trial court would not have acted to deprive defendants of their rights had the courts been aware of certain facts.[229] Some courts, however, have not allowed *coram nobis* because in their view the trial court must have known whether or not the defendant had counsel, and, if not, why not.[230] The advantages of *coram nobis* are that an application is not limited by a specific time period and that use of the writ shortens materially the process of redress by presenting the allegations to the original trial court.[231] Unfortunately, it is not so familiar to lawyers generally as is the writ of error or appeal, whichever is in use in a particular jurisdiction, or the writ of habeas corpus. If *coram nobis* were more widely used, it would limit the tendency to resort to habeas corpus in state and federal courts.[232]

[227] North Dakota, South Dakota, Louisiana, and California. See *People* v. *Shapiro,* 85 C.A. 2d 253, 194 P. 2d 731 (1948); *State* v. *Tennyson,* 73 N.D. 262, 14 N.W. 2d 168 (1944).

[228] See Orfield, *Criminal Procedure from Arrest to Appeal,* pp. 522–525.

[229] See *Bojinoff* v. *People,* 299 N.Y. 145, 85 N.E. 2d 909 (1949), which allowed an application for the writ at any time; *Irwin* v. *State,* 220 Ind. 228, 41 N.E. 2d 809 (1942), which held that a delay of four years in applying was excessive.

[230] *People* v. *Williams,* 293 Ill. App. 92, 11 N.E. 2d 640 (1937).

[231] A 1922 conviction was attacked successfully in *People* v. *Richetti,* 109 N.Y.S. 2d 29, 97 N.E. 2d 908 (1951).

[232] In Indiana, where *coram nobis* was used extensively and supposedly abused, an act was passed in 1947 establishing a presumption of waiver of the right to institute the writ after a five-year period from judgment. It was held invalid in *State* v. *Blackford Circuit Court,* 229 Ind. 3, 95 N.E. 2d 556 (1950). In 1949 Congress adopted a revised motion to vacate judgment and sentence which had the effect of a writ of *coram nobis.* See 28 U.S.C.A. (1950), § 2245.

ERROR AND APPEAL

There are, in addition, the two normal review routes, the common-law writ of error and the modern statutory appeal, which vary in form from state to state. Only their main outlines can be considered here.[233] Except where its original function has been decidedly altered, the writ of error, upon application to a higher court, issues to the lower court, which is ordered to send up its record so that errors of law appearing there may be discovered and judgment in the case reversed if substantial errors are found. Appeal is generally broader and gives the higher court a chance to review the entire cause, both as to facts and as to law in order to determine if the judgment is correct.

Treating both remedies together, we perceive that serious difficulties exist. First, there is only a short period of time, varying from state to state, within which a defendant can apply to the higher court. Moreover, if a defendant went through trial without counsel he will customarily fail to acquire counsel in the ten- to thirty-day period usually allowed. A tremendous number of defendants thus have this normal remedy cut off. A second difficulty rises from the inadequacy of the common-law record, which, where the appellate court holds that the errors must appear on the record, does not usually show the denial of counsel;[234] in a state where a request for counsel is required, the common-law record is again silent. The Illinois courts have been soundly criticized for the status of their records before the adoption of Rule 27–A. A third problem with writs of error or appeal is the necessity in most states of sending up to the higher court a bill of exceptions, that is, a list of the allegedly erroneous actions and rulings by the court to which the defendant objected and to which, upon being overruled, but still unsatisfied, he took an "exception," so that the dispute would be preserved for review by the higher court. But if the defendant did not have counsel, it is extremely unlikely that he

---

[233] See *Corpus Juris Secundum*, Vol. IV, for a full analysis of all aspects of these writs.

[234] A recital of appearance, plea, verdict, and judgment, and a statement that the defendant was "advised of his rights" composes the common-law record.

would have been sufficiently alert to interpose "objections," to save "exceptions," and to insure a complete record for review purposes.

For all these reasons the normal method of obtaining review is usually unsatisfactory to those who claim a deprivation of counsel. This is unfortunate since the advantage of writs of error or appeal, when compared with collateral attack through habeas corpus, is that the higher courts do not apply the presumption of regularity to lower-court judgments on appeal to the same degree that they do to such judgments on collateral attack. In most states today appeal has become a common procedure in which the original trial is prolonged until the judgment is pronounced free from substantial error, and thus higher courts look with less skeptical eyes on appellants than on petitioners for the writ of habeas corpus.[235]

HABEAS CORPUS

Finally, there is the ancient and widely used writ of habeas corpus. Since there is a substantial body of material covering this writ and the complex problems which rise from its use, all that need be said about it here is that it is treated by the courts as an extraordinary writ; it can be sought at any time from any judge, whether sitting in session or not; and it is designed, in its modern form, as an instrument for testing the validity of a detention, whether that detention resulted from arrest, court judgment, or other means.

The use of the writ in right-to-counsel cases is based upon the theory that the failure of the court to afford counsel for the defense is an omission of an act necessary to complete the court and to establish jurisdiction. A conviction obtained by a proceeding with an incomplete court is a nullity and is void, and one held pursuant to such a judgment is illegally deprived of his freedom.[236]

Because the writ may be sought from a sequence of courts,

---

[235] Recurrent themes in habeas corpus denials are the burden of the petitioner in a collateral attack, the presumption of regularity of the judgment, and the presumption that the trial court was fair.

[236] See *Wilcoxon v. Aldredge*, 192 Ga. 634, 15 S.E. 2d 873 (1941), for an excellent discussion of these points.

starting with the lowest court of record, and a denial of the writ can be appealed, and because the claim of a denial of counsel, if sustained, means that new trials must follow, the courts have been very careful to surround the application for the writ with such hazards that the petitioner succeeds in relatively few cases. Courts declare that the preponderance of evidence must support the petitioner [237] and add presumptions in favor of the validity or regularity of the judgment and in favor of the official rectitude of civil officers to the already heavy burden of the petitioner.[238]   Some courts have developed a disconcerting habit of dismissing the application with a simple notation that no grounds were stated for the issuance of the writ or for a hearing.   And if no appeal is allowed and the Supreme Court refuses to hear the facts through a commissioner, the remedy is virtually useless.[239]   In 1949 Illinois, a state whose review procedures had been widely criticized, placed in operation a Post-Conviction Hearing Act, which seemingly empowers trial courts to hold hearings and correct any serious constitutional errors in earlier proceedings by granting a new trial.   Unfortunately, in practice the act has not yet proved successful.[240]

In spite of its difficulties, habeas corpus remains the only remedy available to most of those who belatedly discover that they may have been deprived of their right to counsel.   And though it is utilized by many prisoners who have only the most frivolous claims, it seems clear that had the remedy not existed the subject of the right to counsel would never have assumed so prominent a place in the recent thinking of bench, bar, and litigants as it has.   Through the extensive use, and even abuse, of this extraordinary remedy forces have been set in motion which are already bringing about improvements in judicial pro-

[237] *Bradley* v. *Amrine*, 157 Kan. 451, 141 P. 2d 380 (1943).

[238] *Bissell* v. *Amrine*, 159 Kan. 358, 155 P. 2d 413 (1945).

[239] This is, or was, the situation in Illinois.   In response to the United States Supreme Court's request for enlightenment concerning Illinois remedies, the Illinois court surveyed state procedures in *People* v. *Loftus*, 400 Ill. 432, 81 N.E. 2d 495 (1948): A writ of error required a bill of exceptions; the trial court knew the facts about counsel and thus destroyed the possibility of *coram nobis;* and no appeal was available on habeas corpus within Illinois.   The Illinois court failed to mention that the basis of decision was never given on habeas corpus, and that it customarily refused to hear cases with factual issues.

[240] See later discussion, Chap. VI.

cedure. The creation of more effective postconviction remedies should materially lessen recourse to this writ.

PAYMENT OF COUNSEL

Payment of counsel is a subject intimately connected with the duty to appoint counsel and the quality of service furnished by counsel. It is a well-established American principle that one should be paid for work done at the request of, and for the benefit of, others. Nevertheless, from an early date, members of the legal profession, like medical practitioners in analogous circumstances, have given freely of their services to those facing criminal prosecution. Willingness to serve for absurdly low fees and upon insubstantial promises must be classed with the "volunteered" defense as evidence of legal humanitarianism.

But as the practice of law has become a mass-production enterprise in large cities and as the nation has moved toward industrialization and urbanization, the close contact which lawyers once enjoyed with the general public has been broken, or at least severely weakened. It seems fair to say that the conviction in criminal cases of a great number of undefended persons is especially an urban phenomenon, and that the rural bar has generally taken care of indigent defendants.

The duty of defending prisoners without prospect of payment seems unfair to most attorneys; to some it is a real hardship. Their objection is that most people will not perform useful tasks without pay; when charitable medical care is mentioned, the answer is that doctors can give a short time each day or each week to needy individuals and still maintain a substantial income, whereas lawyers, once appointed, must devote all or nearly all of their time to a pending case, sometimes with the prospect of the trial lasting for weeks.

Whether resulting from the greater influence of state bar associations upon state governments or from some other cause, statutory provisions of a sort exist in most states for the payment of appointed counsel, but appointed counsel in federal courts continues to go unrewarded by Congress. Payment varies in the states, as one would expect, from the adequate (or even generous) to the inadequate, from the possible one-thousand-dollar fee in New York capital cases to the possible five-dollar

fee for lesser service in Arizona.   Some states give payment in
capital cases only.[241]   A larger number have provided for payment in both capital and lesser cases, and where the amount is
flexible within limits, they place on the court the duty of ap-
proving specific allowances in each case.[242]   If an appointed or
elected officer known as a public defender is charged with the
duty of defending all indigents accused of crime, statutes either
set his salary or allow some public body to set it.[243]

In eighteen states there is no provision for payment of counsel in any case.   In general, it can be said that the payments allowed by the various states are far below the fees which most
attorneys would charge, although numerous exceptions to such

[241] E.g., Alabama: $50–$100, *Ala. Code*, 1940, Tit. 15, § 318; Florida: $100 limit
for trial, $100 for appeal, *Fla. Stat.*, 1941, § 909.21; Mississippi: $25 plus $50 for
expenses, *Miss. Code of 1942*, Tit. 11, § 2505; Pennsylvania: $500, *Purdon's Pa.
Stat. Ann.*, 1930, Tit. 19, § 784; North Carolina and New Jersey: fees fixed by the
court, *Gen. Stat. of N. C.*, 1943, § 15–4, N. J. Sup. Ct. Rules, Super. and Co. Cts.
(1948), Rule 2:12–1. See Emery A. Brownell, *Legal Aid in the United States*
(Rochester, N. Y.: Lawyers Co-operative, 1951), Appendix C, for a table covering
all states.

[242] Arizona: $5–$100, *Ariz. Code Ann.*, 1939, § 44–905; Iowa: $5–$20 per day
limit, *Code of Iowa*, 1950, Vol. II, §§ 775.4–775.6; Maryland: $100 limit, *Md. Code*,
1939, Art. 26, § 8; Minnesota: $25 per day limit, *Minn. Stat. Ann.*, 1949, § 611.07;
Montana: $25–$100, *Rev. Code of Mont.*, 1935, c. 73, § 11887; Nebraska: $100 limit,
Rev. Stat., 1943, § 29–1803; New Hampshire: $150 limit, *Rev. Laws*, 1942, c. 428,
§ 5; New Mexico: $25–$100, *N. M. Stat.*, 1941, § 42–1103; New York: up to $1,000
in capital cases, *McKinney's Consolidated Laws of N. Y.*, 1942, Code Crim. Proc.,
§ 308; Ohio: $50–$250, *Page's Ohio Gen. Code Ann.*, 1939, § 13439–3; Oregon:
$5–$150, *Ore. Code*, 1943, § 26–804; Rhode Island: $10–$15 per day, *Gen. Laws of
R. I.*, 1938, c. 625, § 63; South Dakota: $25–$50, *S. D. Code*, 1939, *Jud. Proc. Crim.*,
§ 34.1901; Washington: $10 per day, *Rem. Rev. Stat.*, 1932, Tit. 14, § 2305; Wis-
consin: $25 per day limit, *Wis. Stat.*, 1947, § 357.26; Wyoming: $15–$50, *Wyo. Comp.
Stat.*, 1945, § 10–806; Colorado, Idaho, and Michigan: the judge sets the compensation, *Colo. Stat. Ann.*, 1935, c. 48, § 502; *Idaho Code*, 1932, § 19–1513; *Mich.
Stat. Ann.*, 1938, Code Crim. Proc., § 28.1253.

[243] In California the public defender's salary is set by the County Board of
Supervisors, *Deering's Gen. Laws*, 1944, Act 1910, §§ 1–8. In Connecticut the
defenders are appointed by county judges for five-year terms and receive amounts
fixed by the president judge of each county; these sums vary from $900 to $9,000,
Gen. Stat. of Conn., 1949, Tit. 65, § 8796. In Illinois the salaries are fixed by
county boards, although the defenders are appointed by the judges, *Ill. Rev.
Stat.*, 1947, Tit. 34, §§ 163d, 163g. In Minnesota the salaries of the defenders
are fixed by the judges who appoint them, *Minn. Stat. Ann.*, 1949, § 611.12.
In Nebraska the elected defenders receive $100 or less per case, *Neb. Rev. Stat.*,
1943, § 29–1804. In Oklahoma the defenders, appointed by the judges, receive
$150 per month, *Okla. Stat.*, 1941, Tit. 22, § 464. In Virginia the defenders
are appointed by the judge and salaries are fixed by city councils, *Va. Code
of 1942 Ann.*, Tit. 41, § 4970.

a statement can be found. Yet if payment were set at too high a rate, there would be an inevitable scramble for appointment; an absurdly low figure, however, has the effect of causing most appointments to go to the younger lawyers or to the less successful of the older lawyers. Certainly the rate of payment should not be arbitrary. Perhaps the best method would be to allow the trial judge, who should have a rather accurate conception of the amount of effort put into a case, to fix the compensation within limits proposed by a city or county board consisting of elected public officials, judges, and representatives of the bar association.

In the absence of a statutory provision there is no duty upon a county to pay appointed counsel. This attitude is based on the argument that the attorney is discharging a public duty,[244] a duty as an officer of the court,[245] or a burden assumed with a lawyer's oath,[246] or simply that there is no obligation on the part of the county.[247] Two exceptions to this reasoning are provided by the highest courts of Indiana and Wisconsin. In each, statutes which denied any duty of the counties to pay attorneys appointed by the court were held invalid.[248] The subject of payment for appointed counsel will undoubtedly receive increased attention as the practice of appointing counsel becomes more general. Certainly the present situation is highly unsatisfactory.

SUMMARY

A survey of any problem or principle of law throughout the forty-eight states quickly destroys any tendency to talk about "the law," and what it is. Generalization reached by citing numerous statutes and cases tends to obscure the reality of the law in action in Paducah, Kentucky, for example, or in the Bronx in New York. Broad statements about the right to counsel fail to convey the differences in thinking and motivation between legislatures and courts in generous California and New

[244] *Posey & Tompkins* v. *Mobile County,* 50 Ala. 6 (1873).
[245] *Weatherby* v. *Pittmann,* 24 Ga. App. 452, 101 S.E. 131 (1919).
[246] *Johnson* v. *Whiteside County,* 110 Ill. 22 (1884).
[247] *Pardee* v. *Salt Lake County,* 39 Utah 482, 118 P. 122 (1911).
[248] *Knox County Council* v. *State ex rel. McCormick,* 217 Ind. 493, 29 N.E. 2d 405 (1940); *County of Dane* v. *Smith,* 13 Wis. 585 (1861).

York and formerly indifferent Illinois; between Indiana, which reads a broad right into its constitutional provision, and Florida and others, which hark back to the American Revolution and the historical antecedents of the right in order to limit it as narrowly as possible.

With a few exceptions the state courts have interpreted the counsel provision in their constitutions to mean nothing more than the right to appear with retained counsel. Yet from the earliest period under the colonial legislatures the states have attempted through statutes to aid the indigent defendant by extending to him the assistance of counsel. All states have provided for appointment in capital cases, and thirty-four have placed on the judge a duty to appoint in felony cases. At the same time it should be recognized that the courts of many of these thirty-four states have frustrated or limited the legislative action by a narrow and technical reading of the statute. Thus in Illinois and in other states which have stipulated the appointment of counsel on request, the appellate courts have upheld the trial courts in their callous policy of refusing to inform a defendant of his right to counsel. An existing defect in state statutes is the absence of a clear direction that courts must inform the defendant of his right.

State courts have succeeded similarly in narrowing the practical enjoyment of the right to counsel by an eagerness to discover a "waiver of counsel" in various acts or omissions of the defendant. Presumably, the failure of a court record to note a waiver of counsel would be construed unfavorably to the prosecution, but courts have allowed other evidence to be adduced to show that the defendant waived counsel. This matter of the waiver of counsel is one of the most confusing aspects of the whole problem, yet it is one which would seemingly permit a clear and simple solution. The lack of accurate or detailed court records has contributed materially to the confusion, although the fundamental cause has been the indifference and carelessness of judges who have acted on the principle that they could do no wrong.

Even where retained or appointed counsel appears, various forms of the denial of the right to counsel may occur. The right to a reasonable time in which to prepare for trial is part of the right to counsel, so that a denial of a request for a continuance may, in some instances, result in a reversal of conviction, although usually the exercise of discretion by the trial judge has been upheld. Reversal has also occurred when counsel has been absent at a stage in trial, or when the court has limited the argument of counsel. If there is a conflict in the interests of co-defendants, the court commits error if it appoints one counsel to serve both defendants.

Another frequent complaint of unsuccessful defendants is that their counsel was ineffective. State courts have looked with scant sympathy on these claims, however, regardless of whether the counsel was retained or appointed.

A more difficult problem arises from the question of where and when the right to counsel exists. There is no right to appointed counsel in state civil cases as a rule, and this includes habeas corpus proceedings. Furthermore, there is no right to counsel in minor cases. For practical purposes, the right to retained or appointed counsel in criminal cases begins at arraignment and ends at judgment. A good argument can be made that the right should accrue earlier in the criminal process, within a reasonable period after arrest, but the courts have not yet agreed on this.

Payment of appointed counsel varies strikingly, from five dollars to one thousand dollars, depending on the service and the state. A more realistic examination of this problem is essential if the right to counsel as extended in theory is to become equally substantial in practice.

The ways of asserting and protecting the right to counsel are not adequate. The conventional methods of alleging error in trial procedure are ineffective because of time limitations and because the unadvised defendant is not usually aware that a right has been infringed. Better court records will generally make an appeal possible, and the writ of habeas corpus is always available, although surrounded with presumptions and burdens of proof which are disadvantageous to the petitioner in the vast majority of cases.

It is suggested that under the pressure exerted by United States Supreme Court decisions that have already been handed down, and by those future ones which will follow principles now established, the states will inevitably be forced to adopt measures concerning counsel for state trials which will eventually approximate in practice the right enjoyed in federal trials under the Sixth Amendment provision. In self-defense, states like Michigan and Illinois have taken action after adverse Supreme Court decisions. While states such as Alabama, Florida, and Maryland may move more slowly and less willingly, recent decisions in these states nonetheless reflect the influence of the United States Supreme Court decisions.

The problems of when a court must advise an accused concerning counsel and of what shall constitute a competent waiver require prompt state action. Justice and logic demand that a defendant be informed of whatever benefits of counsel a state provides for him and that the court conduct more than the usual cursory examination of the accused before accepting a waiver of counsel. If the defendant shows a disposition to plead guilty the judge must be certain that he has the requisite mental ability and experience to know what he is doing. However, once a defendant is found competent to waive counsel, he should be held competent to plead guilty. The problems involving waiver will decrease as the practice of making a full record of the judge's interrogation becomes more common, and as judges spend a few extra minutes in ascertaining the essential facts about defendants brought before them.

What is to happen in those states which do not provide for the appointment of counsel in cases less than capital, but where defendants insist on asking the court to appoint counsel? There is a harshness in the unanswered request for legal assistance which is foreign to American law, and it is not mere sentimentalism to urge that this need not be so. The president of the American Bar Association has urged lawyers to extend the work of legal-aid societies in order to "avoid a demand for socialization of the legal profession." [249] And whatever the merits of extending legal assistance in civil suits where money and property are involved, the desirability of providing adequate legal defense for those who may lose their liberty is even more compelling.

[249] Address by President H. J. Gallagher, Annual Convention of the Illinois Bar Association, *New York Times*, June 23, 1950, p. 17, col. 1.

Certain states have created an example which all might follow with advantage. But here, as in other matters of law, the decisions of the federal courts will bring about change and advance in piecemeal fashion. Yet advance there must be in the conduct of state courts if the hand of the United States Supreme Court is to be restrained.

CHAPTER V

RIGHT TO COUNSEL, DUE PROCESS, AND THE FEDERAL COURTS

THE cases and problems arising under the counsel provision of the Sixth Amendment in the federal courts and under state constitutional and statutory counsel provisions in state courts have been considered thus far. It is now necessary to examine the restrictions and standards imposed on state criminal proceedings in respect to counsel by the due-process clause of the Fourteenth Amendment as construed and applied by the United States Supreme Court. After a brief survey of due-process antecedents, the leading Supreme Court counsel cases will be analyzed in order to make possible a statement and criticism of the present doctrine of the right to counsel in state trials. Finally, ways of minimizing the difficulties and confusions inherent in the existing doctrine will be suggested.

MEANING OF DUE PROCESS

Problems of interpretation lurk in almost any legal principle or verbal formulation of a right, but it is safe to say that none has surpassed "due process of law" as a source of discussion and argument. The expression originated formally as a statutory phrase in 1355: "No man of what state or condition he be, shall be put out of his land or tenements, nor taken, nor imprisoned, nor disinherited, nor put to death, without he be brought to answer by due process of law." [1] It had the same meaning as the earlier phrase "law of the land" found in Section 39 of Magna Carta (in 1225). Both signified that certain established modes of trial were to be followed. [2] Without opposition it was included in the Fifth Amendment.

[1] 28 Edw. 3, c. 3, cited in E. S. Corwin, *Liberty against Government* (Baton Rouge, La.: Louisiana State Univ. Press, 1948), p. 91.
[2] E. S. Corwin, *ibid.*

Others have told the story of how this phrase, which originally embodied procedural safeguards, became, as part of the Fourteenth Amendment, a substantive protection for American business and industry in the era after the Civil War.[3]   However, in spite of the extensive use of this clause to restrict attempted exercises of state police power, its procedural connotations were not completely ignored in the decades following 1868.

In *Davidson v. New Orleans* a property owner attempted unsuccessfully to challenge a tax assessment as unreasonable and in excess of benefits conferred.   The Supreme Court, speaking through Justice Miller, said that where, according to state law, "the party aggrieved has, as regards the issues affecting his property, a fair trial in a court of justice, according to the modes of proceeding applicable to such case," no deprivation of property without due process occurs.[4]   While this tolerant attitude toward state actions affecting property and tax rates was soon to be replaced by a more hostile one, the Court retained this fundamental assumption that state procedures must be fair to comply with due process, but need not have specified features.

In the 1884 case of *Hurtado v. California,* where a California constitutional provision replacing indictment by information was upheld by the Court, Justice Matthews, in a rather lengthy statement, said that due process was "that law of the land in each state, which derives its authority from the inherent and reserved powers of the state, exerted within the limits of those fundamental principles of liberty and justice which lie at the base of all our civil and political institutions, and the greatest security for which resides in the right of the people to make their own laws, and alter them at their pleasure." [5]   In order to conform to due process, no particular English or federal precedent

[3] See E. S. Corwin's *Commerce Power versus States Rights* (Princeton, N. J.: Princeton Univ. Press, 1936); and his *Twilight of the Supreme Court* (New Haven, Conn.: Yale Univ. Press, 1934); Rodney L. Mott, *Due Process of Law* (Indianapolis, Ind.: Bobbs-Merrill, 1928); Charles G. Haines, *The Revival of Natural Law Concepts* (Cambridge, Mass.: Harvard Univ. Press, 1930); Benjamin F. Wright, *American Interpretations of Natural Law* (Cambridge, Mass.: Harvard Univ. Press, 1931); Benjamin Twiss, *Lawyers and the Constitution* (Princeton, N. J.: Princeton Univ. Press, 1942). All these books provide excellent accounts from varying viewpoints. The volume of periodical literature is immense.

[4] *Davidson* v. *New Orleans,* 96 U.S. 97, 24 L. Ed. 616 at 620 (1878).

[5] *Hurtado* v. *California,* 110 U.S. 516 at 535, 4 S. Ct. 111, 28 L. Ed. 232 at 238 (1884).

need be followed, but, rather, "Any legal proceeding enforced by public authority, whether sanctioned by age and custom, or newly devised in the discretion of the legislative power, in furtherance of the general public good, which regards and preserves these principles of liberty and justice, must be held to be due process of law." [6]   States were free to differ in establishing judicial proceedings, so long as fairness marked those that were established.

It is true that the Court soon repudiated the canon of statutory construction used by Matthews in the Hurtado case, namely, that the enumeration in the Bill of Rights of a long list of rights, in addition to the due-process clause of the Fifth Amendment, indicated that the due-process clause when used in the Fourteenth Amendment should be interpreted as excluding any of the other rights specifically mentioned in the first eight amendments.[7]   Sixteen years later, in the Minnesota rate cases, the Supreme Court read into the due-process clause of the Fourteenth Amendment a restriction on a state's taking private property for public use without just compensation,[8] although Justice Bradley in his dissent, joined by Gray and Lamar, pointed out that the Court was remaking the Constitution. More recent and more dramatic repudiation of the canon has come since 1925, as the rights of the First Amendment have been drawn into the "liberty" protected by the Fourteenth Amendment.[9]

But the inclusion of a few rights of a substantive nature did not lead to any change in the Court's view of procedural due process.   In surveying the various changes which the states had made from time to time in their judicial procedures, Justice Brown could say in *Holden* v. *Hardy:* "While the cardinal principles of justice are immutable, the methods by which justice is administered are subject to constant fluctuation, and . . . the

---

[6] 110 U.S. 516 at 537, 28 L. Ed. 232 at 239.   Both official and lawyers' edition citations will be used in specific references.

[7] 110 U.S. 516 at 534–535, 28 L. Ed. 232 at 238.

[8] *Chicago, Milwaukee & St. Paul Railway Company* v. *Minnesota,* 134 U.S. 418, 10 S. Ct. 462, 33 L. Ed. 970 (1890).

[9] See the cases cited in E. S. Corwin, *The Constitution and What It Means Today,* 10th ed. (Princeton, N. J.: Princeton Univ. Press, 1948), pp. 194–201, footnotes.

Constitution of the United States, which is necessarily and to a large extent inflexible and exceedingly difficult of amendment, should not be so construed as to deprive the states of the power to so amend their laws as to make them conform to the wishes of the citizens . . . without bringing them into conflict with the supreme law of the land." [10]   Further, he said, due process meant that there were "certain immutable principles of justice which inhere in the very idea of free government which no member of the Union may disregard" and gave as an example: ". . . no man shall be condemned in his person or property without due notice and an opportunity of being heard in his defense." [11]

In *Twining* v. *New Jersey* the Court, proceeding on the assumption that a New Jersey statute permitting a judge to comment on a defendant's failure to testify violated the privilege against self-incrimination, went on to hold that the Fourteenth Amendment did not embody the Fifth Amendment due-process provision.[12]   Justice Moody repeated the "immutable-principle-of-justice" phrase used by Justice Brown in *Holden* v. *Hardy* and the description of due process from the Hurtado case and *Re Kemmler:* ". . . that law of the land in each state, which derives its authority from the inherent and reserved powers of the state, exerted within the limits of those fundamental principles of liberty and justice which lie at the basis of all our civil and political institutions." [13]   While the privilege against self-incrimination was not one of these principles and hence not to be included in the Fourteenth Amendment, Moody, who had a reputation for forthright statement, cautiously added: ". . . it is possible that some of the personal rights safeguarded by the first eight amendments against national action may also be

[10] *Holden* v. *Hardy,* 169 U.S. 366 at 387, 18 S. Ct. 383, 42 L. Ed. 780 at 789 (1898).

[11] 169 U.S. 366 at 390, 42 L. Ed. 780 at 790.

[12] *Twining* v. *New Jersey,* 211 U.S. 78, 29 S. Ct. 14, 53 L. Ed. 97 (1908). Compare Moody's natural-law analysis with that of Justice Murphy, dissenting separately, in *Adamson* v. *California,* 332 U.S. 46 at 68, 67 S. Ct. 1672, 91 L. Ed. 1903 at 1946 (1947), where Murphy insisted that although the Bill of Rights should be incorporated by the due-process clause of the Fourteenth Amendment, there were other, undefined rights which might well receive protection through the Court's use of that phrase.

[13] 211 U.S. 78 at 102, 53 L. Ed. 97 at 107.

safeguarded against state action, because a denial of them would be a denial of due process of law." [14]

Again, in *Hebert* v. *Louisiana*,[15] Justice Van Devanter repeated that due process required that state action "whether through one agency or another, shall be consistent with the fundamental principles of liberty and justice which lie at the base of all our civil and political institutions . . . ." [16]

Finally, the theme recurred in Cardozo's analysis in *Palko* v. *Connecticut,* where a statute permitting appeals by the state in criminal cases was upheld.[17]   The rights of the First Amendment and the right of an accused to have counsel were protected by the Fourteenth Amendment, he said, not because they were specifically enumerated in the Bill of Rights, but because they were "implicit in the concept of ordered liberty."   The dividing line, he asserted, between those rights which are protected by the due-process clause, and those which are not, is determined by asking if the right in question is "of the very essence of a scheme of ordered liberty." [18]   To abolish some rights, such as trial by jury and grand-jury indictment, "is not to violate a principle of justice so rooted in the traditions and conscience of our people as to be ranked as fundamental," he continued, and "few would be so narrow and provincial as to maintain that a fair and enlightened system of justice would be impossible without them." [19]   A hearing, he said, was as much a part of "liberty" as it was of "due process," and he justified the absorption of the rights of the First Amendment by the Fourteenth because "neither liberty nor justice would exist if they were sacrificed."   In each case it was necessary to take stock by asking if the denial of a given right imposed a hardship on the defendant "so acute and shocking that our polity will not endure it." [20]

The attack on this position as a "natural-law" perversion of

[14] 211 U.S. 78 at 99, 53 L. Ed. 97 at 106.
[15] *Hebert* v. *Louisiana,* 272 U.S. 312, 47 S. Ct. 103, 71 L. Ed. 270 (1929).
[16] 272 U.S. 312 at 316–317, 71 L. Ed. 270 at 273.
[17] 302 U.S. 319, 58 S. Ct. 149, 82 L. Ed. 288 (1937).
[18] 302 U.S. 319 at 325, 82 L. Ed. 288 at 292.
[19] *Ibid.*
[20] 302 U.S. 319 at 326, 82 L. Ed. 288 at 292.

the historical purposes of the Fourteenth Amendment reached its climax in Justice Black's dissent in *Adamson* v. *California,* where Black concluded that the use of natural-law phrases allowed the Court to "roam at will in the limitless area of their own beliefs as to reasonableness, and actually select policies, a responsibility which the Constitution entrusts to the legislative representatives of the people." [21]

Apart from Black's criticism, it is fair to ask whether any applicable standard emerges from the use of such vague phrases. Ignoring laymen and even the practitioners of law, who after all have no formal share in the process of adjudication, what norms capable of guiding judges can we draw from the phrase "implicit in the concept of ordered liberty"? The age-long struggle between those who emphasize "liberty" and those who stress "order" is basic in the history of philosophy and government. The uneasy balance which any society achieves between "liberty" and "order" reflects the outcome of the endless political and economic struggles among groups which deem their interests vital. The system of law that results from this crude process of compromise, and the assurance that new and peacefully attained compromises are possible, can be referred to as a "scheme of ordered liberty."

From his philosopher's chair Cardozo was suggesting that judges must draw the line in those close cases which come before

[21] *Adamson* v. *California,* 332 U.S. 46 at 68, 67 S. Ct. 1672, 91 L. Ed. 1903 at 1917 (1947). Obviously, his attack could have been directed with equal effectiveness against his colleagues Murphy and Rutledge. It is interesting to recall Black's disregard of the historical background in *Johnson* v. *Zerbst,* 304 U.S. 458, 58 S. Ct. 1019, 82 L. Ed. 1461 (1938). A seemingly complete refutation of Black's historical reconstruction has been supplied by Charles Fairman, "Does the Fourteenth Amendment Incorporate the Bill of Rights? The Original Understanding," 2 *Stanford L. Rev.* (Dec., 1949), 1. The Court's interpretation of the Fourteenth Amendment is analyzed in Stanley Morrison, "Does the Fourteenth Amendment Incorporate the Bill of Rights? The Judicial Interpretation," 2 *Stanford L. Rev.* (Dec., 1949), 140. The deaths of Murphy and Rutledge and the evidently contrary views of their successors seem to have "killed" the controversy. Grand-jury indictment and civil-jury requirements appear no longer desirable to a substantial number of states. These, as well as the other, less objectionable provisions of the Bill of Rights, would have to be incorporated, under Black's view. Rutledge and Murphy wanted the Fourteenth Amendment to mean all things—both to include the rights in the first eight amendments and to protect any others found desirable.

the Court by deciding either that our polity cannot "endure the shock" of denying a claim of freedom or that the requirements of order are so strong that the individual's cry for liberty must go unanswered. This thesis is a philosopher's creation, but practical men are faced with the necessity of applying the vague principles which Cardozo enunciated. Using and repeating his phrases, the judges before rendering judgment must consider the claimed right, the number who claim it, the effect of granting the right on the practical administration of justice and on the political relationships existing in a federal system, and the historical arguments for and against it. From such an amalgam of considerations they must then decide whether the right should be protected. Conscience and sentiment will play at least as important a role as logic and wisdom.

When all this is said and note is taken of the criticisms of so amorphous a standard, what are the alternatives? Incorporate the Bill of Rights in the Fourteenth Amendment, said Justice Black, and give to historical events their long-overdue meaning. But if his reading of history is wrong, what then? If one includes the whole Bill of Rights, one imposes various outmoded procedural rules in order to protect those having present value, and illogically decrees that the judicial procedures of 1789 be fastened on all the states as the result of an attempt in 1868 to gain equal treatment of Negroes in southern states.

The other alternative is to adopt the selective theory, under which it is necessary to wait for cases involving each claim of right under the due-process clause. The history of this process would indicate that few indeed are the cases in which there is a clear denial by a state of one of the rights in the first eight amendments. In using this method one may ask, furthermore, whether it is possible to be more definite than Cardozo was in the Palko case. To make history, or general practice, or any other rigid standard the test of what should be included in due process would defeat the very desirable possibility of state experiment. Moreover, it is precisely to decide what is "unfair" and "unjust" that we create judges, specialists in choosing between competing values in a practical world. The search for mechanical standards is a will-o'-the-wisp sought by those who feel that "natural law" is the enemy of true law.[22]   But, pressed hard, Black and Douglas, as well as their more yielding brothers Murphy and Rutledge, would admit that conscience and moral sentiment play their substantial part in decisions.   It is because a specific set of mechanical rules coincided with their basic feelings that they became "anti-natural-law" thinkers for the time and purpose at hand.

Yet it is valid to criticize the Court when it applies an amorphous rule to a variety of specific factual situations without enlightening observers or lower courts concerning the crucial points in the cases, as the fair-trial adherents have done in so many instances, thus defeating the very purpose of law and diminishing confidence in the efficacy of appellate tribunals.   As a general concept the requirement that state procedures be fair is a reasonable one.   But the results of its application by the Court to the counsel problem have been far from satisfactory.

ANTECEDENTS OF POWELL V. ALABAMA

By 1932 the procedural protection furnished by the due-process clause of the Fourteenth Amendment amounted to a guarantee of a fair trial.   The absence of one or more elements of the Bill of Rights would be held a denial of due process only if it resulted in an unfair judicial proceeding.[23]   Thus the states had been allowed to dispense with grand-jury indictment,[24] jury trial in criminal and in civil cases,[25] and the privilege against self-incrimination.[26]

Before 1932 there had been no Supreme Court cases in which the right to counsel figured prominently.   In a federal decision involving a person charged with conspiracy to lynch a Negro,

[22] Murphy and Rutledge, dissenting in the Adamson case, expressed the dilemma of those who want the assurance of mechanical standards *and* the pleasures of "free will" in the judicial process.   See the discussion above.   Since judges do intervene, it would seem more discreet for them to expand the meaning of single phrases from time to time than to undertake wholesale constitutional reconstruction and revision.   Black would avoid future judicial "interventions" by one supreme intervention now.

[23] *Moore* v. *Dempsey*, 261 U.S. 86, 43 S. Ct. 265, 67 L. Ed. 543 (1923).

[24] *Hurtado* v. *California*, 110 U.S. 516, 4 S. Ct. 111, 28 L. Ed. 232 (1884).

[25] *Maxwell* v. *Dow*, 176 U.S. 581, 20 S. Ct. 448, 44 L. Ed. 597 (1900).

[26] *Twining* v. *New Jersey*, 211 U.S. 78, 29 S. Ct. 14, 53 L. Ed. 97 (1908).

there was a dictum that the "judge and jury must hear counsel in the prisoner's defense" in Alabama courts.[27]   In another federal case a circuit court decided that the Sixth Amendment did not apply to the states.[28]   An overconfident declaration may be found in *Downer* v. *Dunaway,* where a circuit court said: "It goes without saying that an accused who is unable by reason of poverty to employ counsel is entitled to be defended in all his rights as fully and to the same extent as is an accused who is able to employ his own counsel to represent him."[29]

Passing references to counsel were made in two leading Supreme Court decisions.   In *Frank* v. *Mangum,* where Frank's claim that his Georgia trial was mob-dominated was rejected by the Court, Holmes dissenting, the Court said that Frank had "had a public trial, deliberately conducted, with the benefit of counsel for his defense."[30]   In *Moore* v. *Dempsey,* Holmes, for the Court, asserted that where mob pressure affected the actions of counsel, jury, and judge, there was an obvious departure from due process.[31]   Finally, the Supreme Court reversed a summary conviction for contempt out of court in *Cooke* v. *United States,* declaring that the proper procedure in such cases included "the assistance of counsel if requested."[32]   Thus by 1932 no case dealing with the duty of appointing counsel had yet emerged, though the converse, an appointment of counsel for a defendant who had sought a continuance in order to get his own lawyer, had been upheld.[33]   But at this time a series of events occurred in Alabama which led eventually to the

[27] See *Ex parte Riggins,* 134 F. 404 at 417 (1904), which involved a petition for habeas corpus. The court was speaking of the rights which the murdered Negro should have enjoyed, and one of these was the right to be defended at a trial.

[28] *Perkins* v. *Sheriff,* 23 F. 2d 892 (1927).

[29] *Downer* v. *Dunaway,* 53 F. 2d 586 at 589 (1931). This case involved an indifferent and inactive counsel appointed one hour before trial in a mob-dominated situation.

[30] *Frank* v. *Mangum,* 237 U.S. 309 at 344, 35 S. Ct. 582, 59 L. Ed. 969 at 987 (1914).

[31] *Moore* v. *Dempsey,* 261 U.S. 86, 43 S. Ct. 265, 67 L. Ed. 543 (1923). Counsel, apparently through fear, failed to perform even obvious duties.

[32] *Cooke* v. *United States,* 267 U.S. 517 at 537, 45 S. Ct. 390, 69 L. Ed. 767 at 774 (1925). The court hearing the contempt action had failed to give the contemner an opportunity to retain counsel.

[33] *Ching* v. *United States,* 264 F. 639 (1920).

present controversy concerning the extent of the right to have counsel.

POWELL V. ALABAMA [34]

The Powell case belongs in the same category as the Mooney and the Sacco-Vanzetti cases. All three aroused furious discussion and agitation within and beyond the limits of the United States, provided copious material for left-wing protest, and in the opinion of most observers did little to enhance the reputation of American justice.

The Powell case had its inception on March 25, 1931, when a fight occurred between a group of seven white boys and an undetermined number of Negro youths on a southward-moving train in Alabama.[35] With the exception of one boy named Gilley, the white boys were forced from the train. They informed local authorities, who wired ahead requesting the removal of the Negroes. Of the large number of Negroes supposedly on the train only nine were found when the train was searched at Pointed Rock. The youths were removed from the train and taken by a sheriff's posse to Scottsboro, the county seat. Two other persons found on the train proved to be white girls wearing overalls, Victoria Price and Ruby Bates. Apparently, after a leading question by a station agent named Hill, the girls each told a story of being raped by the Negro youths and identified Patterson, Weems, Norris, Powell, Robertson, Wright, and Montgomery as the leading participants,[36] with two others as witnesses.

Taken to Gadsden for safekeeping, all nine of the prisoners were returned on March 31 for indictment and arraignment on charges of rape. The record at this proceeding showed repre-

[34] *Powell* v. *Alabama*, 287 U.S. 45, 53 S. Ct. 55, 77 L. Ed. 158 (1932).

[35] The facts narrated here are from the record presented to the Supreme Court, and from the opinion of Justice Sutherland in the Powell case.

[36] The origin and reasons for the girls' story are examined in Quentin Reynolds' *Courtroom, The Story of Samuel S. Leibowitz* (New York: Farrar, Straus, 1950), p. 268, and in Haywood P. Patterson and Earl C. Conrad's rather sensational *Scottsboro Boy* (Garden City, N. Y.: Doubleday, 1950), pp. 6–10. In Appendix 4 of *Scottsboro Boy*, Ruby Bates tells her story. In Appendix 5 the opinion of Judge James E. Horton, granting a motion for a new trial after Patterson's second conviction, is a devastating attack on the veracity of the girls' testimony.

sentation by counsel and pleas of not guilty, although the circumstances of this representation were never clarified. In the Scottsboro courthouse, with the state militia on guard, a new arraignment occurred on April 6, when the trial of eight of the Negroes began, at which time no one answered for the defendants or appeared for them. A Mr. Roddy from Tennessee addressed the court, stating that interested persons had asked him to do what he could, although he had not been retained, and he indicated that he wanted to appear along with counsel whom the court might appoint.

In response to Roddy's statement the court replied: "I appointed all the members of the bar for the purpose of arraigning the defendants and then of course I anticipated them to continue to help them if no counsel appears." After expressing this optimistic thought and assuring Roddy that he could help, the judge addressed the local lawyers present and inquired, "Well, are you all willing to assist?" To which the apparent spokesman of the group assented by saying that they had all done what they could. One lawyer seemed to resent appointment if Roddy were to appear. After an indefinite colloquy among the spokesman for the lawyers, Roddy, and the judge, who was evidently highly uncertain of his proper course, the judge concluded: "All right, all the lawyers that will, of course, I would not require a lawyer to appear if . . . ." At which point an attorney named Moody said that he would help Roddy, to which the court replied, "All right," thus ending the discussion.[37]

The nine defendants were divided into groups for trial. Eight were convicted in the four trials completed on that same day. Appeals of seven of the eight to the Alabama Supreme Court were denied, the exception being that of a thirteen-year-old named Williams. The only dissenter in the Alabama Supreme Court was Chief Justice Anderson, who thought that haste, the military atmosphere, mob hostility, and lack of adequate representation added up to less than fair trials in all the cases.[38]

Walter Pollak, who had been retained by the International

[37] 287 U.S. 45 at 53–56, 77 L. Ed. 158 at 163–164.
[38] *Powell* v. *State*, 141 So. 201 at 214–215.

Labor Defense, presented the petitioners' cases, now consolidated into one case, to the United States Supreme Court. His brief alleged several types of unfairness, such as mob hostility, judicial partiality, and the denial of equal protection through exclusion of Negroes from the jury; then it emphasized the denial of the right to counsel. Cooley was cited, and the fact that this had been a capital case was heavily underscored.[39] Pollak stressed the youth, illiteracy, and ignorance of the defendants, which, when coupled with their low status in a strange community, required that they be given a reasonable opportunity to contact their families and obtain counsel. He reminded the Court that Justice Anderson had referred, in his dissent, to the likelihood of counsel appearing had sufficient time been allowed.[40] Finally, he said, the appointment made was illegal and ineffective. It was illegal because the Alabama statute stipulated the appointment in capital cases of not more than two counsel, and ineffective because insufficient time had been allowed to an inexperienced, out-of-state lawyer and an aging, halfhearted local attorney.

The defense thus set forth three basic positions: First, there was insufficient opportunity to retain counsel; second, the appointment of counsel was not properly made; and third, the defense was formal rather than real. In some ways the first position was stronger because the legal right to retain counsel was generally acknowledged. Its only weakness in this case lay in the six days' delay during which defendants took no action to get counsel; many trials proceed with equal dispatch. Since the Alabama Court had determined that the Alabama statutory requirement concerning appointment of counsel had been fulfilled, there was the issue of whether due process demanded an appointment of counsel in an effective manner. Here on this second ground the facts supported the defendants, although the law was vague. The competency of counsel, the third ground, had been the basis of state and federal cases, but had proved most difficult to urge successfully. In the opinion of the Supreme Court, delivered by Justice Sutherland, it was the first and, to a greater extent, the second position (lack of effective

[39] Brief for Petitioner, pp. 48–50.
[40] *Ibid.*, pp. 30–52.

appointment of counsel) which constituted a denial of due process.

Sutherland's opinion for the Court ranged widely over history and the precedents before expressing in powerful, cogent terms the elements which must be present in fair judicial proceedings. Due process always requires the observance of certain fundamental personal rights associated with a hearing, he said, and "the right to the aid of counsel is of this fundamental character." [41] The right to retain counsel, he continued, had always been protected in the United States as a part of a hearing, and in the cases now before the Court the "failure of the trial court to give them [defendants] reasonable time and opportunity to secure counsel was a clear denial of due process." [42] Sutherland did not stress this point, however. It was obvious that many indigents, and, in particular, Negro indigents, could not afford counsel, regardless of the opportunity to retain. He moved on to the main ground: "But passing that, and assuming their inability, even if opportunity had been given to employ counsel, as the trial court evidently did assume, we are of opinion that, under the circumstance just stated [ignorance and the like] the necessity of counsel was so vital and imperative that the failure of the trial court to make an effective appointment of counsel was likewise a denial of due process." [43] After examining the various reasons why this was so, he concluded: "All that is necessary now to decide as we do decide, is that in a capital case, where the defendant is unable to employ counsel, and is incapable adequately of making his own defense because of ignorance, feeble-mindedness, illiteracy, or the like, it is the duty of the court, whether requested or not, to assign counsel for him as a necessary requisite of due process of law, and that duty is not discharged by an assignment at such a time or under such circumstances as to preclude the giving of effective aid in the preparation and trial of the case." [44] The third point, concerning incompetent counsel, was not discussed.

Apart from the legal holding, Sutherland's opinion contains

[41] 287 U.S. 45 at 68, 77 L. Ed. 158 at 170.
[42] 287 U.S. 45 at 71, 77 L. Ed. 158 at 171.
[43] *Ibid.*
[44] *Ibid.*

an eloquent argument that there cannot be a fair hearing unless an accused has counsel: "Even the intelligent and educated layman has small and sometimes no skill in the science of law . . . . He requires the guiding hand of counsel at every step in the proceedings against him." [45] This statement about defendants in capital criminal cases could be applied equally well to all criminal defendants. And though uneducated and illiterate youths were involved in the case at issue, Sutherland in effect placed all but a few rare laymen in the same category as the defendants. In reality he was urging the expansion of the right to counsel, previously defined as the limited right to retain one's own counsel, when he concluded: "In a case such as this, whatever may be the rule in other cases, the right to have counsel appointed, when necessary, is a logical corollary from the constitutional right to be heard by counsel." This principle, taken together with his gratuitous remarks about the plight of unaided defendants in criminal cases, could be broadened by generous judges into a sweeping rule that counsel must be appointed in virtually all criminal cases if indigents are to have a fair hearing.

Butler dissented, giving as a reason his unwillingness to upset a state conviction affirmed by the Alabama Supreme Court with only one justice dissenting. The informality of appointment of counsel was not a decisive factor, he argued, and the record showed that everyone had done his duty. He pointed out, in addition, that three of the defendants had made statements claiming that one or more of the other defendants had committed the act charged. Finally, if the Court agreed that there had been a denial of the opportunity to retain counsel, its opinion should stop there and not go so far as to declare that a duty to appoint counsel must be fulfilled by the state.[46]

The Supreme Court decision was on the whole well received. The *New York Times* said that the willingness of the highest court to protect the humblest citizens had been demonstrated again, and that the fact that Sutherland, "who has often been called the most 'reactionary' member of the Supreme Court," delivered the opinion showed that it was not an act of "weak

[45] 287 U.S. 45 at 69, 77 L. Ed. 158 at 170.
[46] 287 U.S. 45 at 73–77, 77 L. Ed. 158 at 173–174.

sentimentalism."[47]   Some of the contemporary statements revealed a misconception of the rationale of the decision by stressing that the Court had ruled out mob-dominated trials.[48]

Commentators were rather cautious in estimating its effect. One opinion was that no logical distinction could be made in the future between the right to counsel in capital and in noncapital cases, and that the Supreme Court would say so when the proper case was presented.[49]   Another called the decision a further retreat from the Hurtado doctrine, prophesying that the required standard in state criminal cases would be that established by the Supreme Court.[50]   A similar and more laudatory statement approved the test of "fundamental principles of liberty and justice" as a desirable revolt from the mechanical reasoning of the Hurtado case,[51] and still another regarded the decision as a weapon which would be used to intervene in state proceedings only to correct "the plainest and most palpable abuse of some fundamental right."[52]   A narrow rule that due process was violated only when the absence of counsel resulted in an unfair trial was preferable, said another writer, to any rule which required the appointment of counsel in order that due process be observed.[53]   Some of the commentators surveyed state provisions, and one writer noted that although judges had appointed counsel in several instances when the aid of counsel had not been sought, it had been thought that appointment ordinarily rested on nothing more than a moral duty.[54]   In general, the writers expressed approval of the apparent willingness of the Supreme Court to use the Fourteenth Amendment's due-process clause as a means of building up a body of fundamental rights through a case-by-case process.[55]

[47] New York Times (editorial), Nov. 8, 1932, p. 20, col. 2.

[48] See the statements of Walter White, Morris Ernst, and Roger N. Baldwin, New York Times, Nov. 8, 1932, p. 13, col. 1.

[49] M. S. C., 31 Mich. L. Rev. (Dec., 1932), 245, 252; [unsigned note], 17 Minn. L. Rev. (March, 1933), 415.

[50] [Unsigned note], 32 Col. L. Rev. (Dec., 1932), 1430.

[51] S. M. F., 7 So. Calif. L. Rev. (Nov., 1933), 90.

[52] [Unsigned note], 81 Univ. of Pa. L. Rev. (Jan., 1933), 337–338.

[53] [Unsigned note], 18 Iowa L. Rev. (March, 1933), 383.

[54] Bertram Edises, 21 Calif. L. Rev. (July, 1933), 484.

[55] Irwin J. Kaplan, 23 J. Crim. L. and Crim. (Jan.–Feb., 1933), 841; [unsigned note], 31 Mich. L. Rev. (Dec., 1932), 245.

Contemporary adverse criticism was directed primarily at the alleged invasion of state criminal procedure and secondarily at the delay which would follow from the inevitable future practice of seeking certiorari from the Supreme Court; it was also concerned with the probable overburdening of the Supreme Court by a great volume of criminal reviews.[56]   Ready answers to these objections were available.   The Supreme Court had been reluctant to intervene in state proceedings following the Frank and Moore cases.   Moreover, delay which helps to insure justice is obviously warranted, and, with certiorari the Court could ignore cases which lacked merit.   It was "the vicious practice of rushing defendants through rapid trials in which the right to counsel and other constitutional rights are mere formal gestures" [57] which made federal regulation of unfair state criminal trials inevitable.

Generally, then, the doctrine announced in the Powell case was approved as being well within the letter and the spirit of the Fourteenth Amendment, and as a principle calculated to check those states which became careless in the conduct of judicial proceedings.

APPLICATION OF THE POWELL RULE

The lack of cases in which the petitioner claimed a failure to appoint counsel or to appoint effective counsel in the years immediately following the Powell case suggests that states were for the most part careful in capital cases.

There were a few cases beween 1932 and 1942 in which denials of due process in state criminal proceedings were charged. A lower federal court held in *Yung* v. *Coleman* that a prisoner had a right to private consultation with his attorney,[58] but in the more important case of *Brown* v. *Mississippi* the Supreme Court ignored the claim that an ineffective appointment of counsel had been made only one day before trial and decided the case on the basis of a coerced confession.[59]   In another case a lower court disregarded caution and stated that due process

[56] Kaplan, *op. cit.*
[57] *Ibid.,* p. 844.
[58] *Yung* v. *Coleman,* 5 F. Supp. 702 (1934).
[59] *Brown* v. *Mississippi,* 297 U.S. 278, 56 S. Ct. 461, 80 L. Ed. 682 (1936).

included the rights of "trial before a jury" and "to be represented by counsel." [60]

A lower federal court was given an opportunity in 1937 to
extend the Powell rule to noncapital cases, but it abstained.
In this case a Massachusetts defendant had requested and had
been refused counsel in a noncapital case. Since state law
specified an appointment only in capital cases and since no
"special circumstances" existed in the case, the court held that
the defendant possessed only an unexercised right to retain his
own counsel. The circuit court of appeals affirmed this decision, and the Supreme Court denied certiorari.[61] The significance of this ruling is made clearer when one recalls that in the
very next year, 1938, the Supreme Court in *Johnson* v. *Zerbst*
forcefully declared that the Sixth Amendment counsel provision
required the trial court to advise defendants of their right to
have appointed counsel in all cases. Such a rule was not to be
imposed on the states. In the one lower-court case where a
claimed denial of effective aid of counsel was upheld by the
circuit court of appeals, the record contained a strong hint of
perjured testimony, which undoubtedly influenced the appellate
decision. Moreover, it was a capital case, for which three days'
preparation seemed hardly sufficient.[62]

Doubtless because of the vigorous assertion of the broad
right to counsel in *Johnson* v. *Zerbst* in 1938, the number of
petitions for review by the Supreme Court of state cases involving counsel claims increased beginning in 1940. The Supreme
Court resisted strongly.

In *Avery* v. *Alabama,* where a mentally incompetent defendant received a rather swift trial on a murder charge and
argued that appointed counsel had had insufficient time for
preparation, the claim was rejected by the Supreme Court on
the ground that a substantial defense had been offered.[63] Then
in 1941 the Maryland courts were presented with two cases where
defendants were charged with burglary. In one, the accused
had asked for appointed counsel at arraignment and trial and

[60] *Andrus* v. *McCauley,* 21 F. Supp. 70 (1936).

[61] *Wilson* v. *Lanagan,* 19 F. Supp. 870 (1937); 99 F. 2d 544 (1938); 306 U.S.
634, 59 S. Ct. 486, 83 L. Ed. 1035 (1939).

[62] *Jones* v. *Kentucky,* 97 F. 2d 335 (1938).

[63] *Avery* v. *Alabama,* 308 U.S. 444, 60 S. Ct. 321, 84 L. Ed. 377 (1940).

had been refused.   A ten-day continuance had been granted so that the defendant could retain counsel.   After his conviction without counsel, the defendant sought habeas corpus from a federal district court, which denied his petition because no "associated facts" that would make appointment necessary were shown.[64]   The companion case differed only insofar as the defendant had requested the appointment of counsel at arraignment but failed to repeat his request at the trial.   The district court again rejected the claim of denial of counsel.[65]   Both rejections were affirmed by the circuit court of appeals in split decisions which saw the judges riding off in three directions.[66] One judge thought that in the absence of special circumstances failure to appoint counsel on request was not a denial of due process; the second judge thought that there had been a denial, but that appeal, and not habeas corpus, was the proper remedy; and the third thought that there was a loss of jurisdiction as a result of the denial and that habeas corpus should issue.   The outcome was acceptable to the Supreme Court, which denied certiorari.[67]

In 1941, in *Smith* v. *O'Grady,* the Supreme Court made its first application of the Powell doctrine of due process to a noncapital case in remanding a case for full hearing by the Nebraska Court.   The defendant claimed that he had been tricked into a plea of guilty because of ignorance.   Upon discovering at the time of sentencing that his plea had been entered to a charge carrying a twenty-year sentence rather than to the promised charge with a three-year sentence, he had protested and demanded counsel and had sought to withdraw his plea and obtain a copy of the indictment.[68]   The Nebraska Supreme Court had affirmed a denial of habeas corpus below, on the ground that no cause of action had been shown.   To the United States Supreme Court the allegations, if true, spelled out a denial of due process, and the Court indicated that a hearing was necessary.   Because of the other elements present in the case it is

---

[64] *Gall* v. *Brady,* 39 F. Supp. 504 (1941).
[65] *Carey* v. *Brady,* 39 F. Supp. 515 (1941).
[66] *Gall* v. *Brady, Carey* v. *Brady,* 125 F. 2d 253 (1941).
[67] *Gall* v. *Brady, Carey* v. *Brady,* 316 U.S. 702, 62 S. Ct. 1305, 86 L. Ed. 1770 (1941).
[68] *Smith* v. *O'Grady,* 312 U.S. 329, 61 S. Ct. 572, 85 L. Ed. 859 (1941).

impossible to determine the weight given by the Court to the denial of the request for counsel. The question of a defendant's right to counsel under the due-process clause in a noncapital case was not to be answered clearly until the end of the next term of Court, when *Betts* v. *Brady* was decided.

BETTS V. BRADY [69]

In 1942 Smith Betts was convicted of burglary, by a Maryland court, without a jury. To his request that counsel be appointed, the Carroll County trial judge replied that it was the practice to appoint counsel only in murder and rape cases.[70] Betts pleaded not guilty and, without waiving his right to counsel, defended himself, but failed in his effort to prove an alibi. After a writ of habeas corpus had been sought unsuccessfully in a lower Maryland court, he petitioned Judge Bond, Chief Judge of the Maryland Court of Appeals, who held a full hearing and then denied his claim.[71] Judge Bond's opinion stressed the simplicity of the issue in the case, the maturity and intelligence of the defendant, and the traditional fairness and care shown by Maryland courts in trials without juries. Judge Bond stated finally that he doubted whether counsel could have done anything more for the defendant than had been done and emphasized his belief that a fair trial had been given.[72]

The United States Supreme Court granted certiorari and, after being satisfied that Judge Bond's decision was a final judgment and that petitioner had exhausted his state remedies, proceeded to the merits of the case.[73]

Petitioner's argument was that due process required an appointment for indigents who requested counsel [74] because Cardozo in the Palko case had virtually included the Sixth Amendment counsel provision in the Fourteenth Amendment as an

---

[69] *Betts* v. *Brady*, 316 U.S. 455, 62 S. Ct. 1252, 86 L. Ed. 1595 (1942).

[70] Stipulated facts, Transcript of Record, p. 7. The statute allowed appointments in all cases within the discretion of the judge, *Ann. Code*, 1939, Art. 26, par. 7.

[71] Facts in 316 U.S. 455 at 457.

[72] Opinion of Judge Bond, Transcript of Record, pp. 29–30.

[73] The state agreed that the Supreme Court had jurisdiction and that Betts had exhausted his state remedies, Brief for Respondent, pp. 11–12.

[74] Brief for Petitioner, p. 16.

essential part of liberty, and federal courts had not drawn any distinction between capital and noncapital cases, so that none could be drawn logically under-due process.[75]   He cited *Smith v. O'Grady* as proof that the Supreme Court would treat a non-capital case on the same basis as a capital charge and quoted the broad dicta of Justice Sutherland in the Powell case.[76]

The state's answer emphasized the holding and glossed over the dicta in the Powell case, and cited *Wilson v. Lanagan*,[77] where the Supreme Court had denied certiorari to a petitioner whose case paralleled that of Betts.[78]   Then the long line of procedural due-process decisions from the Hurtado case through the Palko case was examined in order to show that states did not have to adopt any specific form of legal procedure, so long as that used was fair.[79]   Moreover, said counsel for Maryland, it would be difficult to find a workable principle by which to separate cases in which counsel was required and those in which counsel was not required, once you abandoned the existing distinction between capital and noncapital cases.[80]   The proper rule, counsel concluded, was that "the appointment of counsel is a necessary element of due process only to the extent that a fair and just hearing would be thwarted by the failure to appoint counsel and to that extent only." [81]   Thus since the trial was fair, the trial court was under no obligation to appoint counsel, even upon request.[82]

By a six-to-three division, the Supreme Court accepted the argument of Maryland and held that failure to appoint upon request in a noncapital case is not a denial of due process where a fair trial is given.[83]   Roberts, who delivered the opinion of the Court, repeated the familiar statement that the Fourteenth Amendment did not incorporate any Sixth Amendment rights as such, and that it was only *"in certain circumstances,* or *in*

[75] *Ibid.*, pp. 16–19.
[76] *Ibid.*, pp. 20–21.
[77] *Wilson v. Lanagan,* 19 F. Supp. 870 (1937); 99 F. 2d 544 (1936).
[78] Brief for Respondent, pp. 12–17, *Betts* v. *Brady,* 316 U.S. 455, 62 S. Ct. 1252, 86 L. Ed. 1595 (1942).
[79] *Ibid.*, pp. 19–20.
[80] *Ibid.*, pp. 20–22.
[81] *Ibid.*, p. 24.
[82] *Ibid.*, p. 29.
[83] *Betts* v. *Brady,* 316 U.S. 455, 62 S. Ct. 1252, 86 L. Ed. 1595 (1942).

connection with other elements" that a denial of a specific provision of the Bill of Rights was also a denial of due process.[84] The concept "due process" was "less rigid and more fluid" than the concepts indicated in the first eight amendments, he added, and its asserted denial was to be "tested by *an appraisal of the totality of facts in a given case."* [85]   He showed that historically the question of appointment of counsel had been settled by legislative policy in different ways from state to state, demonstrating that "appointment of counsel is not a fundamental right essential to a fair trial," [86] and that "while want of counsel in a particular case may result in a conviction lacking in such fundamental fairness, we cannot say that the amendment embodies an inexorable command that no trial for any offense, or in any court, can be fairly conducted and justice accorded a defendant who is not represented by counsel." [87]   Applied to the facts of this case, he concluded, it was clear that there had been a fair trial on a simple issue with an intelligent, experienced defendant.   Roberts' opinion paralleled Judge Bond's opinion in its entirety.

In a dissent, Justice Black, joined by Douglas and Murphy, admitted that his willingness to incorporate the Sixth Amendment rights was not shared by the majority, but urged that even under the narrower view of due process which prevailed, this defendant and others similarly situated required the appointment of counsel.[88]   Black thought that while the prevailing fair-trial rule gave to the Court excessive and ill-defined supervisory powers, it should be interpreted to mean that in a serious case a denial of counsel to one who requests or needs counsel was a denial of due process.   Harking back to Cardozo's phrase, he declared that a trial where the defendant could not have the aid of counsel because of indigence was shocking to "the universal sense of justice."   It was impossible, he believed, to say that a cause was adequately defended where counsel was absent, and thus to say that a "fair trial" was given was pure guesswork.[89]

84 316 U.S. 455 at 462–463, 86 L. Ed. 1595 at 1601.   Italics mine.
85 316 U.S. 455 at 462, 86 L. Ed. 1595 at 1602.   Italics mine.
86 316 U.S. 455 at 471, 86 L. Ed. 1595 at 1606.
87 316 U.S. 455 at 473, 86 L. Ed. 1595 at 1607.
88 316 U.S. 455 at 474–477, 86 L. Ed. 1595 at 1607–1609.
89 316 U.S. 455 at 477, 86 L. Ed. 1595 at 1609.

Black could have cited the Powell case and argued that less than a zealous defense meant less than a fair trial, and a defense without counsel, it could be maintained, would depart even more from standards of fairness.   Surely the majority, in adopting Bond's position that counsel could have done little or nothing for the defendant, was pursuing a line of reasoning which would inevitably destroy all rights.   Rights are agreed upon in order to insure that justice will be done prospectively, in the ordinary run of affairs.   To hold that an individual can be deprived of rights except in those cases where a retrospective view of events reveals a shocking situation is to defeat the whole rationale of the rule of law.

It has been suggested by E. S. Corwin that the "known high character of the trial judge" may have influenced the Court.[90] While it is true that the trial record reads well, the result here seems explainable by less accidental factors.   The fair-trial doctrine had respectable antecedents extending back at least as far as the Hurtado case.[91]   Moreover, Justices Stone and Roberts undoubtedly had developed a loyalty to its traditions as exemplified by the Palko decision.   Justices Frankfurter, Reed, Jackson, and especially Byrnes, had shown a deep concern for the proper balancing of state and national power in the federal system.   The doctrine as enunciated in this case was satisfactory to them because it was calculated to retain state autonomy, subject only to a gentle supervision by the Supreme Court in order to prevent state "excesses."

Those observers who had anticipated a declaration of a broad right to have counsel appointed in noncapital cases were naturally disappointed.[92]   One critic noted the complex of factors which the Court would have to consider as each case arose, and complained that constitutional guarantees should not depend on so many tenuous distinctions.[93]   Another reiterated that it was illogical to distinguish between capital and noncapital cases,

[90] *The Constitution and What It Means Today,* p. 189, n. 12.

[91] 110 U.S. 516, 4 S. Ct. 111, 28 L. Ed. 232 (1884).

[92] Howard S. Golden, "Right to Counsel," 16 *So. Calif. L. Rev.* (Nov., 1942), 55. The writer depicted the decision as abolishing a long-established principle. Obviously, there was no rule applicable to state noncapital felonies under the Fourteenth Amendment before this decision.

[93] [Unsigned note], 42 *Calif. L. Rev.* (Sept., 1942), 1205, 1207–1208.

though he glossed over the simplicity of the principal case.[94]   A puzzling feature of the decision, on which no comment was made, was Roberts' statement that there had been a statute requiring appointment of counsel in all previous state cases where the claim had been upheld.   Just how this made any difference it is hard to see.   Compliance with a state statute is a matter for state courts to pass on, whereas due-process standards stem directly from the Fourteenth Amendment and are not measured by state statutes.

When the result in the Betts case is added to the holding in *Powell* v. *Alabama,* the right to counsel in state trials in 1942 may be described as follows: Counsel had to be appointed in capital cases where special circumstances existed.   In noncapital cases counsel had to be appointed where special characteristics of the defendant existed, or, if there was a trial without counsel because of the inability of the defendant to retain counsel, there was a duty on the trial court to see that the defendant received a fair trial.   In this amorphous state the right existed, awaiting clarification that was possible only by the presentation of new cases with different fact situations.

APPLICATION OF THE FAIR-TRIAL DOCTRINE AFTER 1942

In marked contrast to the two counsel cases which reached the Court in the ten years following *Powell* v. *Alabama,* nineteen cases in which the issue of the right to counsel was squarely raised were presented to the Supreme Court in the decade after *Betts* v. *Brady.*[95]   Of the nineteen claims of denial of counsel, eight were rejected, seven of which, it should be noted, were in noncapital cases.   Four claims in capital cases and seven in noncapital cases were upheld.   In the following treatment of the cases which were considered by the Supreme Court in this period a division has been made into four categories: capital cases where the petitioner's claim was rejected; capital cases where the claim was upheld; noncapital cases where the claim was rejected; non-

94 [Unsigned note], 91 *Univ. of Pa. L. Rev.* (Aug., 1942), 78, 79.

95 *Loftus* v. *Illinois,* 334 U.S. 804, 68 S. Ct. 1212, 92 L. Ed. 1737 (1948), was sent back to the Illinois Supreme Court to ascertain the precise ground of the court's holding. In 400 Ill. 432, 81 N.E. 2d 495 (1948), the Illinois Supreme Court answered. Since there was no consideration of the merits of the case, it will have no place in the following analysis.

capital cases where the claim was upheld.   After such an analysis it should be possible to trace more accurately the contours of the fair-trial rule, and discern more readily its strengths and weaknesses.

CAPITAL CASE WHERE PETITIONER'S CLAIM WAS REJECTED

In 1928 one Carter was convicted of murder, and in 1945 he sought a writ of error from the Illinois Supreme Court. That court, in affirming his conviction, rejected his claim that he had been denied the assistance of counsel at his trial and cited the common-law record, which contained the usual statement that defendant had been advised of his right to have a lawyer appointed.[96]   The United States Supreme Court, in an opinion by Frankfurter, accepted the view of the Illinois Court and did not grant the petitioner's claim.[97]   Frankfurter, for the majority of five, said that this plea of guilty, understandingly made after the defendant had been advised of his right to counsel by the trial court, seemed competent and was supported by the record.   Further, he said, since only the common-law record had been available to the Illinois Supreme Court, the United States Supreme Court, in reviewing the Illinois decision, could not examine other unrecorded events, although on a different procedure perhaps the Supreme Court might look at these facts.[98]

The dissenters, in an opinion by Douglas, pointed to the Illinois Court's statement that counsel could be waived by a failure to request and said that this was not true in a capital case, because if the defendant was not capable of defending himself it was the duty of the court to appoint without waiting for a request.   It was evasive for the Illinois Court to rely on the absence of a bill of exceptions when the defendant had no one to aid him, said the dissenters, and they wanted to remand the case for a full hearing.[99]

In a separate dissenting opinion Justice Murphy disdained the common-law record and, after looking at all the facts certi-

[96] *Carter* v. *Illinois,* 391 Ill. 594, 63 N.E. 2d 763 (1945).
[97] *Carter* v. *Illinois,* 329 U.S. 173, 67 S. Ct. 216, 91 L. Ed. 172 (1946).
[98] 329 U.S. 173 at 179, 91 L. Ed. 172 at 177.
[99] 329 U.S. 173 at 181, 91 L. Ed. 172 at 178.

fied to the Supreme Court, including an uneducated Negro defendant held incommunicado for fifteen days and a five-page indictment in an alleged murder resulting from a casual highway argument, he concluded that a clear denial of counsel was shown, and that no waiver could be inferred.[100]

The basic contrast in the majority and the dissenting opinions arises from the technical approach of the majority and the expression in the dissenters of a willingness to discard the usual rules when a denial of counsel is the basis of the claim on the theory that without counsel a man cannot protect himself on the trial record—hence why use that record against him?   The Court's opinion included a vigorous reaffirmation of the fair-trial rule, which had been in abeyance since the Betts case.[101] Perhaps it was the impact of the ever-increasing *in pauperis* applications from state convicts which made the majority quick to grasp at answers of a technical nature.[102]

CAPITAL CASES WHERE PETITIONER'S CLAIM WAS UPHELD

Only four successful capital claims were pressed on the Supreme Court after the Powell case.   Two of these came from Missouri in the 1944 term of the Court, with only two factual distinctions between the cases.   In *Williams* v. *Kaiser* the defendant was charged with armed robbery, and he had requested counsel.[103]   In *Tompkins* v. *Missouri,* the companion case, the charge was murder, and the defendant had not requested counsel.[104]   Otherwise, the situation in both cases involved defendants who had pleaded guilty without counsel and who had claimed that they were ignorant, unable to hire counsel, and incapable of defending themselves.

Since the Missouri Supreme Court had denied the petitions

---

[100] 329 U.S. 173 at 183–184, 91 L. Ed. 172 at 179.

[101] See John Raeburn Green, "The Bill of Rights, the Fourteenth Amendment, and the Supreme Court," 46 *Mich. L. Rev.* (May, 1948), 869, for a pertinent review of the application of the fair-trial rule to various claims under the Fourteenth Amendment.

[102] See statistics in the *Report of the Director of the Administrative Office of the United States Courts, 1949* (Washington, D.C.: Government Printing Office, 1950), pp. 71–72.   The number of applications jumped from 147 in 1942 to 528 in 1946, though it tapered off to 417 in 1947 and 443 in 1948.

[103] *Williams* v. *Kaiser,* 323 U.S. 471, 65 S. Ct. 363, 89 L. Ed. 398 (1945).

[104] *Tompkins* v. *Missouri,* 323 U.S. 485, 65 S. Ct. 370, 89 L. Ed. 407 (1945).

without demanding that the state answer the claims, the United States Supreme Court accepted the allegations as true, and held that both cases should be remanded for a full hearing in Missouri. The majority, speaking through Justice Douglas, asserted that regardless of any questions arising from the Missouri statute requiring appointment, the due-process clause required appointment, whether requested or not, for one incapable of defending himself on a capital charge and unable to hire counsel. These defendants were in the same class as those in *Powell* v. *Alabama,* said Douglas,[105] in language reminiscent of that used by Sutherland in the Powell case, and he emphasized both the seriousness and the technical complexities of the charges and the inability of the average man to defend himself against a trained prosecutor.[106] Frankfurter dissented in both cases, and was joined by Roberts in the Williams case. He urged that a nonfederal ground may have been present in each case, such as the insufficiency of the facts shown in the habeas corpus petition to prove inability to hire counsel, and in his dissent in the Tompkins case he expressed his confidence in the correctness of the state courts and their procedures.[107]

The effect of the decisions in these two cases was to place a burden on a state to prove that a competent waiver had been made by the defendant in a capital case. Douglas affirmed that in his opinion a capital case should always be considered one "fraught with difficulties." Henceforth it was to be presumed that the average layman was incapable of defending himself when charged with a serious crime. Whether requested or not, counsel would have to be offered, and only a refusal by a competent adult would relieve the state of its obligation to furnish counsel. Following these decisions, the Missouri Supreme Court in conjunction with its judicial conference made provision for the appointment of counsel in all felony cases, unless an intelligent waiver was recorded.[108]

In the next term the Court agreed in *Hawk* v. *Olson* that the State of Nebraska had denied to Henry Hawk the effective as-

[105] *Tompkins* v. *Missouri,* 323 U.S. 485 at 488, 89 L. Ed. 407 at 413.
[106] 323 U.S. 485 at 488–489, 89 L. Ed. 407 at 413.
[107] 323 U.S. 471 at 479–485, 89 L. Ed. 398 at 404–407.
[108] John Raeburn Green, 46 *Mich. L. Rev.* (May, 1948), 869, 903, n. 138.

sistance of counsel, and remanded the case for a full hearing.[109]
Hawk's unanswered allegations indicated that the public defender had consulted with him for a mere fifteen minutes before arraignment for murder and had tried, without success, to
coerce him into pleading guilty, and that Hawk's motion for a
continuance in order to consult with counsel had been denied.
At this point the public defender had re-entered the proceeding,
which terminated in conviction. In his opinion for a unanimous Court, Jackson not participating, Reed pointed out that
degrees of homicide were involved, that counsel was needed,
and that "effective assistance" was denied between the plea of
not guilty and the calling of the jury.[110] "We hold," said Reed,
"that denial of opportunity to consult with counsel on any material step after indictment or similar charge and arraignment
violates the Fourteenth Amendment." [111]

In 1947 the Attorney General of Illinois confessed error in
the Marino case, in which an ignorant, illiterate, Italian immi-
grant youth of eighteen was convicted of murder and sentenced
to life imprisonment.[112] Though his rights were supposedly
explained to him through an interpreter, who had been the arresting officer, his waiver of jury was not signed and a plea of
guilty had not been formally entered. Three of the justices,
Douglas, Murphy, and the spokesman, Rutledge, were not content with a simple remand, but delivered a strong rebuke to the
Illinois courts on the "procedural labyrinth" which they constructed for those who sought relief from criminal convictions.
It was a "theoretical system of remedies" which was inadequate
in practice.[113] Although Illinois provided the common-law writ
of error, *coram nobis,* and habeas corpus, "only an oracle could
point out the proper procedural road," said Rutledge, who
asserted that in the future the Supreme Court of the United

---

[109] *Hawk* v. *Olson,* 326 U.S. 271, 66 S. Ct. 116, 90 L. Ed. 61 (1945).

[110] 326 U.S. 271 at 278, 90 L. Ed. 61 at 66–67.

[111] *Ibid.* The reaction of the Nebraska Court was quite different from that
of the Missouri Court. It denied Hawk's motion for compliance with the Supreme Court's mandate. See [unsigned note], "State Court Evasion of the U. S.
Supreme Court's Mandates," 156 *Yale L. J.* (Feb., 1947), 574.

[112] *Marino* v. *Ragen,* 332 U.S. 561, 68 S. Ct. 240, 92 L. Ed. 170 (1947).

[113] 332 U.S. 561 at 567–569, 92 L. Ed. 170 at 174–176.

States should not require exhaustion of state remedies before permitting resort to the federal courts.[114]

Had the factual issues of the Marino case been presented, the Supreme Court's answer would undoubtedly have been favorable to the defendant's claim. The case fell squarely within the Powell doctrine because of the special characteristics of the defendant. In addition, the retrospective test could have been applied successfully, since the failure to get a signed waiver and the absence of a recorded plea would tend to deny that the defendant had received a fair trial.

The long-needed criticism of Illinois procedure was applauded by those who were aware of the unsatisfactory situation in that state, and it seemed to presage a less generous attitude toward state reliance on technical errors in petitioners' claims to avoid Supreme Court review.[115] The confession of error by the Illinois Attorney General suggested that this careless trial procedure might not have been unique, as some critics had been contending. Certainly by the time of this, the last of the capital cases, it was evident that in capital cases, at least, the Court was inclined to place on the state the burden of showing that a defendant without counsel had desired to proceed without counsel and that his waiver was competent.

The substantial distinction between the rule applicable to these cases and that to be applied to noncapital cases was clearly expressed only four months later. Justice Burton, in holding that the Fourteenth Amendment did not require advice concern-

[114] 332 U.S. 561 at 570, 92 L. Ed. 170 at 176. In *White* v. *Ragen*, 324 U.S. 760, 65 S. Ct. 978, 89 L. Ed. 1348 (1945), the Supreme Court had declared that Illinois petitioners need no longer seek certiorari from the Illinois Supreme Court's denials of habeas corpus. As the Supreme Court pointed out, every Illinois review procedure had a basic weakness when the issue was the failure to appoint counsel. On a writ of error it was unlikely that a claim involving counsel would appear in a bill of exceptions. *Coram nobis* was virtually useless because if the writ were denied by a lower Illinois court no appeal was possible, and if the Illinois Supreme Court denied the writ, it failed to state the grounds of its refusal, thus making it possible for the state's counsel in hearings before the United States Supreme Court to argue against certiorari, claiming that a nonfederal ground existed.

[115] See Richard J. Faletti, "The Tony Marino Case," 36 *Ill. B. J.* (March, 1948), 356, and David Armstrong, "Adequacy of Remedies in State Courts," 47 *Mich. L. Rev.* (Nov., 1948), 72.

ing counsel or an offer to appoint under the factual circumstances shown in the noncapital case of *Bute* v. *Illinois,* declared: "We recognize that if these charges had been capital charges, the court would have been required, both by the state statute and the decisions of this court interpreting the Fourteenth Amendment, to take such steps." [116]   With capital cases, the Court had moved to a position well in advance of that taken in the Powell case, since the very fact that a case was capital now seemed to make it one of hazard even to the normal intelligent layman.   In such cases counsel must be offered and competently waived before the state can proceed to try a defendant unaided by counsel.

NONCAPITAL CASES WHERE PETITIONER'S CLAIM WAS REJECTED

The decision in *Betts* v. *Brady* had shocked those who had assumed after the Powell case that noncapital cases would be treated like capital cases, once the issue was presented.   Yet even in the disappointing Betts case there was a warning that where defendants were immature or incompetent, or where the case was more complex than that faced by the Maryland court, a different answer might be forthcoming.   As a practical matter, the possibility of increased petitions from convicts was almost as great under the Betts rule as it would have been under a more precise declaration that counsel was required in all cases unless waived.   For now every convict tried without counsel could raise the issue either under the special-characteristics feature or under the complex-charge doctrine, or he could ask for retrospective examination of what the court had done in a trial without counsel.   In the fourteen noncapital cases which came before the Supreme Court between 1942, the year of the Betts case, and 1950, half of the claims were allowed and half rejected.   The claims which failed will be examined first, followed by an analysis of the successful claims.

In one sense the claims rejected met that fate without ever arousing a full debate on their merits.   The first case, *White* v. *Ragen,* was typical. [117]   Appointed counsel had represented

---

[116] *Bute* v. *Illinois,* 333 U.S. 640 at 674, 68 S. Ct. 763, 92 L. Ed. 986 at 1005 (1948).

[117] *White* v. *Ragen,* 324 U.S. 760, 65 S. Ct. 978, 89 L. Ed. 1348 (1945).

White, who alleged serious defects in the preparation and presentation of the case. Without stating a reason the Illinois Supreme Court had denied White's petition for habeas corpus. The United States Supreme Court agreed with the Illinois Attorney General, who asserted that a nonfederal ground could have accounted for the action of the state court. Roberts' opinion, however, indicated displeasure with the Illinois practice and removed one procedural step for future claimants by declaring that it would no longer be necessary for Illinois claimants to petition for certiorari to the United States Supreme Court in order to exhaust state remedies. Thus the rule in *Ex parte Hawk* [118] that certiorari was a necessary step in the exhaustion of state remedies was modified because of the futility of the step when the highest state court failed to reveal its decisional grounds. Claimants could go directly into lower federal courts once purely state remedies had been fully utilized.

A unique situation was presented in *Canizio* v. *New York,* where the claim was rejected by a six-to-two division.[119] In 1931 Canizio had pleaded guilty at arraignment to a charge of burglary. He was nineteen at the time and admittedly had neither counsel nor advice concerning counsel when he entered his plea.[120] Two days before sentencing, counsel appeared for him. The simple question then was whether this belated defense effort amounted to the benefit of counsel. On motion for *coram nobis* the New York court said it did, and the United States Supreme Court agreed.

Oddly enough, in view of his earlier and subsequent statements, Justice Black delivered the opinion of the Court rejecting Canizio's claim. The critical issue in the case was whether the counsel who made a belated appearance for Canizio could have withdrawn the plea of guilty, and asked for a new trial, in which evidence of the withdrawn plea would have been inadmissible. The majority of the Supreme Court, speaking through Black, interpreted the New York law to mean that this action was available to counsel. The dissenters, Murphy and Rutledge, pointed to New York lower-court decisions holding that evidence

---

[118] 321 U.S. 114, 64 S. Ct. 448, 88 L. Ed. 572 (1944).
[119] *Canizio* v. *New York,* 327 U.S. 82, 66 S. Ct. 452, 90 L. Ed. 545 (1946).
[120] As required by New York Code Criminal Procedure (1940), § 308.

of a withdrawn plea of guilty was admissible against the defendant.   Apparently nettled by this confusion concerning New York law, the majority opinion asserted gratuitously that if the dissenters' view of the New York law was correct, the Supreme Court might invalidate that law in a future case.[121]   Certainly Black's opinion glosses over the central point.   A counsel who appears after a plea of guilty is faced with the choice either of withdrawing the plea and risking a consequent conviction with maximum sentence or of allowing the plea to stand in the hope of a lesser sentence.[122]   In either event the defense is handicapped.   Murphy's separate dissent avoided the technical issue: "Constitutional rights as well as due process rest upon something more substantial that [sic] what might have been but was not done." [123]   Since this was a situation where even the fair-trial rule required counsel at arraignment, he maintained that the entire proceeding was nullity from that point on, and it should be declared so.

The explanation for Black's stand is that the case lacked merit, for Black seemed convinced that Canizio had pleaded guilty to one of three charges in order to gain a reduced sentence.   Since the original plea was made voluntarily and counsel saw no reason to withdraw it and fight out the case on its merits, he would not infer that Canizio had suffered injury because of the absence of counsel.   The technical status of a withdrawn plea seemed of little importance in his view.   Black, in other words, had fallen completely into the fair-trial trap, by judging whether rights had been denied after considering the issue of guilt or innocence, an entirely separate question.

In the 1947 case of *Foster* v. *Illinois* the Court returned to its more normal division,[124] when in a five-to-four decision it rejected a claim by an Illinois petitioner of denial of counsel and failure to advise.   The majority viewed the Illinois procedure in a formal light and noted that the highest court there had been presented only with a common-law record on a writ-of-error proceeding.   Since the record recited that the defendant had been advised of his rights and of the consequences of a

121 327 U.S. 82 at 87, n. 2, 90 L. Ed. 545 at 549, n. 2.
122 327 U.S. 82 at 91–92, 90 L. Ed. 545 at 551.
123 327 U.S. 82 at 90, 90 L. Ed. 545 at 550.
124 *Foster* v. *Illinois*, 332 U.S. 134, 67 S. Ct. 1716, 91 L. Ed. 1955 (1947).

plea of guilty, the Court would not presume the contrary, said Justice Frankfurter for the majority, although he hinted discreetly that it might be wise to improve the record in regard to counsel in the future.

The dissenters, Black, Rutledge, Douglas, and Murphy, expressing themselves through separate dissents by Black and Rutledge, attacked on two fronts. Through Black they assaulted the fair-trial doctrine, which, as they said, placed constitutional protections on a day-to-day basis. Only by incorporating the Sixth Amendment protections in the Fourteenth Amendment could this unwise personal approach be avoided, they asserted, and they cited the dissenting opinion in *Adamson* v. *California,* handed down that day, as the "true" interpretation.[125] Rutledge, assuming the success of the fair-trial doctrine, argued that the Illinois practice of not advising in noncapital cases and of appointing only upon request was well known. In such a circumstance, the absence of a recital concerning counsel should be construed against the state, especially since constitutional rights were involved. Rutledge, therefore, presumed state failure rather than an individual waiver of a right in this context.[126] He observed tartly that Frankfurter's fears that the prison gates would swing wide seemed to be the most tangible argument offered by the majority opinion, which he thought extremely naïve in suggesting, as late as 1947, that when an Illinois defendant in a noncapital case was "advised of his rights" one could take it for granted that he was offered counsel, since in more than a score of decisions the Illinois courts had affirmed a practice of silence by the courts, and of no appointment without request.[127] Moreover, Rutledge added, advising a defendant of the consequences of a plea does not solve the problem of what plea should be entered to the specific charge described in the information or indictment.[128] The majority, he concluded, which pro-

[125] *Adamson* v. *California,* 332 U.S. 46, 67 S. Ct. 1672, 91 L. Ed. 1903 (1947). A more effective rejoinder than the Court's opinion in that case is made by Charles Fairman in 2 *Stanford L. Rev.* (Dec., 1949), 1. A good study of the cases is the one presented by Stanley Morrison in 2 *Stanford L. Rev.* (Dec., 1949), 140.

[126] *Foster* v. *Illinois,* 332 U.S. 134 at 143, 91 L. Ed. 1955 at 1961.

[127] See cases cited *supra,* in Chap. IV.

[128] See R. W., "Some Recent Decisions on the Right to Counsel, under the Fourteenth Amendment," 33 *Va. L. Rev.* (Nov., 1947), 731, 735.

claimed the merits of the fair-trial rule, showed in this case a keen disposition to avoid applying it.

On the day that *Foster* v. *Illinois* was announced, the Court rejected the claim of a denial of counsel in *Gayes* v. *New York*.[129] In 1938, at the age of sixteen, Gayes had pleaded guilty without counsel and had answered "No" when asked if he needed counsel. In 1941 he pleaded guilty to another charge, again without counsel, and received a more severe sentence, as a second offender. In the new proceeding in 1947 he challenged his first conviction only, claiming that at the earlier time he had not been aware of his rights, and had been too young to waive counsel. His application to vacate judgment, directed to the first trial court, was denied. Frankfurter affirmed this denial in an opinion supported by Vinson, Reed, and Jackson, with Burton concurring in the result only. The essence of the opinion was that this situation was analogous to the Canizio case since Gayes could have contested his first conviction at the time of his second trial, and, having failed to do so, could not now use this flank attack.[130] The Court, in effect, said that a failure to claim the right acted as a waiver.

But if the defendant had not known of his right to counsel at age sixteen, there is no assurance that at age nineteen he would know of it and claim it, particularly since he lacked the aid of counsel at the second as well as the first trial. The other assumption of the majority, that the petitioner should have attacked the original 1938 conviction at the 1941 trial and appealed a denial, disregards several decisions in the lower New York courts that a sentence based on an improper prior conviction can be attacked only through a motion in the court where the improper conviction occurred.[131] Rutledge's dissent tried to show that a distinction between the facts in this and the Canizio case required a different holding here, first, because Canizio had counsel, at least in the final stages, and, secondly,

---

[129] *Gayes* v. *New York*, 332 U.S. 145, 67 S. Ct. 1711, 91 L. Ed. 1962 (1947).

[130] 332 U.S. 145 at 148–149, 91 L. Ed. 1962 at 1964–1965.

[131] See 332 U.S. 145 at 149, n. 3, and 152, n. 11. The majority glosses over these decisions as emanating from courts "of very limited authority." The minority replies that in the absence of decisions of the highest court these decisions are "the law."

because the defendant used the proper procedure in this case, according to the New York decisions. As one commentator has expressed it, ". . . a youthful defendant was denied review because of his failure to adhere to a procedural technicality on which the Supreme Court itself was split 4–4!" [132]

In the next term of the Court the majority maintained the same position when another Illinois case with a silent record came up for review. In *Bute* v. *Illinois* a man of fifty-seven charged with taking indecent liberties with children had pleaded guilty in a 1938 proceeding.[133]   In his suit, ten years later, the petitioner claimed a lack of advice, failure to offer counsel, speedy trial, and personal ignorance as trial defects. Justice Burton, speaking for the majority of five, took advantage of the facts presented to review the whole train of cases and events involved in procedural due process and the fair-trial standard. Without question, the facts here are closer to those in *Betts* v. *Brady* than to those in any other case. The defendant was mature, pleaded voluntarily, and got a reasonable sentence in a trial which seemed fair; thus the facts of the case furnished a logical excuse for reasserting the majority position against the ever more-biting dissents. The majority opinion is notable also for the unequivocal announcement that in capital cases "failure to appoint counsel to assist a defendant or to give a fair opportunity to the defendant's counsel to assist him in his defense where charged with a capital crime is a violation of due process of law under the Fourteenth Amendment." [134]

The dissenters, speaking through Douglas, took their fling at "the ill-starred" decision in *Betts* v. *Brady,* and reasserted the incorporation theory in regard to the Fourteenth Amendment. Then, applying a view "more hostile to the rights of the individual," the fair-trial standard, they advanced the proposition that the repulsive crime charged in this case, and the difficulties of defending against it, required the aid of counsel. Considerations involving liberty are as important as those involved in capital cases, Douglas asserted. He concluded by proposing a

[132] George E. Grover, "Right to Counsel—Habeas Corpus," 22 *So. Calif. L. Rev.* (April, 1949), 259, 264.

[133] *Bute* v. *Illinois,* 333 U.S. 640, 68 S. Ct. 763, 92 L. Ed. 986 (1948).

[134] 333 U.S. 640 at 676, 92 L. Ed. 986 at 1006.

new test to be used in measuring the need for counsel: ". . . the nature of the charge, and the ability of the average man to face it alone, unaided by an expert in the law." [135]

It can be doubted whether this proposed and unaccepted test would have advanced the dissenters far. In the Betts and Bute cases, the majority obviously felt that "average men," charged with simple crimes, had pleaded guilty with a knowledge of what was involved. Douglas may have hoped that eventually the majority, or at least one or two of them, could be won over to Sutherland's eloquently expressed view that "even the intelligent and educated layman has small and sometimes no skill in the science of law." [136] This attempt to play the fair-trial game has been criticized as an unwise tactic,[137] but to justices interested in broadening the right to counsel in practice, it undoubtedly was frustrating to reiterate theories and arguments which had been rejected consistently. A new formula within the contours of the fair-trial rule would retain the cherished continuity of law, while allowing an advance in practice.

In the same term the Court rejected the claim of Joseph Gryger that he was not advised of the right to counsel nor offered counsel on his conviction as a fourth offender.[138] Gryger's face had become familiar to the Pennsylvania courts, since he had been a defendant on eight occasions before the disputed conviction, with defense counsel on two occasions. The majority plainly refused to believe that Gryger was unfamiliar with his rights, and could find no "exceptional circumstances" present. The only questionable feature of the proceeding, an alleged misconstruction by the judge of the sentence to be imposed, was dismissed as a "mere error of state law," if it occurred as alleged.

Rutledge's dissent seized upon this point. Due process had been violated, he said, because the defendant had suffered a disadvantage due to the lack of counsel.[139] This disadvantage, which arose from the trial judge's assumption that a life sentence was mandatory, rather than discretionary, was as prejudicial to

[135] 333 U.S. 640 at 682, 92 L. Ed. 986 at 1009.
[136] *Powell* v. *Alabama*, 287 U.S. 45 at 69, 77 L. Ed. 158 at 170.
[137] See John Raeburn Green, 46 *Mich. L. Rev.*, 869.
[138] *Gryger* v. *Burke*, 334 U.S. 728, 68 S. Ct. 1256, 92 L. Ed. 1683 (1948).
[139] 334 U.S. 728 at 732–733, 92 L. Ed. 1683 at 1688.

the defendant as the trial judge's misuse of the defendant's record in *Townsend* v. *Burke,* where the case had been remanded.[140] "Perhaps," concluded the dissent with some asperity, "the difference serves only to illustrate how capricious are the results when the right to counsel is made to depend not upon the mandate of the Constitution, but upon the vagaries of whether judges, the same or different, will regard this incident or that in the course of particular proceedings as prejudicial." [141]

To an objective observer, the distinguishing features in this case appear to have been the extensive experience of the defendant, the existence of an unchallenged sentence under which the defendant could be held, and the lack of any such hostility shown by the judge to the defendant as was present in the Townsend case. Finally, there is the feeling that the Court regarded a life sentence as eminently fitting in this case, one which the trial judge would have imposed whether he had deemed a life sentence mandatory or discretionary under the statute; since the Pennsylvania Supreme Court had not held the trial judge's construction to be erroneous, it was improper for the United States Supreme Court to do so. It is worth noting, finally, that this marked the last five-to-four division of the Court on counsel cases.

In *Quicksall* v. *Michigan,* the last noncapital case in this series, a murder conviction was upheld against the claim that a plea of guilty without the aid of counsel was a denial of due process.[142] Capital punishment had been abolished in Michigan, and a life sentence became the most severe punishment possible.[143] The petitioner, who was the survivor of a suicide pact with another man's wife, had served previous penitentiary terms; he was forty-four and of normal intelligence, and the plea had been entered after an exhaustive examination by the trial judge. Ten years later the petitioner "reconstructed" a series of events, including misrepresentation by public officials, interference with counsel, and the like, none of which seemed con-

---

[140] *Townsend v. Burke,* 334 U.S. 736, 68 S. Ct. 1252, 92 L. Ed. 1690 (1948).
[141] *Gryger v. Burke,* 334 U.S. 728 at 736, 92 L. Ed. 1683 at 1689. See criticism of this case, George E. Grover, 22 *So. Calif. L. Rev.,* 259.
[142] *Quicksall v. Michigan,* 339 U.S. 660, 70 S. Ct. 910, 94 L. Ed. 1188 (1950).
[143] *Mich. Stat. Ann.* (Henderson 1938), § 28.548.

vincing either to the Michigan trial judge or the Michigan Supreme Court.[144]   The Supreme Court majority agreed, with Justice Black registering a lone dissent.   Justice Douglas took no part in this, the only counsel case after the elevation of Justices Clark and Minton to the bench.

Too much should not be read into the alignment on this case.   Except that it was a serious case, analogous to the capital cases which would have brought Murphy and Rutledge to the aid of Black, the facts are wholly unfavorable to the petitioner. The record was more complete than is usual, and the defendant's whole attitude in seeking review was one of, What can I lose?   On the other hand, the illogic and unfairness of treating noncapital cases in a manner different from capital ones reaches its highest point in this case.   In the bulk of capital cases, sentences of life imprisonment or less are imposed, and the complexity of a case is not always in ratio to the sentence which may be given.

In view of these seven noncapital cases [145] where the claims of petitioners were denied, it can be said that technical grounds will be used to protect the judgments of state courts where the merits of the claim might otherwise receive a favorable response. The Canizio case is perhaps the outstanding example of this tendency, although *Gayes* v. *New York* and *White* v. *Ragen* illustrate the same point.   The virtually unanimous decision in the Quicksall case, on the other hand, shows a willingness to

[144] *Quicksall* v. *Michigan,* 332 Mich. 351, 33 N.W. 2d 904 (1948).

[145] Two cases in the October, 1951, term contained counsel issues, but since the Court's decisions were based primarily on other considerations, they have not been included in this discussion. In *Gallegos* v. *Nebraska,* 342 U.S. 55, 72 S. Ct. 141, 96 L. Ed. 86 (1951), an ignorant Mexican farm hand had confessed to killing his paramour and was convicted of manslaughter.   The petitioner claimed illegal detention, belated hearing, coerced confession, and tardy appointment of counsel.   Reed's opinion, in which Vinson, Burton, and Clark joined, disposed of the counsel claim by repeating the established rule that in a state trial of a noncapital case due process was not violated by lack of counsel unless some element of unfairness appeared, and the same rule was held to apply to events before trial. In *Palmer* v. *Ashe,* 342 U.S. 134, 72 S. Ct. 191, 96 L. Ed. 154 (1951), the petitioner claimed, eighteen years after a Pennsylvania conviction, that he had pleaded guilty without being offered counsel at a time when he was an ignorant youth with a record showing mental abnormality.   Without an examination of the merits of the case, the Supreme Court remanded it to the Pennsylvania Supreme Court for a full hearing.   Minton dissented and was joined by Vinson, Reed, and Jackson.

deal with a case on its merits. In *Gayes* v. *New York, Foster* v. *Illinois,* and *Bute* v. *Illinois* the narrow majority of five resorted to technical grounds, relying on the implications from the silent Illinois records in the Illinois cases and on a peculiar interpretation of New York appellate procedure in the Gayes case. *Gryger* v. *Burke* can best be explained as an exhibition of majority reluctance to interfere with a state procedure in which a substantially just result was reached.

In all these cases the majority seemed convinced that, whatever errors existed in the proceedings in state courts, no serious injustice had been done. This is the intuitive process which the fair-trial rule makes possible and even encourages. A judgment that a trial was fair is obviously retrospective. The dissenters, who maintained their ranks in the Carter, Foster, Gayes, Bute, and Gryger cases, rejected the fair-trial doctrine as applied by the majority. They regarded the right to counsel as one on which defendants should be able to rely before trial, and would presume an unfair trial where counsel was not offered or furnished by the state. When they seemingly joined hands with the majority in applying the fair-trial rule, it was always with the hope of reading into the law a less flexible standard, one which would require the appointment of counsel in almost all cases, as witness the proposal of Douglas in the Bute case that the ability of the "average man" be made the criterion of the need for counsel. They were less concerned with the question of whether those convicted were guilty than with the manner in which conviction came about, and they saw no reason why the Court should apply the same presumption in favor of the correctness of judicial action that might with propriety be urged on behalf of legislative action under review. The majority assumed a duty to interfere with state judicial proceedings sparingly and reluctantly. The dissenters regarded the protection of the individual and his rights as a principle of judicial duty more compelling than the maintenance of the federal principle in criminal proceedings.

NONCAPITAL CASES WHERE PETITIONER'S CLAIM WAS UPHELD

House v. *Mayo* in 1945 was the first noncapital case to reach the Supreme Court in which the right to retain counsel was clearly presented.[146]   The Florida trial court had denied a request for a continuance in order that the defendant House could retain a counsel who had served him previously, and it had forced him to plead guilty to a charge of which he had no warning.   The Court in a *per curiam* opinion, Justice Roberts dissenting, said that the trial judge's action "was a denial of petitioner's constitutional right to a fair trial, with the aid and assistance of counsel whom he had retained."[147]   No question of appointment of counsel was involved, and the case merely gave an official gloss to what had been long regarded as the minimal scope of the right to counsel.

In the same term, however, the issue of appointment was squarely raised, and in an appealing way.   In *Rice* v. *Olson* an ignorant Indian pleaded guilty to burglary, in a Nebraska court, without being advised of his right to counsel or being offered counsel.[148]   And perhaps best of all from the petitioner's viewpoint, there was a complex jurisdictional question in the case arising from the fact that the alleged crime was committed on an Indian reservation.   Justice Black, who delivered the opinion of the Court, struggled inconclusively for two and one-half pages with this problem in order to show how serious was the defendant's need for counsel.[149]   Moreover, the Nebraska Supreme Court had said, in effect, that a plea of guilty where the defendant failed to request counsel "absolutely" implied a waiver.   This was not so, Black answered, because the Fourteenth Amendment required a different presumption, one more easily rebutted.[150]   The three dissenters, Roberts, Jackson, and Frankfurter, the last of whom delivered the opinion, said that the allegations presented to the Nebraska Court were too meager to permit the inference of a denial of due process by that court, since allowable state grounds existed.   Reed and Chief Justice Stone joined with the almost inevitable bloc of Douglas, Murphy, Black, and Rutledge to uphold the claim.   Worthy of comment, also, was the action by the Court in treating a plea of guilty under

---

[146] *House* v. *Mayo,* 324 U.S. 42, 65 S. Ct. 517, 89 L. Ed. 739 (1945).
[147] 324 U.S. 42 at 46, 89 L. Ed. 739 at 742.
[148] *Rice* v. *Olson,* 324 U.S. 786, 65 S. Ct. 989, 89 L. Ed. 1367 (1945).
[149] 324 U.S. 786 at 789–791, 89 L. Ed. 1367 at 1370–1371.
[150] 324 U.S. 786 at 788, 89 L. Ed. 1367 at 1369.

the Fourteenth Amendment as it had treated guilty pleas under the Sixth Amendment in *Walker* v. *Johnston*,[151] not as a conclusive waiver, but as a waiver only after all the facts and circumstances in the case were considered.[152]

A unanimous Court had no difficulty upholding the claim of Rene De Meerleer that in 1932 he had been denied due process in a one-day proceeding at which he pleaded guilty to murder. Seventeen at the time, he was neither offered counsel nor advised of the consequences of his plea. This "speedy" procedure, it was held, did not constitute a fair "hearing." [153] The importance of the absence of counsel is difficult to assess, however. Had counsel been present, it is unlikely that the speed of the proceeding alone would have been fatal, unless counsel had moved for and had been denied a continuance. With counsel, the other defects, such as the failure to advise the defendant of the consequences of the plea, would not have arisen. This case was well within the established doctrine of due process, for unfairness was stamped on every aspect of the proceeding.[154]

The first five-to-four decision where the petitioner prevailed was in the 1948 case of *Wade* v. *Mayo*.[155] Wade, an eighteen-year-old defendant, claimed that he requested and was refused appointed counsel. Two days after trial and conviction, counsel then retained by Wade petitioned the trial court for habeas corpus and appealed the subsequent denial to the Florida Supreme Court. In its decision upholding Wade's conviction the Florida Supreme Court did not make clear its ground, although from subsequent cases it was obvious that the basis was the reliance on *Betts* v. *Brady* and the belief that the state was not required to provide counsel in any noncapital cases. Wade's counsel did not appeal the conviction, believing it fruitless in view of the Florida Court's attitude, nor did he petition for certiorari to the United States Supreme Court. A year later

151 *Walker* v. *Johnston*, 312 U.S. 275, 61 S. Ct. 574, 85 L. Ed. 830 (1941).

152 See [unsigned note], "Plea of Guilty Not an Absolute Waiver of Counsel," 31 *Minn. L. Rev.* (Jan., 1947), 195.

153 *De Meerleer* v. *Michigan*, 329 U.S. 663, 67 S. Ct. 596, 91 L. Ed. 584 (1947).

154 Frank H. Roberts, "Right of an Accused to Have Counsel Appointed by the Court," 45 *Mich. L. Rev.* (June, 1947), 1047.

155 *Wade* v. *Mayo*, 334 U.S. 672, 68 S. Ct. 1270, 92 L. Ed. 1647 (1948).

Wade turned to the federal district court, which said that the failure to appoint counsel was a denial of due process. The circuit court of appeals reversed on the ground that no case had been cited in which failure to appoint counsel in a noncapital case was held a denial of due process "unless the law of the state requires such an appointment." [156]

The United States Supreme Court upheld the petitioner on the preliminary question of whether he had exhausted state remedies and on the merits of the case, and reversed the court below. Justice Murphy, for the majority created by Frankfurter's defection from the fair-trial ranks, said that a decision on the merits had been obtained in Florida by one of the alternative routes. [157] To the more difficult question of why certiorari had not been sought in order that state remedies be exhausted, as *Ex parte Hawk* [158] seemingly required, Murphy answered with the rather mysterious comment that "no hard and fast rule" is justified, since respect for the highest state court is no longer a problem once that court has passed on the merits. [159] Moreover, he said, the discretionary nature of certiorari made it possible to refuse without reason, and, in a phrase that expressed the essence of his outlook, he commented: "The prevention of undue restraints on liberty is more important than mechanical and unrealistic administration of the federal courts." [160] Furthermore, he argued, there was no danger of excessive interference by federal judges with state-court decisions since in only 1.3 per cent of the total number of petitions filed in federal district courts in 1943, 1944, and 1945, had convictions been reversed and release ordered. [161] On the merits of the case Murphy was on firmer ground. "To the extent that there is a constitutional right to counsel in this type of case," he said, "it stems directly from the Fourteenth Amendment, and

---

[156] *Mayo v. Wade*, 158 F. 2d 614 at 617–618 (1946).

[157] *Wade v. Mayo*, 334 U.S. 672 at 678, 92 L. Ed. 1647 at 1652.

[158] *Ex parte Hawk*, 321 U.S. 114, 64 S. Ct. 448, 88 L. Ed. 572 (1944).

[159] 334 U.S. 672 at 681, 92 L. Ed. 1647 at 1653. This departure from *Ex parte Hawk* was in turn overruled by *Darr v. Burford*, 339 U.S. 200, 70 S. Ct. 587, 94 L. Ed. 761 (1950), where the Court held that a petition for certiorari to the United States Supreme Court was ordinarily a required step in exhausting state remedies.

[160] 334 U.S. 672 at 681, 92 L. Ed. 1647 at 1653.

[161] 334 U.S. 672 at 682, 92 L. Ed. 1647 at 1653.

not from state statutes," and the trier of the facts (the district court) can best determine the capacity of a defendant to defend himself.[162]

The dissent of Reed, with the concurrence of Vinson, Jackson, and Burton, stressed the procedural confusion which would result from this peculiar limitation on "the doctrine of exhaustion of state remedies so clearly expounded in *Ex parte Hawk* . . . ."[163] It was the petitioner's own fault if no state remedy was now available, since he had obtained counsel in sufficient time to appeal and to seek certiorari. The federal district court should have refused to exercise its discretionary power, they concluded. Rather lamely the dissent defended the decision of the circuit court of appeals by the assertion that *Betts* v. *Brady*, and not the lack of a state statute, had been the basis of that court's ruling, but a reading of the lower court's decision would indicate the contrary.[164]

Here again is a clear clash of viewpoints. The majority, with the unexpected assistance of Frankfurter, concentrates on the failure to appoint counsel, the resulting void conviction, and the wrongful detention pursuant to that conviction. Hence, it says, this is a logical case for the granting of the flexible writ of habeas corpus. The dissent emphasizes the failure of petitioner, aided by counsel, to pursue the proper procedure in asserting the deprivation of right and evolves what amounts to a doctrine of forfeiture of rights because of that failure. The majority's interest in individual rights and its willingness to disregard procedural rules to protect them are laudable, but it confuses the whole process of claiming constitutional rights by permitting the petitioner to flout the procedural guidelines so clearly set forth in *Ex parte Hawk*.[165]

On the day that *Wade* v. *Mayo* was handed down, the Court upheld the petitioner's claim in *Townsend* v. *Burke*.[166] This six-to-three decision, in a case which was free of technical pro-

---

[162] 334 U.S. 672 at 683–684, 92 L. Ed. 1647 at 1654–1655.

[163] 334 U.S. 672 at 688, 92 L. Ed. 1647 at 1657.

[164] *Mayo* v. *Wade*, 158 F. 2d 614 at 617–618 (1946).

[165] *Ex parte Hawk*, 321 U.S. 114, 64 S. Ct. 448, 88 L. Ed. 572 (1944). See E. W. Rothe, Jr., "Exhaustion of State Remedies," 47 *Mich. L. Rev.* (March, 1949), 720, for comment on this point.

[166] *Townsend* v. *Burke*, 334 U.S. 736, 68 S. Ct. 1252, 92 L. Ed. 1690 (1948).

cedural difficulties, turned on the use that the trial judge made of the defendant's record of previous convictions at the time of sentencing. In addition, there was a certain amount of hostility and facetiousness in the judge's conduct. All this would have been of no significance except that the defendant, a mature man, had not been advised of his right to counsel or offered counsel. The crucial conversation in the record was as follows:

> Court: "*1933, larceny of automobile.* 1934, larceny of produce. 1930, larceny of bicycle. 1931, entering to steal and larceny. *1938, entering to steal and larceny in Doylestown.* Were you tried up there? No, not arrested in Doylestown. That was up on Germantown Avenue, wasn't it? You robbed a paint store."
> Defendant: "No. That was my brother."
> Court: "You were tried for it, weren't you?"
> Defendant: "Yes, but I was not guilty."
> Court: "And in 1945, this. 1936, entering to steal and larceny, 1350 Ridge Avenue. Is that your brother too?"
> Defendant: "No."
> Court: "*1937, receiving stolen goods, a saxophone?* What did you want with a saxophone? Didn't hope to play in the prison band then, did you? Ten to twenty in the penitentiary." [167]

On two of the italicized charges the defendant had been found not guilty and on the other he had been discharged by the magistrate. Whether he had been overreached by the prosecutor, who submitted misinformation, or harmed by the judge's misuse of the record, the majority concluded that the defendant "while disadvantaged by lack of counsel . . . was sentenced on the basis of assumptions . . . which were materially untrue," a result which "is inconsistent with due process of law . . . ." [168] The Chief Justice, Reed, and Burton dissented without opinion. The majority's position is clear. The state is not required to appoint counsel for all defendants, but if it chooses to permit a defendant to proceed undefended, it must guard him against any serious error. If the prisoner suffers a

[167] 334 U.S. 736 at 739–740, 92 L. Ed. 1690 at 1693. Italics mine.
[168] 334 U.S. 736 at 741, 92 L. Ed. 1690 at 1693.

serious disadvantage without counsel, a violation of due process occurs.[169]

This poses a difficult problem for states which have not acknowledged the desirability and necessity of providing counsel for indigents. By swinging Jackson and Frankfurter over to their side in this case, the foes of the fair-trial rule utilized the fair-trial rule in order to achieve a result which may go a long way toward scuttling that much-maligned standard. If a judge wants to protect himself against reversal after this decision, he must either appoint counsel or assume a more active role in the conduct of a case than is traditional in state courts. A further illogic exists in this retrospective test of the right to counsel in that the accused must discover errors or misconduct in the proceedings in order to show that he should have had counsel, and yet without counsel he is ill-equipped to discover such defects. In a retrial of this case, for example, no counsel need be appointed for Townsend; the cat-and-mouse game could take place again.[170]

Two cases in the 1948 term complete the list of noncapital cases where the petitioner succeeded. One is analogous to the Townsend case and was decided on the same principle. In *Gibbs* v. *Burke* a mature man with six previous convictions was tried and convicted without counsel or an offer of counsel.[171] On a plea of not guilty, Gibbs had conducted his own defense. Without detailing the defects which he alleged, we can say that they consisted of various erroneous actions by the judge, hostility by the judge, incompetent and inadmissible evidence, incorrect rulings in law, and other prejudicial elements. In an opinion by Justice Reed the Court held that a fair trial had not been extended to a defendant handicapped by lack of counsel. To the question of how states were to decide when counsel should be furnished, Reed answered: "We cannot offer a panacea for the difficulty . . . . The due process clause is not susceptible of reduction to a mathematical formula." [172] Gibbs's trial lacked "fundamental fairness because neither counsel nor ade-

---

169 334 U.S. 736 at 739, 92 L. Ed. 1690 at 1692.
170 See George E. Grover, 22 *So. Calif. L. Rev.* (April, 1949), 259, 269.
171 *Gibbs* v. *Burke*, 337 U.S. 733, 69 S. Ct. 1247, 93 L. Ed. 1686 (1949).
172 337 U.S. 733 at 780–781, 93 L. Ed. 1686 at 1691.

quate judicial guidance or protection was furnished at the trial." [173] Black and Douglas concurred, but wanted *Betts* v. *Brady* overruled. Murphy and Rutledge concurred in the result.

There is reason in the plaintive request by the State of Pennsylvania for more exact judicial guidance, and yet one can sympathize with the fair-trial adherents on the Supreme Court, who had attempted to reconcile the retention of the control which the states had always exercised over criminal procedure with the requirements of fairness. In spite of the experience and the bad record of the defendant in this case, it is obvious that he was not given a fair trial. The vital function of defense counsel is to prevent errors in the proceeding, as well as to present facts favorable to his client, and it comes with ill grace, then, for a state to claim that it can deny the aid of counsel and, in addition, to deprive the defendant of a fair and proper trial while he is undefended. [174]

In *Uveges* v. *Pennsylvania,* the conviction of a seventeen-year-old defendant on a plea of guilty was reversed. [175] Here again confusion is introduced into the decision because of a dispute between majority and dissenters concerning the claims which had been presented to the Pennsylvania Supreme Court and were thus reviewable on certiorari. Frankfurter's dissent, with Jackson and Burton concurring, stresses what he considers an unwarranted assumption by the majority that the Pennsylvania Court had before it, and rejected, a claim of denial of counsel. He would rather infer that a lack of particularity in the Uveges claim explained that Court's denial. The majority opinion, delivered by Justice Reed, seems explicit, however, in disclaiming any reliance on facts not considered by the Pennsylvania Court. The facts presented revealed that an inexperienced youth of seventeen was allowed to plead guilty to charges carrying a maximum penalty of eighty years and that there was no attempt to explain the consequences of the plea. The division within the majority was indicated by Reed's statement: "Some members of the Court think that where serious offenses are

[173] 337 U.S. 733 at 781, 93 L. Ed. 1686 at 1692.
[174] See comment by Charles Myneder, 48 *Mich. L. Rev.* (Feb., 1950), 521.
[175] *Uveges* v. *Pennsylvania,* 335 U.S. 437, 69 S. Ct. 184, 93 L. Ed. 127 (1948).

charged, failure of a court to offer counsel in state criminal trials deprives an accused of rights under the Fourteenth Amendment . . . . Others of us think that when a crime subject to capital punishment is not involved, each case depends on its own facts." [176]

There is some confusion when the two rules are applied to the facts of this case, which Reed fails to clarify. "Under either view . . . , the facts in this case required the presence of counsel," he said, and then emphasized the age, the inexperience of the defendant, and the failure of the trial court to advise him of his rights or to offer counsel.[177] This seemingly amounted to a holding that youth and inexperience were factors which made appointment, or at least an offer, of counsel mandatory. Had Reed stopped there, his position would be clear. But he continued, saying, "Whatever our decision might have been if the trial court had informed him of his rights and conscientiously had undertaken to perform the functions ordinarily entrusted to counsel, we conclude that the opportunity to have counsel in this case was a necessary element of a fair hearing"— which clearly implies that facts and events at the trial, in addition to age and inexperience, were decisive in impelling Reed and Vinson to join the "Bill-of-Rights" bloc.[178]

Frankfurter's complaint against this intervention in state proceedings, however, and his tart comment, "After all, this is the nation's ultimate judicial tribunal, not a super-legal-aid bureau," came with ill grace from one who had warmly supported the fair-trial rule in his opinions in *Carter* v. *Illinois*,

[176] 335 U.S. 437 at 440–441, 93 L. Ed. 127 at 131.

[177] 335 U.S. 437 at 441–442, 93 L. Ed. 127 at 132.

[178] It could be, as Frankfurter claimed, that while disavowing any use of facts in addition to those before the Supreme Court of Pennsylvania, the majority was influenced by such facts. The Brief for Petitioner painted a picture of a hasty and indifferent judicial proceeding, evidenced by failure to advise the defendant of his right to retain counsel or of the consequences of the plea or of the specific charges (p. 10). None of the nine indictments was signed by the district attorney, nor were any of the pleas signed by the defendant (pp. 10–11). Testimony of witnesses was unsworn and added little toward a conviction (Transcript of Record, pp. 43–44). The assistant district attorney told the court that the accused was charged with sixty-seven burglaries, seven firearm violations, and three miscellaneous charges, though nine indictments had been prepared (Brief for Petitioner, p. 24). No indication was given by the court or the record that the one plea of guilty was to be applied to four indictments (Brief, p. 25).

Foster v. *Illinois,* and *Gayes* v. *New York.* If the sense of injustice of some of his fellow fair-trial adherents has proved to be more tender than his own, it seems but the inevitable result of attempting to apply the vague standards of this doctrine, with its stress on subjective factors. His desire to assume the correctness of state-court judgments again evades reality. It is because errors occur in courts of justice that a system of review is necessary. A presumption of regularity can easily be erected into a dogma which would destroy whatever meaning the fair-trial rule ever possessed. A fair-trial rule is in itself a confession that not all trials conform to existing concepts of fairness.[179]

Yet the equivocal remarks of the majority are equally liable to criticism. The necessity of applying a vague standard does not require the use of vague language in explaining why in a specific case one of two possible solutions was chosen. The opinion seems at one moment to declare that age and inexperience are the factors which proved decisive and that both schools of thought on the majority side unite on that basis, but then in a mysterious sentence it implies that no counsel would be needed if a fair trial were given. In other words, we are uncertain whether the defendant needed counsel because of his characteristics, or because he suffered a disadvantage during his trial while lacking counsel. Such opinions do little to inform either trial judges or potential litigants.

Note on the Due-Process Clause and the Lower Federal Courts

No attempt will be made to treat the details of the lower federal courts' application of due process to the counsel problem. Obviously they have experienced some difficulty in their efforts to decipher the content of the fair-trial doctrine and to apply the rule as developed in the Supreme Court decisions. Since they perform a creative task only where the highest court has not spoken, the brief analysis here will merely point out certain of their difficulties and indicate the few aspects of the right to

---

[179] Oddly enough, the practice within Pennsylvania has varied widely. In certain counties, Luzerne, for example, judges have made a practice of appointing counsel to advise on pleas and to defend indigents throughout their trials. In Philadelphia and Allegheny (Pittsburgh) a different system has prevailed, as the Uveges case and the Gibbs case would prove.

counsel to which the lower federal courts have applied the due-process clause without guidance from the Supreme Court.

One difficulty has arisen from the belief of some lower courts that the counsel requirement under due process depended on the statutory pattern in the individual states.[180] This belief was natural after *Betts* v. *Brady*, where Roberts muddied the water by emphasizing in his review of the precedents that a state law had required appointment of counsel in all the previous cases in which petitioners were successful.[181] Lower-court confusion was inevitable as a result.[182]

Another problem concerned the significance of a plea of guilty when the defendant was without counsel. There had been until 1948 a tendency to regard a plea of guilty as a conclusive waiver.[183] But *Wade* v. *Mayo* destroyed that assumption.

Perhaps the only area where the lower courts have been under siege on a matter not clarified by the Supreme Court is that of competency of counsel and effective appointment of counsel. It will be recalled that *Powell* v. *Alabama* turned on the lack of an effective appointment of counsel.[184] A third, and undiscussed, point in that case was the character of the aid rendered by counsel once appointed.

As a result of *Powell* v. *Alabama* and, perhaps more directly, of *Hawk* v. *Olson*, where appointed counsel rendered no assistance, the lower federal courts have had a number of cases in which it was alleged that the counsel appointed was incompetent and that a lack of due process resulted. Unless the charge of inefficiency is well documented, the claim will fail.[185] In ex-

---

180 See *Coates* v. *Lawrence*, 46 F. Supp. 414 (1942); *Hoelscher* v. *Howard*, 155 F. 2d 909 (1946); *Commonwealth ex rel. Billman* v. *Burke*, 74 F. Supp. 846 (1947).

181 *Betts* v. *Brady*, 316 U.S. 455 at 463–464, 63 S. Ct. 1252, 86 L. Ed. 1595 at 1602–1603 (1942).

182 *Wade* v. *Mayo*, 334 U.S. 672, 68 S. Ct. 1270, 92 L. Ed. 1647 (1948), ended the doubts.

183 See *Flansburg* v. *Kaiser*, 55 F. Supp. 959, 144 F. 2d 917 (1944).

184 *Powell* v. *Alabama*, 287 U.S. 45, 53 S. Ct. 55, 77 L. Ed. 158 (1932).

185 See *Sweet* v. *Howard*, 155 F. 2d 715 (1946), where counsel had had forty years' experience, and *Achtien* v. *Dowd*, 117 F. 2d 989 (1941), where a white defendant claimed that a Negro appointed counsel was inefficient. In *Hawk* v. *Hann*, 103 F. Supp. 138 (1952), the energetic petitioner Hawk—of *Ex parte Hawk*, 321 U.S. 114, 64 S. Ct. 448, 88 L. Ed. 572 (1944), and *Hawk* v. *Olson*, 326 U.S. 271, 66 S. Ct. 116, 90 L. Ed. 61 (1945)—after being rebuffed in the Nebraska courts, finally convinced a federal court that he had received only

ceptional cases, where it is clear that appointed counsel did little or nothing for the defendant, a gross failure by counsel will be held a denial of due process.[186]   With retained counsel it seems safe to say that only shocking mental incompetence or total lack of action on behalf of the defendant will result in a reversal.[187]

Failure to permit defendant to retain counsel,[188] or to allow sufficient time for counsel to prepare has been held a denial of due process,[189] as has a waiver of counsel by a district attorney,[190] and an appointment of a codefendant's lawyer to represent an ignorant sharecropper after a trial had begun.[191]   A refusal to appoint counsel for appeal, on the other hand, was upheld as not violative of due process.[192]

A subject that has aroused controversy is whether a state court can exclude out-of-state counsel for reasons which seem satisfactory to the state court.   A 1950 decision by a circuit court of appeals indicates that the due-process clause requires that an out-of-state attorney in good standing in his state of origin must be admitted when retained in a criminal case, and that he can be excluded only for good cause.[193]

In conclusion, it can be said that while some federal courts

---

perfunctory assistance from a public defender and a retained counsel who was not granted a postponement.

[186] *United States ex rel. Foley* v. *Ragen*, 52 F. Supp. 265 (1943); *United States ex rel. Hall* v. *Ragen*, 60 F. Supp. 820 (1945).

[187] *Tompsett* v. *Ohio*, 146 F. 2d 95 (1944); *Amrine* v. *Tines*, 131 F. 2d 827 (1942); *Andrews* v. *Robertson*, 145 F. 2d 101 (1944); *United States ex rel. Feely* v. *Ragen*, 166 F. 2d 976 (1948); *Farrell* v. *Lanagan*, 166 F. 2d 845 (1948).   Certiorari was denied in all cases where sought.

[188] See *Melanson* v. *O'Brien*, 191 F. 2d 963 (1951), where a Massachusetts court failed to advise a defendant of his rights, and the defendant had been informed by an assistant district attorney that it would be impossible to obtain a postponement so that the accused could retain counsel.

[189] *Jones* v. *Kentucky*, 97 F. 2d 335 (1938).

[190] *Voight* v. *Webb*, 47 F. Supp. 743 (1942).

[191] *Mitchell* v. *Youell*, 130 F. 2d 880 (1942).

[192] *Kelly* v. *Ragen*, 129 F. 2d 811 (1942).

[193] The difficulty arose from the out-of-court activities and comments of O. John Rogge and other defense counsel in the "Trenton Six" case. See *New York Times*, July 22, 1950, p. 32, col. 7.   The New Jersey court rule says that "any counsellor from any other of the United States, of good standing there, may, at the discretion of this court, be admitted, *pro hac vice*, to speak in any cause in this court in which he may be employed," Rules Governing the Courts of New Jersey (1948), 1:7-4(b).   The decision in *Cooper* v. *Hutchinson*, 184 F. 2d 119 (1950), is equivocal, but seems to hold that a hearing and cause shown should have preceded the court ruling.

have been vigorous in their condemnation of state criminal trials which violate due process,[194] it seems evident from the relatively small number of cases in which habeas corpus has been granted by the district courts that a suspicious eye is cast on claims made by convicts challenging state convictions.[195] Lower-federal-court decisions are invulnerable for the most part if they are based on a factual finding. But if the district courts misconstrue the existing fair-trial standard by unwarranted assumptions concerning either the meaning of state statutes or the scope of due process [196] or the effect of a plea of guilty,[197] they are taking a serious chance of being reversed. It seems reasonable to assert that the lower courts have been given a greater opportunity to intervene as the result of the Uveges and Betts cases. One suspects that there has been a greater number of trials without counsel in which serious errors occurred than the few cases on the point would suggest. The necessity of scrutinizing state trial records in some detail is not likely to prove appealing, however, to the lower courts. Finally, it is safe to predict that with the increasingly evident tendency of the states to correct their trial procedure in respect to counsel, the opportunities for intervention by the federal courts on any theory of due process will decrease and the threat of national "interference" with state-court procedures will disappear.

SUMMARY AND CONCLUSIONS

The early cases of *Frank* v. *Mangum* (1914) and *Moore* v. *Dempsey* (1923) showed that the United States Supreme Court would intervene when state criminal proceedings departed markedly from commonly held standards of justice. But in a long line of decisions dating back to the Hurtado case, the Court also expressed its unwillingness to use any part of the Fourteenth Amendment to fasten specific modes of trial or particular pro-

---

[194] *Mitchell* v. *Youell*, 130 F. 2d 880 (1942); *Voight* v. *Webb*, 47 F. Supp. 743 (1942), where Judge Schwellenbach lashed the Washington trial court; *United States ex rel. Hall* v. *Ragen*, 60 F. Supp. 820 (1945); *United States ex rel. Mills* v. *Ragen*, 77 F. Supp. 15 (1948); *Spence* v. *Dowd*, 145 F. 2d 541 (1944).

[195] Murphy in *Wade* v. *Mayo* states that only 1.3 per cent of habeas corpus applications were granted, 334 U.S. 672 at 682, 68 S. Ct. 1270, 92 L. Ed. 1647 at 1653 (1948).

[196] *Andrus* v. *McCauley*, 21 F. Supp. 70 (1936).

[197] *Flansburg* v. *Kaiser*, 55 F. Supp. 959, 144 F. 2d 917 (1944).

cedural elements on any of the states. In the Twining case Justice Moody gave a hint of what was to come when he said: "It is possible that some of the personal rights safeguarded by the first eight amendments against national action may also be safeguarded against state action, because a denial of them would be a denial of due process of law." [198]

This prophecy seemed to be approaching realization in respect to the counsel clause of the Sixth Amendment when *Powell* v. *Alabama* was decided in 1932. While it is true that the Sixth Amendment counsel requirement had never been the subject of a Supreme Court decision, and that it was by statute that provision was made for the appointment of counsel for indigents in capital cases, still the practice of appointing counsel at least on request in all federal felony cases was well-established, and counsel was appointed in all felony cases without request in most federal courts.

After the Powell case it was anticipated that the doctrine of the right to appointed counsel would be extended to all felony cases when the opportunity arose. But in 1942 in *Betts* v. *Brady* the Court refused to go so far. In short, it declared that only in certain circumstances, with the defendants who had particular characteristics and where a fair trial could not be had without the appointment of counsel for the defense, must counsel be appointed. But other than being reminded of the vague duty of observing standards of fairness, states were told that they were free in all cases to decide if counsel should be appointed. The Supreme Court would appraise the "totality of facts" in each case to see if the state action constituted "a denial of fundamental fairness, shocking to the universal sense of justice . . . ." [199] In contrast to this position, a bloc consisting of Justices Black, Douglas, and Murphy, to be augmented shortly by Justice Rutledge, urged the incorporation of the Sixth Amendment counsel provision within the Fourteenth Amendment. Failing this, they maintained that the requirements of a fair hearing demanded that counsel be appointed unless waived by a competent defendant.

[198] *Twining* v. *New Jersey,* 211 U.S. 78 at 79, 29 S. Ct. 14, 53 L. Ed. 97 at 106 (1908).
[199] *Betts* v. *Brady,* 316 U.S. 455 at 462, 86 L. Ed. 1595 at 1609 (1942).

In the cases to which this fair-trial doctrine was applied in the period after *Betts* v. *Brady* the alignment of the Court revealed certain curious features. In eleven of the nineteen cases the claim of the petitioner was upheld, but in four of these cases a majority of the fair-trial adherents, Roberts, Reed, Frankfurter, and Jackson, opposed the decision.[200] In other words, the adherents of the fair-trial rule—Chief Justice Stone originally, with Chief Justice Vinson and Justice Burton joining later—thought that a valid claim of denial of counsel had been shown in only seven of the nineteen cases, rather than in eleven, as was held by the full court. Yet in all the successful cases the language of the decisions spells out an application of the fair-trial rule.

As would be expected, the four "incorporators"—Black, Douglas, Murphy, and Rutledge—voted to uphold the petitioners' claims in spite of the use of a doctrine which they found repugnant. There was one exception to this conformity when Black and Douglas joined the fair-trial bloc in the Canizio case and rejected the claim of denial of counsel where counsel appeared before sentencing. In five of the cases where petitioners failed, the "incorporators" dissented, and in the Quicksall case Black dissented alone, Douglas not sitting, when the bloc had been reduced through death to two.[201] In the nineteen cases there were only three unanimous decisions, which shows the difficulty of applying the fair-trial doctrine.[202] In twelve of the nineteen cases the fair-trial adherents voted as a unit.[203] Murphy and Rutledge were unswerving in their support of all petitioners, and Douglas and Black were close behind. This will

---

[200] *Rice* v. *Olson, Wade* v. *Mayo, Townsend* v. *Burke, Uveges* v. *Pennsylvania.*

[201] *Carter* v. *Illinois, Foster* v. *Illinois, Gayes* v. *New York, Bute* v. *Illinois,* and *Gryger* v. *Burke* were the five. In *White* v. *Ragen* the Court unanimously rejected the claim on the theory that an adequate state ground existed. The Quicksall decision and the Canizio split complete their action on dissents.

[202] *White* v. *Ragen, Hawk* v. *Olson, De Meerleer* v. *Michigan.*

[203] Frankfurter was the least consistent, breaking away to dissent in *Williams* v. *Kaiser* and *Tompkins* v. *Missouri* and to join the "incorporators" in forming a majority in *Wade* v. *Mayo* and *Townsend* v. *Burke;* Reed helped form a majority twice, by leaving his fellows in *Uveges* v. *Pennsylvania* and *Rice* v. *Olson;* Jackson, once, in *Townsend* v. *Burke;* Vinson, twice, in *Townsend* v. *Burke* and *Uveges* v. *Pennsylvania.*

suffice to show the nature of the Court alignment when counsel questions were presented.

The difficulties of discerning a logical or consistent pattern in the Court's application of the fair-trial rule have dismayed observers, who have condemned it as a "nebulous standard," [204] a complex "ex post facto" standard,[205] and an "arbitrary and capricious" rule.[206]   Obviously, it lacks the essential qualities of a good rule of law: clarity of meaning, facility in application, and satisfying results.   Apart from a statement concerning the right to appear with retained counsel, clarified by the decisions in *House* v. *Mayo* and *Hawk* v. *Olson,* the Court has shown a disinclination to set forth any guide rules to indicate the proper road through the procedural maze.

Apparently, an offer of counsel must be made in all capital cases, but this has been said as a dictum in noncapital cases rather than directly, in cases where the issue was squarely raised.[207]   In noncapital cases only a number of imprecise elements indicate the dangers which a state must face if it conducts a trial without counsel or an offer of counsel.   Youth is significant, but no rule is evident in regard to it.[208]   Ignorance, illiteracy, and inexperience are of great importance in determining whether appointment is necessary, but it is not obvious just how these factors are to be shown.   In *Rice* v. *Olson* they loomed large, but in addition there was in that case a difficult technical question on which no layman could have been qualified.   In the Uveges case the petitioner claimed that he was ignorant and "frightened," and the record seemed to support him.   In *Canizio* v. *New York* a claim of ignorance was fruitless.   Although "inexperience" can be brushed aside if the defendant has had previous court experience,[209] yet such previous "experience" can be rejected if the latest proceeding contains sub-

[204] See 33 *Va. L. Rev.* (Nov., 1947), 731.

[205] See 22 *So. Calif. L. Rev.* (April, 1949), 259.

[206] See J. R. Green, 46 *Mich. L. Rev.* (May, 1948), 869, 898.

[207] *Bute* v. *Illinois, Williams* v. *Kaiser, Quicksall* v. *Michigan.*

[208] Youth was stressed in *Wade* v. *Mayo* and in *De Meerleer* v. *Michigan,* where the defendants were aged eighteen and seventeen, respectively.   Yet in *Gayes* v. *New York* the defendant was sixteen, and in *Canizio* v. *New York* the defendant was eighteen at the time of conviction.

[209] *Quicksall* v. *Michigan* and *Gryger* v. *Burke.*

stantial error.[210]   On the surface, there is a greater simplicity in the Court's application of the fair-trial rule where it reverses convictions in trials without counsel because of an error or errors in the proceedings, but *Gryger* v. *Burke* shows that in this matter, also, there is a lack of consistency.

All that one can conclude is that the Court will decide whether an offer or an appointment of counsel was necessary by looking at the characteristics of the defendant and the nature of the case,[211] and at the record of the trial as it unfolded.   Presumably, the Court should be able to decide whether or not the appointment of counsel was necessary by examining the situation in which the trial judge found himself at the time of arraignment.   But if the Supreme Court has performed its task in this way it is difficult to understand why it has failed to enunciate a more precise set of subordinate rules to guide trial courts at this important stage.

Seemingly there have been two ideas dominating the thinking of the fair-trial-rule partisans.   First, there has been an evident desire to avoid a doctrinaire position which would interfere with the freedom of the states to alter existing judicial procedures and to create new ones.   Excessive intervention in state proceedings would inevitably result in the demand that the Supreme Court prescribe the rules to govern criminal trials. To avoid this possibility the Supreme Court has used various technical explanations, such as the existence of a nonfederal ground,[212] a belated appearance of counsel who could have withdrawn a plea of guilty,[213] an opportunity to challenge a first conviction at a second trial,[214] the limitations of a common-law record,[215] a strong presumption of the regularity of a proceeding buttressed by a recital of "advised of their rights" in the record,[216] and inferences that a defendant knows his rights.[217]

[210] *Gibbs* v. *Burke* and *Townsend* v. *Burke.*
[211] The Court talks of the simplicity of the murder charge in *Quicksall* v. *Michigan* and the complexity of the murder charge in *Hawk* v. *Olson.*
[212] *White* v. *Ragen.*
[213] *Canizio* v. *New York.*
[214] *Gayes* v. *New York.*
[215] *Bute* v. *Illinois* and *Carter* v. *Illinois.*
[216] *Foster* v. *Illinois.*
[217] *Quicksall* v. *Michigan.*

But at the same time it maintained the practice of reviewing state procedures.

Secondly, there has been the desire to develop certain standards of fairness and correctness which could be applied to state proceedings in order to prevent injustice. It should be remembered that this was the same Court which had demonstrated tender concern for the "liberty" of the individual as expressed through speech, press, assembly, and religion. To protect the citizen in his soapbox utterances and yet to ignore an unfair judicial proceeding by which his very life or liberty might be lost would have been alien to the thinking of all Court members. Thus, where the whole conduct of the trial seemed lacking in fairness, as in *De Meerleer* v. *Michigan, Rice* v. *Olson, Marino* v. *Ragen,* and *Gibbs* v. *Burke,* a majority of the Court was willing to vote for reversal.

The lower federal courts have interfered with state-court proceedings infrequently and with reluctance, and the small number of cases in which certiorari has been granted shows conclusively that the Supreme Court is similarly hesitant. Yet the very vagueness of the fair-trial test has encouraged recourse to the lower federal courts and to the Supreme Court by state convicts.[218] And the unfortunate illusion of "interference" in state proceedings is heightened by the ambiguity of this test and the extreme difficulty of discerning logic or consistency in the cases that have been decided. Both state and lower federal courts have expressed a need for a readily applicable standard, which they would be happy to accept in place of the present chaotic and equivocal rule.[219] Both state appellate courts and lower federal courts have been reluctant to upset state convictions because the law has been so indefinite and subjective. Defendants, trial courts, and laymen have been confused to a much greater extent than have the higher courts, it is safe to conclude.

A desirable solution, then, would have two qualities. First, it should not lead to excessive interference with state criminal

[218] Forty per cent of the 1,356 causes presented to the Supreme Court in 1946 were from state convicts. *In forma pauperis* applications now constitute about one third of all applications.

[219] See *Newman* v. *State,* 148 Tex. Cr. 645, 187 S.W. 2d 559 (1945); *Potter* v. *Dowd,* 146 F. 2d 244 (1949).

procedure, as the incorporation theory expressed in *Adamson v. California* would do.[220]   Secondly, it should improve the fairness of state trials.

A suggestion that the right to counsel at a trial be conceived of and protected as part of "liberty" has been advanced by a writer having extensive experience with the counsel problem.[221] A more unusual position holds that equal protection is violated by trials where the defendant is not represented by counsel because of indigence.[222]   A different, more obvious approach would be a declaration that "due process" under our present system of procedure and modern concept of "fairness" requires an offer of counsel to indigents.[223]   The advantages of this method would be that it uses a procedural concept to make a procedural advance; it would inform trial courts of their duty, and it comes closer to the established precedents and pronouncements of the Court.   There is nothing to prevent a reiteration of the fair-trial doctrine as part of due process and then a pronouncement that future state trials to be "fair" must include counsel for the defense unless counsel is competently waived.

A more practical solution, from a different viewpoint, is that the states should adopt a rule similar to federal Rule 44, which requires an offer of counsel, and appointment unless counsel is competently waived.[224]   This suggestion, one that rarely appeals to those who demand immediate change, has already been adopted by some of the states which have experienced, or which have foreseen, the difficulties likely to result from the application of the fair-trial rule.   Missouri, Michigan, and Illinois in the first category and West Virginia and New Jersey in the second are examples of states which have attempted reform by enunciat-

220 Some writers want the counsel provision alone incorporated, without much concern for the peculiar principle of constitutional interpretation thus established. See R. W., 33 *Va. L. Rev.* (Nov., 1947), 731; 23 *Tex. L. Rev.* (Dec., 1944), 66; 90 *Mo. St. L. J.* (Summer, 1948), 529.

221 Green, 46 *Mich. L. Rev.* (May, 1948), 869.

222 J. Tussman and J. ten Broek, "Equal Protection of Law," 37 *Calif. L. Rev.* (Sept., 1949), 341. This is certainly a long distance from the original intention of the equal-protection clause. See John P. Frank and Robert F. Munro, "The Original Understanding of Equal Protection of the Laws," 50 *Col. L. Rev.* (Feb., 1950), 131.

223 See 48 *Mich. L. Rev.* (Feb., 1950), 521.

224 Bennett Boskey and John H. Pickering, "Federal Restrictions on State Criminal Procedure," 13 *Univ. of Chic. L. Rev.* (April, 1946), 266.

ing a precise standard in respect to counsel in order to avoid the possibility of day-to-day reversals by the United States Supreme Court. Perhaps this will be the means by which the Supreme Court will escape the necessity of rethinking the question of counsel in state trials. It would increase respect for the principle of local rule if states were to initiate reforms in the conduct of criminal proceedings after receiving warnings from the Supreme Court, rather than merely repeat the cry of "interference" and permit undesirable state practices to remain. State courts, either through their rule-making power or, where that is insufficient, through influence in state legislatures, should, with the aid of bar associations, bring state counsel provisions up to a level commensurate with federal practice today.

CHAPTER VI

RIGHT TO COUNSEL IN PRACTICE

THE large number of appellate decisions concerning counsel reviewed in the previous chapters does not fully reveal the magnitude of the actual problem of furnishing counsel for indigents. It seems fair to conclude that at least as many claims of denial of counsel are never appealed to higher courts as are, and that an even greater number of potential claims are never pressed in any court. The same indigence which resulted in the initial loss of the right to counsel continues to act as a restraint on possible corrective action. Nevertheless, it is evident that the intensity of the controversy in the higher courts concerning the scope of the right is having, and will continue to have, substantial influence on the actions of trial courts. For whatever trial judges or disgruntled laymen may think of the wisdom of certain Supreme Court decisions, the doctrines set forth by that Court are the law, and will be followed to the fullest extent possible. It has been the lack of easily applied rules which has made the task of the trial courts more difficult.[1]

Obviously, with present incomplete data, no one can trace with precision the defects and accomplishments of American trial courts as they attempt to conform with the legal rules concerning counsel announced by the highest Court. The discussion to follow is hardly more than a sketch of selected important phases of the practical problem, such as the demand for improvement, the ascertainment of the need for counsel in individual cases and the administration of the right to it, the

---

[1] This is not to say that all trial courts have been aware of the problem. Unless his decision is reversed, a typical trial judge is inclined to proceed with business as usual. The lower bench is not filled with constitutional scholars, and, particularly in state lower courts, there is a tendency to dismiss the counsel problem as "theoretical." It is only when a rule or a mandate from the highest state court is directed at the lower courts that they awaken.

three methods of handling appointment (assignment from the private bar, assignment from legal-aid bureaus, and the public defender), and, finally, a new postconviction remedy by which claimed denials of the right to counsel and other constitutional rights are to be tested in Illinois.

CALL FOR ACTION

In spite of the alertness of appellate courts in protecting trial rights, most realistic observers of the judicial system are aware that true reform must take place on a systematic basis at the trial or pretrial level. Consequently, prominent jurists, lawyers, criminologists, and scholars have proposed and demanded a constructive program for the appointment and payment of counsel in criminal cases to replace the existing defective system. There have been various spokesmen on the Supreme Court from Sutherland to Rutledge who have emphasized the necessity of having appointed counsel for the defense of indigents. An experienced lower-court judge, Alexander Holtzoff, has gone on record in favor of an official system of paid public defenders, commenting: "The existing methods of securing representation by counsel for indigent defendants are often inadequate and frequently operate in a haphazard manner. The right of counsel is essential in our system of jurisprudence and should be carefully and zealously guarded." [2]

Two members of the private bar have waged a vigorous fight over the years in an effort to improve the lot of the indigent defendant. Mayer C. Goldman has lectured widely and has written a book in support of the public-defender idea; he has done more perhaps than any other individual to encourage the movement which has resulted in the adoption of this system in various states and cities.[3] Reginald Heber Smith, of the Boston bar, not only made the first scholarly examination of the defects of the law as applied to indigents, and of the possible solutions, but he has also been largely responsible for awakening the somewhat lethargic American Bar Association to the need for corrective action. Legal-aid societies and legal-reference

[2] Alexander Holtzoff, "Defects in the Administration of Justice," 9 *F.R.D.* (1949), 303, 305.

[3] See Mayer C. Goldman, *The Public Defender* (New York: Putnam's, 1917).

plans have been his especial concern.[4]   Both Goldman and
Smith have emphasized the necessity for ascertaining and filling
the need for counsel where indigent defendants appear.

Various organizations of a legal nature have also made definite efforts to suggest reforms.   The American Law Institute,
in its Code of Criminal Procedure, advocated the appointment
of counsel in all cases unless the defendant desired to retain his
own counsel or objected to any appointment.[5]   The Wickersham Commission in its 1931 report sharply criticized the existing methods of appointing counsel for indigents, though its
recommendations were rather equivocal and its evaluation of
proposed reforms showed a strong tendency to maintain the
status quo.[6]   In 1937 the Conference of Senior Circuit Judges
approved the principle of public defenders in large districts and
of assigned counsel in others.[7]

The most recent display of interest in the counsel problem
has been that of the Survey of the Legal Profession, directed by
Reginald Heber Smith, under the auspices of the American
Bar Association.   The survey naturally devoted considerable attention to the problem of the indigent civil and criminal litigant.
In the report on *Legal Aid in the United States*, written by
Emery A. Brownell, the need for legal aid in criminal litigation
is shown to be substantial, and Brownell urges the extension of
the various forms of legal aid to criminal cases.[8]   The report
on "Legal Aid in Criminal Cases," prepared by Martin V.
Callagy fully documents the public need in criminal proceedings.[9]

All these proposals would have had little effect in themselves

[4] See Reginald Heber Smith, *Justice and the Poor* (New York: Carnegie
Foundation, 1919). Smith's articles on the same theme have appeared in the
American Bar Association Journal and other periodicals from time to time.

[5] *Code of Criminal Procedure* (Official Draft) (Philadelphia: American Law
Institute, 1930), c. 8, § 203.

[6] National Commission on Law Observance and Enforcement, *Report on
Prosecution* (Washington, D.C.: Government Printing Office, 1931), pp. 30–33.

[7] See 23 *J. Amer. Judic. Soc.* (Dec., 1939), 131–132.

[8] Emery A. Brownell, *Legal Aid in the United States* (Rochester, N. Y.: Lawyers Co-operative, 1951), especially pp. 35–40, 83–85, 146. This is the definitive
work covering the need for, and methods of supplying, legal aid in the United
States.

[9] Martin V. Callagy, "Legal Aid in Criminal Cases," 42 *J. Crim. L., Crim. and
Pol. Sci.* (Jan.—Feb., 1953), 587.

had it not been for the sudden growth after 1940 in the number of petitions from convicts who alleged a denial of counsel. Both state and federal courts were flooded with these claims. Although the problem was more serious in Illinois, New York, and California, there were difficulties in Oklahoma, Texas, Missouri, and many other states. Moreover, the expanded scope of due process made inevitable a recourse to the federal courts by state convicts who were disappointed in the state courts.

The director of the Federal Bureau of Prisons, James V. Bennett, has estimated that about one half of the four hundred petitions for habeas corpus presented in 1948 by federal prisoners were based on claims of lack of counsel or of indifferent or inefficient representation by appointed counsel.[10] In 1949 Chief Justice Vinson said that nearly one half of the matters presented to the Supreme Court were applications from prisoners seeking postconviction relief.[11] He emphasized the need for more effective posttrial procedures in the states, maintaining that "a well-defined method by which prisoners can challenge their convictions," with allegations "aired in open hearings," would eliminate many of the petitions to the Supreme Court based on trivial grounds.[12] Another judicial figure has complained that the writ of habeas corpus is being abused, and he suggests a modification of the generous features of that ancient writ in order to limit its misuse.[13] The number of *in forma pauperis* petitions sought has increased since 1939, and the percentage granted has diminished.[14] Conspicuous, too, has been the excessive proportion of these petitions which have emanated from Illinois convicts, an "honor" which drew sharp comment in the

---

[10] James V. Bennett, "To Secure the Right to Counsel," 32 *J. Amer. Judic. Soc.* (April, 1949), 177, 179. Bennett's experience causes him to place his finger on arraignment as the vital step in criminal proceedings, since most convicts' complaints concern the events at that time.

[11] Address: "Work of the Federal Courts," reprinted in 70 S. Ct. xiii.

[12] *Ibid.*, p. xvi.

[13] See Louis E. Goodman (district-court judge), "Use and Abuse of the Writ of Habeas Corpus," 7 *F.R.D.* (1947), 313. Between January 1, 1937, and June 15, 1947, 180 Alcatraz convicts filed 368 petitions for the writ, with the four leading petitioners having filed sixteen, fifteen, fourteen, and nine petitions each.

[14] Of the 117 sought in 1939, eighteen were granted; of the 528 sought in 1946, eight were granted; and of the 443 sought in 1948 eighteen were granted. See *Report of the Director of the Administrative Office of the United States Courts, 1949* (Washington, D.C.: Government Printing Office, 1950), pp. 71–72.

Marino case [15] and critical articles in the Illinois legal periodicals, although other states have had their share of criticism, as the previously discussed Supreme Court decisions clearly reveal.[16]

It is apparent from these criticisms and suggestions that three main problems require solution: first, it must be made plain when and under what circumstances counsel must be appointed. Secondly, there must be some efficient, regularized method of furnishing counsel when counsel is appointed. And thirdly, there is a need in many jurisdictions for an improved system of appeal from convictions in which a denial of the right to counsel has occurred. If workable solutions are found for the first two problems, however, the significance of the third will inevitably diminish. With approximately sixty per cent of defendants in criminal cases unable to employ counsel because of indigence, these problems constitute a substantial challenge.[17]

ADMINISTRATION OF THE RIGHT TO COUNSEL [18]

FEDERAL COURTS

The Supreme Court's decisions in *Johnson* v. *Zerbst,* 1938, and in *Walker* v. *Johnston,* 1941, contained a number of pronouncements concerning counsel which are embodied in Rule 44 of the Federal Rules of Criminal Procedure effective September 1, 1946. After that date federal district courts had no excuse for failing to advise defendants of their rights or for failing to offer counsel to indigent defendants. It seems clear that federal-district-court judges have performed this duty in a conscientious manner. The most common method followed is to tell the defendant in easily understood language what the charge against him means and then to ask if he has seen, or talked to, an attorney. If he has not, the judge asks whether he wants

---

[15] *Marino* v. *Ragen,* 332 U.S. 561, 68 S. Ct. 240, 92 L. Ed. 170 (1947).

[16] E.g., *Williams* v. *Kaiser* dissent, *Gayes* v. *New York, Rice* v. *Olson, Canizio* v. *New York, Wade* v. *Mayo, Uveges* v. *Pennsylvania.*

[17] See Brownell, *op. cit.,* p. 83. This was the estimate of a committee of experts reporting to the Survey of the Legal Profession.

[18] The material which follows is based on personal observation of court procedure and on interviews with judges, prosecutors, and attorneys in one or more districts in New Jersey, Pennsylvania, Michigan, Indiana, Ohio, Missouri, and Illinois.

to see one and if he has money or property with which to pay an attorney. If the answer is "Yes" to the first and "No" to the second question, the judge says that he will appoint counsel who will serve without cost to the defendant. This offer is usually accepted. But if the defendant says he does not want counsel, further questioning takes place to determine his age, education, experience, and mental ability, before a waiver is accepted. There is some indication that a few federal judges appoint counsel regardless of the wishes of the defendant, apparently on the theory that it is easier to make an appointment than to examine each defendant with the care necessary to ascertain if a waiver is competent.[19]

The usual reason for rejecting an offer of appointed counsel is the defendant's wish to "plead guilty and get it over with." In many cases he hopes to get a lighter sentence, a hope which has often been planted by the district attorney to save the time and the expense of trial. There exists a danger, however, that the defendant's willingness to plead guilty may arise from his consciousness of wrongdoing, but that he may not have any accurate understanding of the technical charge against him, so that he may be pleading guilty to a more serious charge than his acts really warrant. And occasionally a defendant fancies that he is the legal equal of the prosecutor and tries to present his own case. Thus one can sympathize with the judge who protects himself by appointing counsel in all cases in an attempt to avoid erroneous pleas and to prevent inadequate defense by a person who tries to act as his own counsel.

Unquestionably, the chief hazard still confronting federal-district judges as well as state judges is the acceptance of a plea of guilty from an uncounseled defendant. There is no iron-clad assurance that a defendant is competent to plead guilty and waive counsel or that he is pleading guilty wisely to the specified charges. Without requiring counsel in every criminal case, which no one has seriously suggested,[20] there would seem to be a duty on the judge to question and advise the defendant in

[19] It is true, of course, that a satisfactory rationale of peremptory appointment is the due-process requirement. In other words, the judge can argue that any defendant or, at least, this defendant, is incompetent to waive.

[20] Under the public-defender system in a large city, however, this is what results.

greater detail than is done at present if claims of denial of the right to counsel are to be eliminated, or at least decreased. Moreover, while a judge is not expected to act as a confidant, it may be submitted that judges are frequently too formidable in their attitude toward the accused and that they are prone to employ language which is beyond the ready comprehension of an uneducated defendant.

STATE COURTS

Of the procedure in state courts it is impossible to speak with assurance. Illinois Rule 27–A, promulgated by the Illinois Supreme Court in 1948, has resulted in a vigorous examination of defendants. In Sangamon County, Illinois, the judge usually asks all defendants, "Do you have counsel?" If the answer is "No," he then asks, "Can you afford to hire a lawyer?" If the prisoner says "Yes," the arraignment is postponed. If he says "No," the judge says, "I am going to ask the public defender to help you. Do you object to my appointing him?" If the defendant answers "No," a postponement is granted for consultation. If he says that he does not want counsel and wishes to plead guilty, the judge asks, "Do you want counsel to advise you about your plea?" If the answer is again "No," the judge asks the following questions: "How old are you?" "Have you ever been in a mental institution?" "Have you ever had any mental trouble or long illness?" "How many years of schooling have you had?"

If then the judge is not yet certain that the appointment is necessary because of incompetency and if the defendant continues to insist that he does not want counsel, the judge says, "You are charged with larceny, in that . . . . [Here he mentions the actual crime allegedly committed, with the time and the place.] If you plead guilty, you can be sentenced for a minimum of ———— and a maximum of ————." Then if the defendant shows any hesitancy or if the judge has any doubt of the defendant's understanding or other possibly limiting characteristics, an appointment of counsel is made and arraignment is postponed; or if a penitentiary sentence would result from a plea of guilty, an appointment is usually made regardless of the willingness of the defendant to enter such a plea.

This extremely cautious procedure is a very fine implementation of the letter and the spirit of the Illinois rule, and is
in striking contrast to the old Illinois judicial practice of forcing the indigent defendant to take the initiative at arraignment.
In Sangamon County concern for the defendant's rights extends
to collateral proceedings in which a convict appears and is ready
to proceed on his own behalf. In most instances the judge
appoints counsel, regardless of the defendant's protestations.[21]
The Sangamon process is substantially similar to that used in
Chicago, with one significant difference. There, when defendants appear at arraignment they are advised by the judge of their
right to retain counsel and a continuance is granted if they
answer that they wish to do so. But if the defendant has no one
in mind and cannot afford counsel, the public defender is appointed, even though the accused wishes to defend himself. A
private attorney will be appointed, however, if an objection is
made to the public defender, with the public defender being
assigned as assistant when only inexperienced private attorneys
are available.

I observed some very penetrating questioning of defendants
in Indiana and in Michigan. The attitude of the two criminal
court judges in Indianapolis was particularly noteworthy in that
they seemed almost aggressive in their attempts to protect the
defendants. The judges appoint counsel in almost every case
and refuse pleas of guilty in the absence of counsel if there is
the slightest doubt concerning the reliability of the plea.

In 1945 the trial judge in Ann Arbor, Michigan, operating
under a system of paid appointment of counsel from the private
bar, began to question defendants in detail before accepting
pleas of guilty. Rule 35-A, adopted by the Supreme Court of
Michigan in 1948, added nothing to the procedure he had been
following.[22]

In other courts and other states equally careful examinations

[21] Apparently, lawyer inmates of the penitentiary sometimes prepare competent pleadings and compile the proper record for their fellows, who are instructed in their use. After such preparation, the petitioner probably feels that
he would be more competent in his own cause than a strange assigned counsel
who appears indifferent by his standard.

[22] It should be noted that there had been some headshaking by veteran officials because of the judge's concern for the accused, since it was more than the
law required. After the De Meerleer case the criticisms ceased.

of the defendant are conducted, but a waiver is permitted if the judge is satisfied that the defendant is aware of the consequences of his plea. In those cities with legal-aid societies, such as New York, it is customary for the court to appoint a lawyer from the legal-aid society when the defendant expresses a desire for counsel. In serious cases it is likely that a member of the society has already talked to the accused by the time of arraignment.[23] It is fair to say, in addition to the specific comments above, that in New Jersey an equally detailed and cautious procedure is followed. Observation of practices in these states would tend to show a dearth of undefended persons and an extreme reluctance by judges to accept a waiver.

OBJECTIONS TO THE RIGHT TO COUNSEL

It should not be thought that such a careful procedure is followed in every court. Some trial judges have strong contempt for the theory that every accused is entitled to an adequate defense. They voice, in one or more ways, the feeling that too many defendants escape conviction under the present system, and express surprise that anyone should want to take any action which might protract trials by affording counsel where not-guilty pleas are entered, or which might prevent pleas of guilty by appointment of counsel before a plea is made.

Some of these judges will admit that the professional criminals, the "syndicate representatives," the hired gunmen, and the veteran safe-crackers, are well aware of their rights and will say nothing until they see their lawyers. In fact, it is not uncommon in some cities for a "mouthpiece" to appear at precinct headquarters before the suspect is brought in. The undefended criminals, for the most part, are perpetrators of amateur crime, simple assault, petty larceny, or grand larceny involving slightly more than the statutory sum, or they are first or youthful offenders. In other words, the criminals most dangerous from the viewpoint of society are rarely, if ever, tried without coun-

---

[23] In a letter of July 3, 1950, Mr. Domenic Della Volpe, of the Criminal Division of the New York Legal Aid Society, outlined the procedure in New York. He added that virtually all the complaints received from convicts relate to alleged defects in trials held at least ten years before, which would tend to show that the New York courts became more careful as the number of petitions from convicts increased.

sel, while those who might be saved, or who at least are worth saving, are unaided. It would merit study to ascertain the reaction in the minds of defendants in Maryland, for example, when the judge responds to a request for counsel, "We don't appoint for noncapital felonies." Whether the trial judge acts fairly or not is beside the point. The prosecution has three advantages which the defendant lacks: investigation of the facts, preparation for the trial, and effective presentation. Guilty or not, a man found guilty after this type of proceeding will inevitably feel that society has done him a great wrong.

In the larger cities in Pennsylvania, and apparently in several other states where the statutes do not require appointment in noncapital cases, it has been unusual for an appointment to be made, and, when made, the appointment has resulted from a request by the defendant. In a number of medium-sized counties the judges have followed a rule of thumb in determining if, and when, counsel should be appointed. Since substantial payment is provided only in capital cases in most states, the judge is naturally reluctant to appoint unless he feels that the defendant "deserves" aid. This seems to mean, in practice, that a youthful or inexperienced first offender will receive appointed counsel if a fairly serious offense is charged. But when a "repeater" stands before him, even a generous judge is apt to slur over his statement that counsel will be appointed if the defendant requests. In other words, a prejudgment is made of the defendant's case. This is a rather ironic situation since, though a defendant's previous record is excluded, with certain exceptions, from the consideration of the jury, it may nonetheless play a decisive role in preventing the appointment of counsel whose aid and advice might be vital in determining what the plea shall be and whether jury trial is desired.

Moreover, it is readily apparent that the trial judges resent what they regard as the intrusive decisions of the United States Supreme Court and often express a willingness to hazard a reversal by that Court so long as the state supreme court sanctions the local procedure. Under these circumstances there can be no foreseeable end to the postconviction claims of criminal defendants.

RIGHT OF DEFENDANT TO WAIVE COUNSEL

An interesting and somewhat ironic question which emerges from the foregoing brief description of current practices and which should be mentioned here is whether the right to defend oneself may not be violated by some of the judges who insist on appointing counsel regardless of the defendant's wishes. Most state constitutional provisions extend to the defendant either the right to be heard by himself, or by counsel, or both, or the right to appear and defend in person, or by counsel, or both.[24] It has always been assumed that a defendant had the right to defend himself unless he were suffering from some disability, and no interpretation of due process by any of the federal courts has suggested that the right to counsel could not be waived by a competent defendant; since indictment and trial by jury can be waived, there would seem little reason to insist that the right to counsel cannot be waived. At the same time, one can sympathize with trial judges faced with a stubborn defendant who refuses counsel. If the defendant pleads not guilty, the judge is forced to play a more active role than is usual in our state courts to prevent serious error unfavorable to the accused. While no decision has held that errors in a procedure where the defendant refused counsel are fatal, the possibility exists that a materially unfair trial will always violate due process. If, on the other hand, the defendant pleads guilty without counsel, the judge has no assurance that his plea is proper unless he asks the defendant a long series of questions to ascertain his competency.

It is safe to predict, however, that somewhere a convict will soon initiate a claim based on the "right to defend in person," with some slight chance of successfully arguing either that the appointment itself violated the constitutional provision or that errors occurred as the result of actions by an unwanted appointed counsel. The latter ground might be necessary in those eleven states whose constitutional provisions fail to mention the right to defend "in person."

[24] E.g., Illinois, *Const.*, Art. II, § 39; New York, *Const.*, Art. I, Bill of Rights, 36; Indiana, *Const.*, Art. 1313. Thirty-seven states have one or the other provision.

APPEARANCE OF COUNSEL

A problem which should also be considered here concerns the stage of a criminal proceeding at which counsel should appear. Attention to this problem may seem premature after a discussion which has revealed large numbers of undefended or unadvised defendants, or both, in most states. Would it not be wiser, however, for judicial and bar officials and legislators to consider the question before it arises at some later date through postconviction complaints?

We know now that an increasing number of convictions are being attacked on the ground that conviction resulted from statements or confessions by the accused which were not "voluntary" in character. To be sure, no court has yet held that a confession or statement given by the defendant was "involuntary" solely because it was taken without advice of counsel, or after waiver of counsel. Nevertheless, in the Watts case the lack of counsel, coupled with the lack of legal arraignment and the excessively long period during which the accused was held incommunicado, invalidated the confession and resulted in an expensive retrial. In other cases, too numerous to cite, the absence of counsel has been a factor which, when added to various departures from normal procedure, has resulted in reversal. Without laboring the issue, it seems clear that the absence of counsel renders criminal judgments less secure than they would be if counsel had been present, and so introduces an additional hazard into criminal procedure.

From a different viewpoint, that of the accused and of counsel who may be retained or appointed at arraignment or later, it is frequently true that the possibility of an effective defense has been eliminated as the result of official action between arrest and the appearance of counsel.[25] In one large Midwestern city the case "checklist" of the public defender contained space for one of two entries under confessions—"voluntary," or "involuntary." The public defender who had constructed the "checklist" asserted that this issue was a complicating factor in almost every defense, for if the confession or statement by the defendant is to be attacked it places a heavy burden on counsel.

[25] See Brownell, op. cit., pp. 140–142.

Moreover, if a form of physical persuasion has been used to induce a confession, physical evidence in support of the defendant's claim will often have vanished by the time of arraignment, when, in many cases, counsel appears for the first time. Even a brief survey of the law-enforcement methods used in the various states reveals frequent recourse to illegal methods in the treatment of suspects. It is equally clear that these practices are less frequently followed when counsel appears promptly.

No one questions the necessity or the right of police and prosecutor to interrogate the accused. But it would seem that admissions which are voluntary would be made within a reasonable time after arrest; statements elicited from the accused after prolonged detention and other forms of pressure are always subject to suspicion. While the only true question in each instance is whether the statement was voluntary, a counsel who attempts to attack a statement with nothing more than the word of the accused as evidence of coercion is doomed to defeat. To attack a coerced statement or confession effectively, counsel must appear earlier than he does at present.

Finally, when counsel is not appointed until arraignment, he frequently must go to trial with little or no preparation, depending on the condition of the docket. Although most judges will grant a motion for continuance in a very serious case, it is commonplace for a judge to appoint counsel, to give him a very brief time for consultation, and then to allow the trial to begin. This is not true, generally, where public defenders, legal-aid lawyers, or even paid private lawyers are appointed, but it is inevitably the rule where unpaid lawyers are appointed.

This leads to the question of what corrective action is possible. Though one decision and one writer advocate a holding that the right to counsel arises upon arrest,[26] it is unlikely that the police will be willing to accept such a view and the duty it imposes at the present time. It does seem possible at this date

26 *Suter* v. *State,* 227 Ind. 648, 88 N.E. 2d 386 (1949), dealt with a defendant on a burglary charge who repeatedly asked if he could call a lawyer. The writer of an unsigned note, 26 *Ind. L. J.* (Winter, 1951), 234, suggests that the duty to advise be placed on the police or else on the magistrate who conducts the preliminary hearing. When I presented this comment to police officials they invariably insisted that they were working in each case to ascertain the "true" story before defendants saw lawyers, hence they could not assume a conflicting duty.

to place upon the magistrate at the preliminary hearing the duty of advising an accused that he has the right to retain counsel, and if it clearly appears that the defendant is without means and desires the aid of counsel, it should be the duty of the magistrate to notify the president judge of the local court of record, who could then make an immediate appointment. The advantages accruing from appointment at this stage are clear. A plea of guilty could be accepted at arraignment without fear of challenge on the ground of insufficient advice. If a plea of not guilty were entered, then the trial could proceed without delay and without danger of attack on the ground of ineffective preparation or insufficient time for preparation. Finally, the caliber of the defense which the appointed counsel could offer would be substantially higher than is possible under the present system. Facts could be investigated, the defendant's witnesses could be discovered and subpoenaed, and the state's case, in general, could be subjected to critical scrutiny.

This change in appointment could be accomplished through amendment of existing statutes which require magistrates to advise defendants of their right to retain counsel and of the statutes which call for appointment at arraignment. To prevent administrative errors from destroying the validity of later proceedings, it could be provided that if upon arraignment the defendant should appear without counsel and without having waived counsel competently, it should be the duty of the judge to appoint counsel and postpone arraignment for at least one week. Only by this or a similar measure will it be possible to extend the effective aid of counsel in a criminal case to those unable to afford it.

DEFENSE BY ASSIGNED COUNSEL

Both trial and appellate courts, as well as those persons participating in the criminal trial of an indigent defendant, are vitally interested in the quality of the counsel appointed, once the need for appointment has been established. One can go further, and show that the bar as a group and society as a whole are or should be interested in the solution of this problem. The right to counsel loses substance if the formality of appointment is confused with the provision for an effective defense. The traditional solution, that of appointing private members of the bar, is the first solution worth examining.

COUNSEL FROM THE PRIVATE BAR

At the outset, two generalizations concerning the traditional method of appointment of counsel should be made, although the proof of both rests solely on observation. First, in murder cases, indigent defendants have commonly received adequate defense counsel, for the notoriety, the opportunity for personal publicity as well as public service, and the fascination of defending the life of an accused have combined to make many able and experienced attorneys available for the defense in such cases.[27] (Whether this has proved true, however, in certain communities where racial tension exists is doubtful.)

The second generalization is that in rural or small-town communities the concern of the bar and the people has been more evident, and a real effort to provide counsel has been the rule. This has resulted either from the volunteering by attorneys, the creation of an informal "system" of appointment by the small local bar, or the actions of judges whose contacts with the bar are more intimate and whose powers are in many ways more persuasive than those of their city colleagues.

In murder cases a tangible incentive for attorneys has been added to those previously enumerated, because some payment is provided for such service on appointment in virtually all states. In the Western states there is usually a small payment in noncapital felonies, also, but in the bulk of the Southern and Eastern states no provision for payment is made in such cases.

The difference in attitude and action between city and small-community courts is merely one more example of the social losses accompanying the growth of cities. As relations between citizens became impersonalized, a corresponding mechanization of bar relationships took place, so that lawyers lost their former sense of duty to the public and the judge became just another civic official. The very size of the indigent segment of a city population frightened away many persons who might have aided poor individuals in a more leisurely, rural setting.

In noncapital cases, furnishing counsel has been and is, there-

[27] See Reginald Heber Smith, *Justice and the Poor*, pp. 112–114.

fore, largely an urban problem. Where statutes require appointment, the judge often tries to parcel out the duty with an eye to fairness, but an especially heavy load is likely to fall on young attorneys. Thus the defense burden is frequently placed on the least-skilled members of the bar, who are opposed by prosecutors of wide experience in criminal matters. A further difficulty arises from the well-known tendency of modern lawyers to avoid criminal practice, thus making it ever harder for the judge to appoint experienced criminal lawyers, if this is his objective. Moreover, it seems patently unfair to fasten the entire duty of gratuitous service to indigent defendants on the members of the relatively small criminal bar. It has the effect of further diminishing the quantity and quality of membership in a portion of the bar which needs to be strengthened. In general, the system of providing counsel by appointment from the private bar has been found to be defective.[28]

Would the problem disappear if the legislature were to grant substantial fees? One reason for a negative answer is that such action would create a fund for the maintenance of the least capable element of the criminal bar, since the better criminal lawyers could earn more from "retained" cases. In addition, it is feared that if the fees were substantial a political "disposition" of appointments would follow, with a consequent weakening of the dignity of the courts. Something more than adequate payment seems necessary if the system of assignment from the purely private bar is to work efficiently and equitably.

Nevertheless, it is fair to say that payment in some form is essential for any effective system of counsel, whether provided by appointment from the private bar, by the public defender, or by the legal-aid bureau. While the common argument that political considerations would influence the appointments cannot be dismissed lightly, it is hardly likely that the resulting situation would be worse than the present one under the unpaid system.[29]

[28] Brownell, *op. cit.*, pp. 136–143. My own observations would support this judgment.

[29] In Detroit, where appointments are made by the judge who is serving as president judge that month, there undoubtedly is some rewarding of political supporters, but there seems to be substantial agreement that the standard of service rendered is relatively high. In contrast, one encounters widespread cynical

New Jersey has recently established a scheme of private appointment which represents the most ambitious effort to date to retain the traditional system.   Although no payment is provided for any of the attorneys appointed in noncapital cases, there is a rotation plan for assigning all attorneys who are active members of the various county bars.   This plan, which originated in 1948 in Essex County, has now been embodied in the amended New Jersey Supreme Court rule on counsel and is followed in all New Jersey counties.[30]   In effect, the rule requires appointments in noncapital cases to be made in rotation from an alphabetical roster.   One advantage arising from this equitable distribution of labor is that it decreases the number of periods when an attorney's income may be lost, since it is estimated that assignment of any one man will not occur more frequently than once in ten months and that trials will not be necessary oftener than once in two and one-half years.   Moreover, since all lawyers serve and since comparison is inevitable, there exists an incentive to perform efficiently.[31]   Finally, appointments made on this basis are not vulnerable to the suspicion with which defendants sometimes greet the appointment of a public defender or even a representative of a welfare agency.[32]

Criticisms which can be made are, first, that the plan represents lawyer and bar interests more than it does defendant interests.   All lawyers are not competent in the criminal field, nor are all suitable as trial lawyers.   Secondly, the infrequency of appointment will not lead to the creation of experienced defenders, and the experienced prosecutor will still be at an advantage.   In short, the form of the right to counsel is observed without an equal concern for its substance, and this defeats the fundamental purpose of extending the right to counsel to indigents, namely, to answer the claim for equal justice under the law.   The New Jersey plan does not achieve that goal, although

---

references to the quality of service rendered by appointed counsel in federal courts.

[30] Rule 2:12–1, as amended, 72 *N.J.L.J.* (Nov. 10, 1949), 377.   See Robert K. Bell, "Legal Aid in New Jersey," 36 *A.B.A.J.* (May, 1950), 355, 357.

[31] See Robert K. Bell, *op. cit.*

[32] See remarks of Justice Robert H. Jackson at the annual meeting of the New York City Legal Aid Society on February 23, 1950, excerpted in 48 *Legal Aid Rev.* (June, 1950), 10, 11.

it is a substantial advance over the haphazard system of appointment at present in effect in most states.

LEGAL-AID SOCIETIES AND VOLUNTARY-DEFENDER ORGANIZATIONS

One of the alternatives to assignment on a purely private basis is to appoint as counsel for indigents an attorney who is a member of, or is paid by, a nongovernmental agency, usually termed a legal-aid society or a voluntary-defender's organization. There is no intention here of attempting an analysis of the variety of forms of these organizations or a description of the multiplicity of functions which they perform,[33] but some mention must be made of their role in criminal cases.

Though there are numerous variations in the methods of financing the plans, there are two methods that are fundamentally distinct. The New York Legal Aid Society has received support through a great number of contributions from the public and from members of the bar, with law firms playing an important role by contributing on behalf of all members on an annual basis. The budget is drawn with a division according to function, criminal or civil, and a further division according to the courts to be served.[34] The second type, where the society is financed entirely by the Community Chest fund, is exemplified by the Voluntary Defender's Office in Philadelphia. It extends the same services as does the criminal division of the New York Legal Aid Society, but relies more heavily

[33] See Reginald Heber Smith, *Justice and the Poor*, Part III, for an excellent account of the early development and expansion of the various societies up to 1919. Valuable treatments of later trends are found in J. S. Bradway and R. H. Smith, eds., "Legal Aid Work," 124 *Annals of the American Academy of Social and Political Science* (March, 1926); J. S. Bradway, ed., "Law and Social Work," 145 *Annals* (Sept., 1929), Part I; J. S. Bradway, ed., "Frontiers of Legal Aid Work," 205 *Annals* (Sept., 1939). Annual reports issued by the New York Legal Aid Society give an accurate picture of the nature and the scope of the work of this, the oldest and largest society, and the *Legal Aid Review*, published monthly by the same society, gives brief accounts of current happenings in legal-aid work. The most valuable and most recent source is Emery A. Brownell, *Legal Aid in the United States;* Chapter VI of this book contains an excellent discussion of public and private defender organizations.

[34] The New York Legal Aid Society's criminal division handled 2,435 cases in the fourth quarter of 1949, and 3,035 cases in the first quarter of 1950, 48 *Legal Aid Rev.* (June, 1950), 14, 15.

on the efforts of the permanent staff than does the New York society, which utilizes volunteer assistance as well.[35]

The chief objection to this volunteer type of organization is financial: during depressions, when the burden of work is greater, the sources of funds decrease and some curtailment of service is necessary.[36] But the advantages of this method of supplying aid to indigents are great. First, the plan enlists the enthusiastic support of the more idealistic members of the bar, who feel that a social contribution should be made. Secondly, and more important, the establishment of a permanent staff of experienced criminal and trial lawyers assures effective aid to the defendant. Thirdly, investigative and clerical services are made available to a degree far beyond what is possible for most private attorneys who might be appointed as defense counsel. Fourthly, the effective work of these private societies has earned them a reputation for conscientiousness and zeal. Since sham defense, perjured witnesses, and bribed jurors have no place in their efforts for indigent defendants, there is a feeling on the part of defendants and the public that a fair and honest presentation will be made. Political factors do not enter into the work of the legal-aid societies. At present the organized bar is trying to extend and improve these legal-aid societies, although the criminal aspect is viewed as only one phase of the larger problem of low-cost or free legal aid for those unable to retain private attorneys.

PUBLIC DEFENDER

The first office of the public defender was established in 1913 in Los Angeles County, California. Today similar offices exist on a state-wide basis in California, Connecticut, Mis-

[35] See Louis Fabricant, "Voluntary Defenders in Criminal Cases," 205 *Annals* (Sept., 1939), 24, and Herman I. Pollock, "The Voluntary Defender as Counsel for the Defense," 32 *J. Amer. Judic. Soc.* (April, 1949), 174.

[36] In 1933 the New York society had 36,000 clients and suffered a deficit of $26,000, which was made up by a few large firms. In that same year the branches at Harlem and Brooklyn had to be discontinued; in prosperous 1949 two new branches were opened. In 1940 fewer clients were served under a slightly larger budget than in 1933, and no deficit was sustained. See *Annual Reports,* 1933, 1940, 1949.

sissippi, Nebraska, Virginia, and Illinois.[37]   Illinois, the most recent addition to the list of state-wide adherents to the plan, had observed its operation in Cook County before enacting legislation extending it to all counties of more than 35,000 population.[38]   Larger cities using the plan are Providence, St. Paul, St. Louis, Tulsa, and Indianapolis.

The public defender is a public official, having assistants and a clerical staff, whose duty it is to defend indigent persons accused of crime.   In addition, statutes may require that he serve indigents making certain types of legal claims, particularly wage claims.[39]

The organized bar has raised substantial objections, and exerted powerful opposition, to the public-defender plan from the very beginning.[40]   Difficult to analyze, but important, have been the vociferous attacks by a certain segment of the criminal bar.   As far back as 1931 the Wickersham Commission noted the existence of a group within the bar which depended for its livelihood on appointments in indigent-defendant cases, and consequently engaged in political activity in return for appointments.[41]   More substantial objections arise from the fear that the public defender, as a public official, will not be motivated by concern for the defendant's plight but will tend to establish a friendly and "workable" relationship with the judge and, more important, with the prosecutor's office, which itself has been a target of extensive criticism.[42]   The standard arguments of the

[37] Donald Freeman, "The Public Defender System," 32 *J. Amer. Judic. Soc.* (Oct., 1948), 74.   See also Brownell, *op. cit.*, Chaps. VI, VIII.

[38] *Illinois Ann. Stat., 1949* (Smith-Hurd, 1950), c. 34, § 163c.

[39] The best general treatment, though dated, is that of Mayer C. Goldman, *The Public Defender*.   Articles in the *Annals* symposia cited above, in footnote 33, cover the public-defender system.   Statutory provisions exist in California: *Deering's Calif. Gen. Laws*. Act 1910, § 1–8; Connecticut: *Conn. Gen. Stats.*, 1949, Tit. 65, § 8796; Nebraska: *Rev. Stat.*, 1943, 29–1804; Minnesota: *Minn. Stats. Ann.*, 1947, 611.12, 611.13; Illinois: *Ill. Ann. Stat.* (1935) as amended 1949, c. 34, § 163c; Virginia: *Va. Code of 1942*, Tit. 41, § 4970a.

[40] See Goldman, *op. cit.*, preface, p. viii.   For a more recent expression of opposition, see William Scott Stewart, "The Public Defender System Is Unsound in Principle," 32 *J. Amer. Judic. Soc.* (Dec., 1948), 115.

[41] U. S. National Commission on Law Observance and Enforcement, *Report on Prosecution* (Washington, D.C.: Government Printing Office, 1931), p. 31.

[42] *Ibid.*, pp. 37–38.

critics which proved decisive in defeating the proposal for a public defender when this was urged at Cleveland in 1931 emphasized the tendency of the public defender to "harden" toward all defendants' stories because of the volume of cases and the resulting lack of enthusiasm, and the unhealthy relationship which would develop between prosecutor, judge, and public defender.[43]

Although it is frequently asserted that public defenders induce a greater number of guilty pleas than do other appointed or retained counsel, there is no apparent support for this claim in the limited statistical data now available.[44] Several observers of, and participants in, the system of unpaid appointment from the private bar now used in the federal courts have commented caustically on the readiness of appointed attorneys to enter pleas of guilty. Part of this is due to the obvious displeasure with which some federal judges greet a not-guilty plea by appointed, or retained, counsel, but certainly the lack of payment creates a less-than-enthusiastic attitude in the attorney, at least in the more minor cases. Where paid appointments are made from the private bar, as in Detroit, there is no evidence that a more effective defense is offered. In fact, some observers suggested that the inexperienced attorneys appointed in several cases did their clients harm by insisting on going to trial rather than advising a plea of guilty, with a consequent lower sentence.

[43] 17 *A.B.A.J.* (March, 1931), 141. This possible defect is not inevitable. I can testify that in Cook County, Illinois, and in Indianapolis the public defender opposes the prosecutor's office as staunchly as private counsel would. If the public defender can increasingly exert influence with the judge, this would seem a desirable counterweight to the well-known influence of the prosecutor.

[44] In one California county approximately 70 per cent of those represented by the public defender pleaded guilty either at arraignment or later, compared with 44 per cent of those who retained counsel. Twenty-five per cent of the clients of retained counsel were convicted by juries, compared with 14.6 per cent of the persons represented by the public defender, and the same percentages were convicted in trials by the judge. See R. H. Beattie, "The Public Defender and Private Defense Attorneys," cited in Donald Freeman, "The Public Defender System," 32 *J. Amer. Judic. Soc.* (Oct., 1948), 74, 78. Compare these statistics with those from the first year's operation of the New Jersey system of private appointment, discussed *supra*, where two thirds pleaded guilty, and about 14.3 per cent were found guilty after trial, a result almost identical with the California findings. See 73 *N.J.L.J.* (Aug. 31, 1950), 299.

Experienced observers have supported the public-defender plan and urged its use in the federal courts.[45] Stress has been placed on the necessity for its adoption because of the shortage of experienced criminal lawyers available for individual appointment and because of the need for experienced lawyers at arraignment, where mental deficiencies in defendants should be detected.[46] Without question, it is more economical than would be any scheme of adequate compensation for case-by-case appointments, and it permits a more thorough investigation and preparation of each case. Whenever it has been used, it has shortened the time which elapses between arrest and trial.[47] Where the system is properly constituted and operated, as in Cook County, Illinois, the reaction of officials and observers has been favorable.[48]

When we survey the three possibilities of providing counsel —continuance of the traditional method, legal-aid groups, and public defender—the choice seems to lie clearly between the last two. Whether the legal-aid society or the public-defender system is the better agency to carry out the task of defending indigents is a question that is hard to answer without more comprehensive data than are now available. Neither plan has been tried in more than a small percentage of our jurisdictions. There is no reason why a public defender, if made independent of the more obvious political controls, should not develop into a very able and devoted public servant. The traditional American distrust of government, already weakened in so many other sectors, can be overcome as the public defenders now serving continue to create and maintain high standards. There has been no serious movement in any of the states which have

[45] Alexander Holtzoff, 9 *F.R.D.* (1949), 303. The Conference of Senior Circuit Judges adopted it in principle in 1937 for use in large districts. See 23 *J. Amer. Judic. Soc.* (Dec., 1939), 131–132.

[46] James V. Bennett, 32 *J. Amer. Judic. Soc.* (April, 1949), 177.

[47] See 17 *A.B.A.J.* (March, 1931), 141. See also Donald Freeman, 32 *J. Amer. Judic. Soc.* (Oct., 1948), 74. The ability to conduct thorough investigations which characterizes the well-organized Cook County Public Defender's Office is indispensable.

[48] I found that the chief complaint was the excessive zeal of the public defender in protecting "criminals." See the comment (Brownell, *op. cit.*, p. 138) on the Los Angeles public defender made by Justice Miller, then Dean of the Southern California Law School, that all agencies which dealt with the public defender—courts, prosecutor, police, and social agencies—had expressed approval.

adopted the plan to discard it. On the contrary, its use has spread. Legal-aid societies likewise have shown a tremendous growth, particularly since World War II, as the national and various state bar associations have tardily recognized that so important a problem as legal service for indigents could not be ignored much longer without endangering the standing of the legal profession. Both the public defender and the legal-aid society offer a tremendous advance over the traditional practice. Through either device the indigent defendant gains a substantial enjoyment of the right to counsel.[49]

POSTCONVICTION REMEDY

One of the principal differences between the English and the American legal systems is the much greater emphasis in our procedure on the right to appeal. The question of whether this has been a desirable development is beyond the scope of this inquiry. It seems obvious, however, that if an appeal is to be a regular feature of a judicial system, it must be designed so as to accomplish its purpose in an efficient and logical way.

Congress attempted to provide an effective substitute for the overused writ of habeas corpus by requiring prisoners to direct a motion to vacate sentence to the court in which they were convicted, so that a hearing might be held by the person best qualified to review the constitutional claims presented.[50]

In certain states, notably Illinois, the postconviction remedy, where a denial of a state or a federal constitutional right was claimed, has been inefficient, unsatisfactory, and irregular in its functioning. In *Marino* v. *Ragen,* the exasperation of three members of the Supreme Court with the Illinois "labyrinth" was expressed in the most vigorous language possible.[51] The very fact that no counsel was present during trial made it highly unlikely that a proper record could be had upon which to base appeal or writ of error. Thus collateral attack was necessary in Illinois. *Coram nobis,* however, or its modern statutory variant, is a writ intended to direct the trial judge's attention to facts not known by him at the time of trial. Unless some

---

[49] Brownell, *op. cit.,* pp. 143–146, reaches the same conclusion.
[50] See discussion of 28 U.S.C.A. (1950), § 2255, in Chap. III, *supra.*
[51] 332 U.S. 561, 68 S. Ct. 240, 92 L. Ed. 170 (1947).

interference by public officials in the right to retain counsel or some misinformation relative to counsel could be shown, *coram nobis* would hardly prove effective, since the judge would know the other facts relating to the nonappearance of counsel. Of course, the writ may be given a broader application and directed to the conscience of the court, as has been done in New York, but Illinois chose not to do this. Habeas corpus was the last possibility, and in Illinois and various other states it became customary to dismiss the applications for this writ without revealing the basis of the dismissal.

Unlike some states, Illinois did not allow an appeal from a denial of the writ, but required an original application to the Illinois Supreme Court. To complete the confusion, that court declared by rule its refusal to hear any application in which factual issues were presented. On certiorari, the existence of a nonfederal ground could be alleged because the basis of the state decision was not evident, so that the United States Supreme Court remained unenlightened and the convict was left with no alternative but to try other state or federal judges, with equally unrewarding results.

To the credit of Illinois, it took action after the Marino case to provide a convenient, simple, and efficient postconviction remedy. By its Supreme Court Rule 27–A it made effective provision for future cases, and by extending the office of public defender to counties of more than 35,000 inhabitants it implemented the formal right to counsel. On August 4, 1949, a "Post-Conviction Hearing Act" became effective, and the Illinois reform effort was complete.[52]

Intended as an additional remedy, and not as a replacement for any of those existing, the Post-Conviction Hearing Act allows a convict to claim, by presenting a petition to the original trial court, that his conviction was invalid because of the denial of a state or federal constitutional right. All relevant facts and proof must be shown, and the petitioner must identify any previous proceedings in which any of the matters now alleged were raised or could have been raised.[53] Matters which are not raised are deemed waived, and the proceeding itself is shaped

[52] *Ill. Rev. Stat., 1951*, c. 38, §§ 826–832.
[53] *Ibid.*, § 827.

by the court after the state's answer is returned. The act seems to guarantee a hearing on the merits of the case and insures that a substantial judgment results.[54] Finally, the judgment thus rendered is subject to appeal within six months from time of entry, and each of the courts states the grounds of its action.[55] Clearly, it is a well-designed piece of judicial legislation.[56] Petitions for certiorari from persons convicted in Illinois were dismissed without prejudice by the United States Supreme Court in the period immediately following the act's passage in order that the new remedy could be pursued.[57]

Unfortunately, as the decision of the United States Supreme Court in the Jennings case shows, the Illinois postconviction statute has not as yet been implemented to achieve the purposes for which it was designed.[58] In each of three Illinois cases (consolidated in the Supreme Court) a convict had petitioned his trial court for a hearing, alleging a denial of constitutional rights, but in each case the petitions were dismissed without a hearing on grounds of *res judicata,* and failure to state a cause of action. The Illinois Supreme Court dismissed writ of error in each case, without argument and without opinion.

The legal principle underlying the action of both trial and appellate Illinois courts was to be found, apparently, in a 1950 decision of the Illinois Supreme Court sustaining the Post-Conviction Hearing Act, in which it was held that the act did not require a rehearing of issues *already adjudicated.*[59] On that basis the Illinois trial courts decided without a hearing that the alleged constitutional issues in these three cases had been disposed of or had been waived at the original trial (*res judicata*) and that the new claims raised were insufficient to state a cause of action. The Illinois Supreme Court's form order

[54] *Ibid.,* §§ 828–829–831.

[55] *Ibid.,* § 832.

[56] See Albert E. Jenner, Jr., "The Illinois Post-Conviction Hearing Act," *Illinois Rev. Stat., 1949* (Smith-Hurd, 1950), p. 199, for an extended discussion of the features of the act.

[57] See *Walker* v. *Ragen* (mem.) 338 U.S. 833, 70 S. Ct. 37, 94 L. Ed. 507 (1949), and memorandum cases cited there. The Seventh Circuit Court had denied habeas corpus because of the existence of the remedy. See also *United States ex rel. Peters* v. *Ragen,* 178 F. 2d 377 (1949).

[58] *Jennings* v. *Illinois* (*Lafrana* v. *Illinois* and *Sherman* v. *Illinois*), 342 U.S. 104, 72 S. Ct. 123, 96 L. Ed. 119 (1951).

[59] *People* v. *Dale,* 406 Ill. 238, 92 N.E. 2d 761 (1950).

dismissing the writs stated simply, "After having examined and reviewed the petition and record in the postconviction hearing the same is found to disclose no violation or denial of any substantial constitutional rights . . . ." [60]

In vacating the judgment and remanding to the Illinois Supreme Court, the United States Supreme Court asked whether an adequate state remedy was afforded by the Post-Conviction Hearing Act. If no adequate remedy existed, petitioners were advised to try a district court. Justice Frankfurter exhibited his usual deference to state courts by urging in a dissenting opinion that the denial of a federal right had not been shown. He thought, moreover, that the majority's opinion offered no guidance to the Illinois Supreme Court. It appears that the Illinois courts could readily satisfy critics by adding to their brief decisions a few well-chosen sentences stating in each case the ground or grounds upon which a decision is based.

The difficulties of Illinois should not deter other states from taking steps to improve their judicial administration. An intransigent state attitude will inevitably result in stronger mandates from the Supreme Court, and little sympathy will be expressed for a claim of "states' rights" when the "state right" supposedly threatened is the right to deny counsel to indigent defendants.

By court rules, or through legislation where necessary, the states must make explicit the duty of a trial judge to ascertain the needs of defendants and to appoint counsel when required for the conduct of a fair trial. The state bar association, judges, and social agencies should work toward the establishment of an efficient means of furnishing counsel, either through an extension of the legal-aid-society principle or through the adoption of the public-defender scheme. Finally, a simple and effective postconviction remedy must be provided in order that the fulfillment of this and other constitutional rights can be sought and achieved in practice. All of these measures will tend to make constitutional rights meaningful, with a subsequent increase in the respect with which citizens regard our courts and our legal system.

[60] 342 U.S. 104 at 107, 96 L. Ed. 119 at 123–124.

CHAPTER VII

SUMMARY AND CONCLUSIONS

THE object of this study has been to examine the meaning and the scope of the right to counsel in federal and state courts under the various forms of law applicable to each. Whether or not a defendant in a criminal proceeding should have the right to retain counsel and whether or not he should have the right to receive the assistance of appointed counsel are ethical or philosophical questions which can be answered readily. But whether or not a defendant actually enjoys these rights under the existing rules of law is a question that raises issues fraught with complications and, as should be evident by now, permits only an answer replete with equivocations and conditions. The substantial body of case law testifies that the counsel problem is more than an academic one. It has vexed the United States Supreme Court more than many of seemingly greater magnitude.

The history of the right to counsel, though lacking in details, has exhibited certain characteristics which can be described. In England the government for a long period was unwilling to sanction assistance for one charged with serious violations of its laws, although in misdemeanor and private cases where the state's interest was slight or nonexistent, a full defense by counsel furnished by the accused was permitted from an early date. With the exception of treason cases, in which counsel was not only allowed but, after 1695, could be appointed if the defendant were indigent, counsel could not appear as a matter of right in English felony cases until a statute of 1836 made full representation by retained counsel possible. It is clear, moreover, that trial judges, who in general had allowed defendants to appear for the purpose of arguing some points of law from early in the eighteenth century, broadened their interpretation of what constituted points of law until by the end of the century counsel could fully defend by modern standards, with the exception of the argument to the jury. In England today indigent defendants are given appointed counsel, although in less serious cases the duty to appoint is discretionary.

In the American colonies, statutes or charters permitted defense by retained counsel in all criminal cases. By custom in Connecticut and by statute in the other states, provision was made for the appointment of counsel in capital cases. Most post-Revolution state constitutions contained a clause concerning the right to retain counsel, although any right to appointed counsel was set forth in legislative enactments. The counsel provision of the Sixth Amendment was probably intended as nothing more than a guarantee of the right to retain counsel; otherwise, the 1790 act of Congress providing for the appointment of counsel in federal capital cases would have been superfluous.

Two developments during the nineteenth century remain to be noted. First, in most federal trial courts a practice emerged of appointing counsel in serious cases where the defendant pleaded not guilty but was unable to retain a lawyer. Secondly, state legislatures began to require appointment of counsel in all felony cases, and in many instances they allowed for payment of the appointed counsel.

The problem of counsel in federal courts was solved in a decisive manner once it arose. After *Powell* v. *Alabama*,[1] decided in 1932, it was only a question of time before the Supreme Court would have to face the issue of what the counsel clause in the Sixth Amendment required in the way of procedure. Lower courts wrestled with the problem ineffectively, but in *Johnson* v. *Zerbst*[2] the matter was finally resolved by the Supreme Court. In this case young, inexperienced defendants pleaded not guilty and were convicted in a trial in which they defended themselves. The Supreme Court held that failure to appoint counsel was a jurisdictional defect and that the subsequent conviction was void. Only where a competent waiver of counsel is shown, that is, one made by a defendant of normal

---

[1] *Powell v. Alabama*, 287 U.S. 45, 53 S. Ct. 55, 77 L. Ed. 158 (1932).
[2] *Johnson v. Zerbst*, 304 U.S. 458, 58 S. Ct. 1019, 82 L. Ed. 1461 (1938).

mental ability who has been fully advised of his rights, can a defendant be tried without counsel, said the Court. In 1941, in *Walker* v. *Johnston,* the Court clarified an old problem when it held that a plea of guilty by a defendant who had not been informed of his right to counsel should not be treated as a waiver of counsel.[3] Moreover, in *Johnson* v. *Zerbst,* the Court had suggested that the trial record should contain the circumstances of waiver or of any other action respecting counsel.

Thus the clear mandate of the Court made imperative the formulation of a rule which district courts could apply readily in all cases. Rule 44 of the Federal Rules of Criminal Procedure, effective since 1946, requires that defendants be advised of their right to retain counsel and be offered counsel through court appointment if they are indigent. The counsel problem in the federal courts is thus substantially solved. Questions involving interference with the right to retain counsel, lack of time for the preparation of cases, denials of motions for continuances, quality of assigned and retained counsel, absence of counsel at one or more stages in the proceeding, and curtailment of the time necessary for argument have arisen and will continue to arise. The answer in most of these situations turns on the manner in which the discretion of the trial judge was exercised and on the appellate court's later judgment of the reasonableness of the action taken. If counsel issues are raised on collateral attack, the petitioner's difficulties are much greater than if they are raised on appeal. Most claims are rejected.

The issue of the right to counsel in state trials as interpreted by state courts is more complicated. In surprisingly few instances—New York, California, Indiana, Georgia, Nevada, New Mexico, and Nebraska being the exceptions—have state constitutional provisions respecting counsel been construed broadly as requiring appointment for indigents. The statutes range from the explicit provisions in California, which cover every aspect of the problem, including the duty to appoint counsel for indigents in all cases, to the less protective Illinois statute specifying appointment upon request, down to the minimal capital-case provisions in Pennsylvania and Massachusetts and in Mississippi and other Southern states.

[3] *Walker* v. *Johnston,* 312 U.S. 275, 61 S. Ct. 574, 85 L. Ed. 830 (1941).

All states supply counsel for indigents in capital cases, though, as many of the trials indicate, the defense furnished is frequently more formal than real. In noncapital cases in those states where the statute provided for appointment on request, as in Illinois, failure to request was deemed a waiver, with no duty on the court to advise the defendant of his rights. Another problem with which many state courts wrestled inconclusively was how to find a waiver of counsel where a statute seemingly required appointment and the trial record was silent concerning waiver. A third substantial question involved the adequacy of the methods of claiming a denial of counsel. In most instances absence of counsel during trial made it unlikely that an adequate record would exist for review on writ of error or appeal. Yet if the claimant tried collateral attack, the courts expressed substantial faith in the rectitude of trial courts and, in many instances, dismissed the petition for habeas corpus or *coram nobis* without much interest in the factual realities of the trial situation.

Generally, Western states have been the most generous, both in providing counsel for indigents and in recognizing the advantages of using state funds to compensate attorneys who were appointed to serve indigents. The public-defender movement, for example, had its origin in California, in 1913. The Eastern and Southern states have, for the most part, taken an indifferent attitude toward indigent defendants in noncapital cases. Yet it is true that in many Pennsylvania and Massachusetts courts, where no statutory provision applies, a tradition of appointing in all serious cases in which a defense is claimed, has existed for a long period. Such a practice, based on the inherent power of a court, has been more prevalent in rural areas than in the large urban districts.

As was true with federal procedure, numerous claims charging inadequate appointed counsel, restrictions on the right to retain counsel, absence of counsel at various stages of trial, curtailment of time for argument, denials of motions for continuances, and other aspects of the right to counsel have been the subject of suits in state courts. Since most of these matters rest within the discretion or purview of the trial court, the judgment is not likely to be reversed unless a very powerful case is set forth. Most claims are denied.

It was not until 1932, when *Powell* v. *Alabama* was decided, that the states learned that the due-process clause of the Fourteenth Amendment was a limitation on their policy regarding counsel in criminal proceedings. In a series of cases dating back to *Hurtado* v. *California,* in 1884, the Supreme Court had proclaimed the freedom of the states to adopt specific modes of trial suitable to each state, the only standard required being that of "fairness." Trial by jury and indictment by grand jury had been found unessential, and with these ancient procedural rights discarded it seemed improbable that any specific trial element would be held to be part of due process.

In *Powell* v. *Alabama* ignorant, illiterate Negro youths were tried and convicted of rape and sentenced to death. In an atmosphere charged with tension, a vague appointment of the entire local bar to defend the nine Negroes was made at arraignment, but confusion marked the "defense" when the trial commenced six days later. Present also as an issue was the likelihood that counsel might have been retained had opportunity been given. But it was on the first ground that the Supreme Court found a denial of due process. In a capital case, said Sutherland, where defendants were illiterate, ignorant, youthful, and strangers in a community, an effective appointment of counsel was essential to a hearing which accorded with due process.[4] The reasoning which led Sutherland to this conclusion, however, was so cogent that it seemed only a matter of time before it would be extended to include virtually all criminal proceedings.

The expected did not happen. In 1942, in *Betts* v. *Brady,* a Maryland trial court refused to appoint counsel at the request of an indigent defendant charged with robbery.[5] The refusal to appoint counsel was not a denial of due process in this noncapital case, said the Supreme Court, because the issue had been simple, the defendant mature, and the trial "fair." The effect of this fair-trial rule was to make the question of appointment

---

[4] *Powell* v. *Alabama,* 287 U.S. 45, 53 S. Ct. 55, 77 L. Ed. 158 (1932).
[5] *Betts* v. *Brady,* 316 U.S. 455, 62 S. Ct. 1252, 86 L. Ed. 1595 (1942).

one to be decided on a case-by-case basis after an examination of the "totality of facts." Under the rule, appointment was necessary only if the defendant had certain characteristics or if unusual circumstances or a complicated charge made an adequate defense without counsel impossible. By emphasizing the fairness of the trial, an additional test was suggested. Thus, where an examination of the trial record revealed a "fair" proceeding for a normal defendant without counsel, the reviewing court could decide that no appointment of counsel had been necessary.

This fair-trial doctrine has proved difficult to apply. So many variables are included within its ill-defined limits that it has failed to provide adequate guidance for state trial courts and has confused state and federal courts called upon to review alleged denials of the right to counsel. Subsequent to *Betts* v. *Brady,* nineteen state counsel cases were presented to the Supreme Court in which the merits of each case were considered. The claims of four of the five petitioners convicted of capital crimes were upheld.[6] Strangely enough, in none of these cases did the Court announce a clear-cut rule to be applied to counsel in capital cases, but, rather, it emphasized additional elements in each case which permitted the use of the Powell doctrine. Through dicta in four noncapital cases, however, the Court made it clear that in capital cases a trial court must offer counsel in every case, and may accept a waiver of counsel only when the defendant is competent in the fullest sense.[7] A different set of assumptions is thus to be employed depending on whether a case is capital or noncapital.

The petitioners' claims have been upheld in half of the fourteen noncapital cases presented to the Supreme Court where the

---

[6] Upheld in *Williams* v. *Kaiser,* 323 U.S. 471, 65 S. Ct. 363, 89 L. Ed. 398 (1945); *Tompkins* v. *Missouri,* 323 U.S. 485, 65 S. Ct. 370, 89 L. Ed. 407 (1945); *Hawk* v. *Olson,* 326 U.S. 271, 66 S. Ct. 116, 90 L. Ed. 61 (1945); *Marino* v. *Ragen,* 332 U.S. 561, 68 S. Ct. 240, 92 L. Ed. 170 (1947). In *Carter* v. *Illinois,* 329 U.S. 173, 67 S. Ct. 216, 91 L. Ed. 172 (1946), the claim was denied, but the defendant had been advised of his right to counsel, according to the common-law record.

[7] *Bute* v. *Illinois,* 333 U.S. 640, 68 S. Ct. 763, 92 L. Ed. 986 (1948); *Wade* v. *Mayo,* 334 U.S. 672, 68 S. Ct. 1270, 92 L. Ed. 1647 (1948); *Quicksall* v. *Michigan,* 339 U.S. 660, 70 S. Ct. 910, 94 L. Ed. 1188 (1950); *Uveges* v. *Pennsylvania,* 335 U.S. 437, 69 S. Ct. 184, 93 L. Ed. 127 (1948).

question of appointment of counsel was involved.[8]   In three of
the successful cases [9] the youth of the defendant was an important
factor, although claims of ignorance, inexperience, and fright
undoubtedly played some part.   Ignorance and a complicated
jurisdictional issue were the main elements in *Rice* v. *Olson*.
In *Townsend* v. *Burke* and *Gibbs* v. *Burke* an examination of
trial records in which indigent defendants had not been offered
counsel revealed material errors to the disadvantage of the defendant.   *House* v. *Mayo* turned on interference by an impatient trial court with the traditional right to retain counsel.

In all but two of the seven noncapital cases in which the
Supreme Court did not uphold claims of denial of counsel, one
or more technical grounds furnished the basis for the decision.
The exceptions were *Bute* v. *Illinois,* where the age of the defendant and the simplicity of the charge permitted an application of the *Betts* v. *Brady* doctrine, and *Quicksall* v. *Michigan,*
where the petitioner's claim clearly lacked merit.[10]   Deficiencies
in the record as presented to the Supreme Court or alternative
grounds for the state court's decision account for *White* v. *Ragen*
and *Foster* v. *Illinois*.[11]   In *Gayes* v. *New York* and *Canizio* v.
New York the Court used a doctrine of forfeiture of the right
to appointed counsel because of the petitioner's failure to raise
the issue at the procedural stages subsequent to the denial.[12]
Yet in *Gryger* v. *Burke* a judge's misinterpretation of the statute
applicable to the sentence was dismissed as an error of state law.[13]

With the exception of the Canizio case, in which Black and

---

[8] *House* v. *Mayo*, 324 U.S. 42, 65 S. Ct. 517, 89 L. Ed. 739 (1945), involved a
denial of the right to retain counsel, but has been included in the analysis.   In
six cases the question of appointment was involved: *Rice* v. *Olson*, 324 U.S. 786,
65 S. Ct. 989, 89 L. Ed. 1367 (1945); *De Meerleer* v. *Michigan*, 329 U.S. 663, 67
S. Ct. 596, 91 L. Ed. 584 (1947); *Wade* v. *Mayo*, 334 U.S. 672, 68 S. Ct. 1270, 92
L. Ed. 1647 (1948); *Townsend* v. *Burke*, 334 U.S. 736, 68 S. Ct. 1252, 92 L. Ed.
1690 (1948); *Uveges* v. *Pennsylvania*, 335 U.S. 437, 69 S. Ct. 184, 93 L. Ed. 127
(1948); *Gibbs* v. *Burke*, 337 U.S. 733, 69 S. Ct. 1247, 93 L. Ed. 1686 (1949).

[9] De Meerleer, Wade, and Uveges.

[10] *Bute* v. *Illinois*, 333 U.S. 640, 68 S. Ct. 763, 92 L. Ed. 986 (1948); *Quicksall*
v. *Michigan*, 339 U.S. 660, 70 S. Ct. 910, 94 L. Ed. 1188 (1950).

[11] *White* v. *Ragen*, 324 U.S. 760, 65 S. Ct. 978, 89 L. Ed. 1348 (1945); *Foster* v.
Illinois, 332 U.S. 134, 67 S. Ct. 1716, 91 L. Ed. 1955 (1947).

[12] *Canizio* v. *New York*, 327 U.S. 82, 66 S. Ct. 452, 90 L. Ed. 545 (1946); *Gayes*
v. *New York*, 332 U.S. 145, 67 S. Ct. 1711, 91 L. Ed. 1962 (1947).

[13] *Gryger* v. *Burke*, 334 U.S. 728, 68 S. Ct. 1256, 92 L. Ed. 1683 (1948).

Douglas voted to deny the claim, the bloc of Douglas, Murphy, Black, and Rutledge was consistent in upholding claims of denial of counsel. They espoused a broad theory which would have incorporated the full Bill of Rights, including the Sixth Amendment counsel provision, within the protective confines of the Fourteenth Amendment. Since the majority of the Court would not retreat from the fair-trial rule of *Betts* v. *Brady,* the successful claims of denial of counsel were marked by an alliance of the four "incorporators" with one or two of the fair-trial adherents. Nevertheless, five-to-four alignments existed in six cases. The tactic of the four incorporators seemed to be one of reading into the fair-trial rule so many conditions favorable to defendants that appointment of counsel would be required in virtually all cases if a trial judge were to have confidence in the invulnerability of the judgment.

Whether this intention of the four incorporators was accomplished or whether the failure of the fair-trial doctrine was inevitable because of ambiguities and variable elements, it is obvious that several of the states began to realize that their existing procedures were proving less than satisfactory upon review by the Supreme Court. By means of state-supreme-court rules in Missouri, Michigan, and Illinois, trial courts were directed to advise defendants of their rights and to offer counsel in all cases. Improved legislation was passed in Virginia requiring appointment of counsel unless it were waived. In the states which had experienced trouble, and in others which had not, judges began to approach the task of possible appointment of counsel with new interest, and they have demonstrated extreme caution in allowing any waivers of counsel. This trend has progressed so far in a few states that there is some possibility of future claims of denial of the right to defend "in person," a right seemingly guaranteed by constitutional provisions in thirty-seven of the states.

Another general problem which needs attention is the method of providing counsel once the necessity of appointment is determined. The traditional solution has been to assign members of the bar on any basis which seemed appropriate to the trial judge. Some judges have called upon young lawyers, or those whose practice was not heavy. Other judges have compiled lists of volunteers who were willing to serve indigent defendants. A few judges have considered the entire local bar available for appointment. Undoubtedly there have been some judges who have habitually designated the most experienced lawyer available, regardless of the wishes of the local bar.

It is fair to say that this system has worked well where capital offenses were charged. Attorneys who shunned appointment in less notorious cases were quite willing to serve in these because of the splendid publicity or the opportunity for public service. It is probably true, also, that indigents in rural areas and small towns have generally been defended regardless of their ability to pay. In such places the local bar assumed the burden as one of its social obligations. But in cities, where the volume of cases has grown while the ties between the bar and the community have weakened, the results of this system have been unsatisfactory.

Prominent judges, lawyers, and scholars have decried the existing method of appointment and have proposed alternatives. New Jersey, under its able Chief Justice Arthur T. Vanderbilt, has improved the traditional haphazard scheme of assignment by providing for rotation of attorneys from the entire county-bar roster.

More radical departures are the criminal defense activities of the legal-aid society and the office of public defender, both of which maintain staffs of experienced criminal lawyers aided by investigatory and clerical personnel. Each plan has certain advantages, and while both have enthusiastic adherents and have shown the power to grow, it is too early to say which will prove stronger, although the resources of the American Bar Association have been thrown behind the legal-aid plan. Each system is such an improvement over the traditional method of appointment that it has continued to spread in the areas where it now exists. The legal-aid society, so efficiently demonstrated in New York and Philadelphia, is expanding throughout those states. The public-defender plan started in Los Angeles in 1913 and has spread throughout California. It was first used in Illinois in Cook County, and has since been made obligatory throughout the state by a legislative act of 1949. The need for increased use of both of these methods is revealed by the reports of the Survey of the Legal Profession.

If the states undertake widespread reform of their existing practices respecting counsel, there will be little need for the Supreme Court to intervene in their proceedings. Review by federal courts would be curtailed substantially if states that have had difficulty with appellate remedies would adopt simple and efficient postconviction acts requiring courts to grant a hearing and to reveal the grounds of decisions in any postconviction proceeding. As Illinois experience has shown, however, no act can solve all problems if intelligent implementation is lacking.

If the states fail to act, the Supreme Court will be compelled to devote an excessive amount of time to a flood of petitions alleging denials of counsel, and, inadequately armed with its fair-trial doctrine, it will have to undertake a re-examination of factual situations as presented on the cold record. The Supreme Court was not designed for this purpose and is ill-prepared to execute this function. In desperation, it may already have been forced to use its discretionary power of certiorari to defeat worthy claims; it has in any event created a confusing situation by its effort to defer to state courts at the expense of litigants, who as a result are forced to pursue their remedy through a complex and circuitous route.

The alternative seems obvious. The Supreme Court, either by declaring that under modern conditions due process in criminal proceedings requires counsel, unless waived, or by formulating a new application of its fair-trial doctrine, should take the firm position that a trial cannot be fair unless counsel assists every defendant who wants or needs the aid of counsel. To say that trials without counsel can be fair is to assume either that the defense which counsel might have presented would not have changed the result in the case or that in certain types of cases counsel serves no useful function. The first assumption is hindsight and unprovable. The second, if true, would convict a portion of the bar of taking money under false pretenses in all those "simple" cases where counsel accepts a retainer but apparently cannot influence the result. We cannot with justice keep the existing "fight" theory of criminal law and force the indigent defendant to fight alone. If our vaunted claim of "equal justice under law" is to be more than an idle pretense, the right to have counsel must be extended in practice to all persons accused of crime.

APPENDIX I

STATE CONSTITUTIONAL PROVISIONS REGARDING COUNSEL*

Right to be heard by himself or by counsel, or both	Right to appear and defend in person or by counsel, or both	Right to have the assistance of counsel	Unique provisions
Ala. (Art. 1, § 6)	Ariz. (Art. 2, § 24)	Iowa (Art. 1, § 10)	Ga. (Art. 1, §§ 2–105): privilege and benefit of counsel
Ark. (Art. 2, § 10)	Cal. (Art. 1, § 13)	La. (Art. 1, § 9)	
Conn. (Art. 1, § 9)	Colo. (Art. 2, § 16)	Mich. (Art. 1, § 19)	Md. (Art. 21, Decl. of Rts.): right to be allowed counsel
Del. (Art. 1, § 7)	Idaho (Art. 1, § 13)	Minn. (Art. 1, § 6)	
Fla. (Decl. of Rts. § 11)	Ill. (Art. 2, § 9)	N.J. (Art. 1, § 10)	N.C. (Art. 1, § 11): right to aid of counsel
Ind. (Art. 1, § 13).	Kan. (B. of Rts. § 10)	R.I. (Art. 1, § 10)	
Ky. (B. of Rts. § 11)	Mo. (Art. 2, § 22)	W. Va. (Art. 3, § 14)	
Mass. (Pt. 1, Art. 12)	Mont. (Art. 3, § 16)		
Me. (Art. 1, § 6)	N.D. (Art. 1, § 13)		
Miss. (Art. 3, § 26)	Neb. (Art. 1, § 11)		
N.H. (B. of Rts. Art. 15)	Nev. (Art. 1, § 8)		
Okla. (Art. 2, § 20)	N.M. (Art. 2, § 14)		
Ore. (Art. 1, § 11)	N.Y. (Art. 1, B. of Rts. § 6)		
Pa. (Art. 1, § 9)	Ohio (Art. 1, § 10)		
S.C. (Art. 1, § 18)	S.D. (Art. 6, § 7)		
Tenn. (Art. 1, § 9)	Utah (Art. 1, § 12)		
Tex. (Art. 1, § 10)	Wash. (Art. 1, § 22)		
Vt. (C. 1, Art. 10)	Wyo. (Art. 1, § 10)		
Wis. (Art. 1, § 7)			

* Virginia has no provision.

237

APPENDIX II

DUTIES OF STATE COURTS UNDER STATUTORY PROVISIONS REGARDING COUNSEL

State	Duty to advise of right to counsel	Duty to appoint counsel				
		Capital cases only	Capital cases and some felonies	Capital cases and all felonies	All cases	On request in non-capital cases
Ala.		×				
Ariz.	×					×
Ark.				×	×	
Cal.	×			×	×	
Colo.				×		
Conn.				×		
Del.				×	×	
Fla.		×			×	
Ga.					×	×
Idaho				×	×	×
Ill.					×	
Ind.				×	×	
Iowa	×				×	
Kan.	×				×	
Ky.					×	
La.		×		×	×	×
Mass.				×		×
Md.					(×)*	
Me.						
Mich.			×		(×)*	×
Minn.					×	
Miss.		×				

State						
Mo.	×		×			
Mont.		×				×
N.C.					×	
N.D.		×		×		×
Neb.						
Nev.		×		×		×
N.H.			×			
N.J.			×			
N.M.						
N.Y.		×				×
Ohio	×	×				
Okla.		×				×
Ore.		×				×
Pa.					×	
R.I.		(×)*				
S.C.					×	
S.D.		×				
Tenn.			×			
Tex.					×	
Utah		×				×
Va.		×				×
Vt.			×			
Wash.	×		×			
Wis.		×				
W. Va.		×				
Wyo.	×	×				

* Duty to appoint counsel is discretionary in this state.

SELECTED BIBLIOGRAPHY

BOOKS

AMERICAN LAW INSTITUTE, *Code of Criminal Procedure* (Official Draft). Philadelphia: American Law Institute, 1930.

AUMANN, FRANCIS R., *The Changing American Legal System.* Columbus, Ohio: Ohio State Univ. Press, 1940.

BLACKSTONE, WILLIAM, *Commentaries on the Laws of England,* 12th ed., Vol. IV. London: T. Cadell, 1795.

BLOOM, SOL (ed.), *Formation of the Union under the Constitution.* Washington, D.C.: Government Printing Office, 1937.

BROWN, ESTHER LUCILE, *Lawyers and the Promotion of Justice.* New York: Russell Sage Foundation, 1938.

BROWNELL, EMERY A., *Legal Aid in the United States.* Rochester, New York: Lawyers Co-operative, 1951.

CHITWOOD, OLIVER, *A History of Colonial America.* New York: Harper, 1931.

Cobbett's State Trials, comp. T. B. Howell, Vols. XVIII, XIX. London: T. C. Hansard, 1813.

COOLEY, THOMAS M., *Constitutional Limitations,* 1st ed. Boston: Little, Brown, 1868.

CORWIN, EDWARD S., *Commerce Power versus States Rights.* Princeton, New Jersey: Princeton Univ. Press, 1936.

—— *The Constitution and What It Means Today,* 10th ed. Princeton, New Jersey: Princeton Univ. Press, 1948.

—— *Liberty against Government.* Baton Rouge, Louisiana: Louisiana State Univ. Press, 1948.

—— *Twilight of the Supreme Court.* New Haven, Connecticut: Yale Univ. Press, 1934.

CUMMINGS, HOMER, AND MCFARLAND, CARL, *Federal Justice.* New York: Macmillan, 1937.

CURTIS, CHARLES P., JR., *Lions under the Throne.* Boston: Houghton Mifflin, 1947.

EDSALL, PRESTON W. (ed.), *Journal of the Courts of Common Right and Chancery of East New Jersey*. Philadelphia: American Legal History Society, 1937.

ELLIOT, JONATHAN, *Debates on the Federal Constitution*, 2nd ed., Vol. III. Philadelphia: Lippincott, 1901.

FARRAND, MAX, *Records of the Federal Convention of 1787*, Vol. III. New Haven, Connecticut: Yale Univ. Press, 1928.

GOEBEL, J., AND NAUGHTON, T. R., *Law Enforcement in Colonial New York*. New York: Commonwealth Fund, 1944.

GOLDMAN, MAYER C., *The Public Defender*. New York: Putnam's, 1917.

GRICE, WARREN, *The Georgia Bench and Bar*, Vol. I. Macon, Georgia: Burke, 1931.

HAINES, CHARLES G., *The Revival of Natural Law Concepts*. Cambridge, Massachusetts: Harvard Univ. Press, 1930.

Halsbury's Laws of England, Vol. IX. London: Butterworth, 1909.

HELLER, FRANCIS H., *The Sixth Amendment*. Lawrence, Kansas: Univ. Kansas Press, 1951.

JACKSON, RICHARD M., *The Machinery of Justice in England*. Cambridge, England: Cambridge Univ. Press, 1940.

KELLY, ALFRED H., AND HARBISON, WINFRED A., *The American Constitution*. New York: Norton, 1948.

LEAMING, THOMAS, *A Philadelphia Lawyer in the London Courts*. New York: Holt, 1912.

MASON, PAUL (comp.), *Constitution of the State of California, Annotated*. Sacramento, California: 1946.

MOTT, RODNEY L., *Due Process of Law*. Indianapolis, Indiana: Bobbs-Merrill, 1928.

ORFIELD, LESTER B., *Criminal Appeals in America*. Boston: Little, Brown, 1939.

—— *Criminal Procedure from Arrest to Appeal*. New York: New York Univ. Press, 1947.

PATTERSON, HAYWOOD, AND CONRAD, EARL, *Scottsboro Boy*. Garden City, New York: Doubleday, 1950.

PLUCKNETT, THEODORE F., *A Concise History of the Common Law*, 3rd ed. London: Butterworth, 1940.

POORE, BENJAMIN PERLEY (ed.), *Federal and State Constitutions, etc.*, 2nd ed., 2 vols. Washington, D.C.: Government Printing Office, 1878.

PRITCHETT, C. HERMAN, *The Roosevelt Court*. New York: Macmillan, 1948.

RADZINOWICZ, LEON, *A History of the English Criminal Law*. London: Stevens, 1948.

REYNOLDS, QUENTIN, *Courtroom, The Story of Samuel S. Leibowitz.* New York: Farrar, Straus, 1950.

SCOTT, ARTHUR P., *Criminal Law in Colonial Virginia.* Chicago: Univ. Chicago Press, 1930.

SMITH, REGINALD HEBER, *Justice and the Poor.* New York: Carnegie Foundation, 1919.

STEPHEN, SIR JAMES F., *A History of the Criminal Law of England,* Vol. I. London: Macmillan, 1883.

STORY, JOSEPH, *Commentaries on the Constitution,* 3rd ed., Vol. II. Boston: Little, Brown, 1858. Fourth ed. (Thomas M. Cooley, ed.), Vol. II. 1873.

SWIFT, ZEPHANIAH, *A System of the Laws of Connecticut,* Vol. II. Windham, Connecticut, 1795.

SWISHER, CARL BRENT, *American Constitutional Development.* Boston: Houghton Mifflin, 1943.

THORPE, FRANCIS NEWTON (ed.), *Federal and State Constitutions, etc.,* 7 vols. Washington, D.C.: Government Printing Office, 1909.

TWISS, BENJAMIN, *Lawyers and the Constitution.* Princeton, New Jersey: Princeton Univ. Press, 1942.

VANDERBILT, ARTHUR T. (ed.), *Minimum Standards of Judicial Administration.* New York: New York Univ. Press, 1949.

WARREN, CHARLES, *A History of the American Bar.* Boston: Little, Brown, 1911.

WRIGHT, BENJAMIN F., *American Interpretations of Natural Law.* Cambridge, Massachusetts: Harvard Univ. Press, 1931.

—— *A Source Book of American Political Theory.* New York: Macmillan, 1929.

PUBLIC DOCUMENTS

Annals of Congress, Vol. I. Washington, D.C.: Gales and Seaton, 1834.

U.S. *Federal Rules of Criminal Procedure for the United States District Courts.* Washington, D.C.: Government Printing Office, 1945.

U.S. *Report of the Director of the Administrative Office of the United States Courts, 1949.* Washington, D.C.: Government Printing Office, 1950.

U.S. NATIONAL COMMISSION ON LAW OBSERVANCE AND ENFORCEMENT, *Report on Criminal Procedure.* Washington, D.C.: Government Printing Office, 1931.

—— *Report on Prosecution.* Washington, D.C.: Government Printing Office, 1931.

ARTICLES

ABRAHAMS, ROBERT D., "The English Legal Assistance Plan," 36 *American Bar Association Journal* (Jan., 1950), 1.

ARMSTRONG, DAVID, "Adequacy of Remedies in State Courts," 47 *Michigan Law Review* (Nov., 1948), 72.

BELL, ROBERT K., "Legal Aid in New Jersey," 36 *American Bar Association Journal* (May, 1950), 355.

BENNETT, JAMES V., "To Secure the Right to Counsel," 32 *Journal of the American Judicature Society* (April, 1949), 177.

BOSKEY, BENNETT, AND PICKERING, JOHN H., "Federal Restrictions on State Criminal Procedure," 13 *University of Chicago Law Review* (April, 1946), 266.

BOWMAN, OTTO M., "The Right to Counsel in a Criminal Proceeding," 12 *Oregon Law Review* (April, 1933), 227.

BRADWAY, J. S. (ed.), "Frontiers of Legal Aid Work," 205 *Annals of the American Academy of Social and Political Science* (Sept., 1939).

—— "Law, and Social Work," 145 *Annals of the American Academy of Social and Political Science* (Sept., 1929).

—— AND SMITH, R. H. (eds.), "Legal Aid Work," 124 *Annals of the American Academy of Social and Political Science* (March, 1926).

CALLAGY, MARTIN V., "Legal Aid in Criminal Cases," 42 *Journal of Criminal Law, Criminology and Police Science* (Jan.—Feb., 1953), 587.

CHAPMAN, GERALD, "Right of Counsel Today," 39 *Journal of Criminal Law and Criminology* (Sept.—Oct., 1948), 342.

FABRICANT, LOUIS, "Voluntary Defenders in Criminal Cases," 205 *Annals of the American Academy of Social and Political Science* (Sept., 1939), 24.

FAIRMAN, CHARLES, "Does the Fourteenth Amendment Incorporate the Bill of Rights? The Original Understanding," 2 *Stanford Law Review* (Dec., 1949), 1.

FALETTI, RICHARD J., "The Tony Marino Case," 36 *Illinois Bar Journal* (March, 1948), 356.

FELLMAN, DAVID, "The Constitutional Right to Counsel in Federal Courts," 30 *Nebraska Law Review* (May, 1951), 559.

—— "The Federal Right to Counsel in State Courts," 31 *Nebraska Law Review* (Nov., 1951), 15.

FOLKERTH, JACK W., "Right to Counsel in a State, Non-capital, Criminal Case," 9 *Ohio State Law Journal* (Summer, 1948), 529.

FRANK, JOHN P., "Court and Constitution: The Passive Period," 4 *Vanderbilt Law Review* (April, 1951), 400.

—— AND MUNRO, ROBERT F., "The Original Understanding of Equal Protection of the Laws," 50 *Columbia Law Review* (Feb., 1950), 131.

FREEMAN, DONALD, "The Public Defender System," 32 *Journal of the American Judicature Society* (Oct., 1948), 74.

GOLDEN, HOWARD S., "Right to Counsel," 16 *Southern California Law Review* (Nov., 1942), 55.

GOODMAN, LOUIS E., "Use and Abuse of the Writ of Habeas Corpus," 7 *Federal Rules Decisions* (1947), 313.

GREEN, JOHN RAEBURN, "The Bill of Rights, the Fourteenth Amendment, and the Supreme Court," 46 *Michigan Law Review* (May, 1948), 869.

GROVER, GEORGE E., "Right to Counsel—Habeas Corpus," 22 *Southern California Law Review* (April, 1949), 259.

HOLTZOFF, ALEXANDER, "Defects in the Administration of Justice," 9 *Federal Rules Decisions* (1949), 303.

—— "Right to Counsel under the Sixth Amendment," 20 *New York University Law Review* (June, 1944), 1.

JENNER, ALBERT E., JR., "The Illinois Post-Conviction Hearing Act," *Illinois Revised Statutes, 1949* (Smith-Hurd, 1950), 199.

LEEK, J. H., "Due Process: Fifth and Fourteenth Amendments," 60 *Political Science Quarterly* (June, 1945), 188.

MANDELKER, DANIEL R., "Right to Counsel in State Cases," *Wisconsin Law Review* (March, 1948), 235.

MORRISON, STANLEY, "Does the Fourteenth Amendment Incorporate the Bill of Rights? The Judicial Interpretation," 2 *Stanford Law Review* (Dec., 1949), 140.

NUTTING, CHARLES B., "Supreme Court, 14th Amendment, and State Criminal Cases," 3 *University of Chicago Law Review* (Feb., 1936), 244.

POLLOCK, HERMAN I., "The Voluntary Defender as Counsel for the Defense," 32 *Journal of the American Judicature Society* (April, 1949), 174.

POUND, ROSCOE, "Problems of the Law," 12 *American Bar Association Journal* (Feb., 1926), 85.

PRESSLEY, HAROLD, JR., "Right to the Assistance of Counsel under the Federal Constitution," 23 *Texas Law Review* (Dec., 1944), 66.

ROBERTS, FRANK H., "Right of an Accused to Have Counsel Appointed by the Court," 45 *Michigan Law Review* (June, 1947), 1047.

ROTHE, E. W., JR., "Exhaustion of State Remedies," 47 *Michigan Law Review* (March, 1949), 720.

SCHWEINBURG, E. F., "Legal Assistance Abroad," 17 *University of Chicago Law Review* (Winter, 1950), 270.

SMITH, REGINALD HEBER, "The English Legal Assistance Plan," 35 *American Bar Association Journal* (June, 1949), 453.

—— "Survey of the Legal Profession," 35 *American Bar Association Journal* (Sept., 1949), 748.

SNIVELY, JOHN R., "The Right of an Accused to the Assistance of Counsel," 32 *Journal of the American Judicature Society* (Dec., 1948), 111.

STEWART, WILLIAM SCOTT, "The Public Defender System Is Unsound in Principle," 32 *Journal of the American Judicature Society* (Dec., 1948), 115.

TUSSMAN, J., AND TEN BROEK, J., "Equal Protection of Laws," 37 *California Law Review* (Sept., 1949), 341.

UNSIGNED NOTE, "Plea of Guilty Not an Absolute Waiver of Counsel," 31 *Minnesota Law Review* (Jan., 1947), 195.

UNSIGNED NOTE, "Right to Counsel in Indiana," 26 *Indiana Law Journal* (Winter, 1951), 234.

UNSIGNED NOTE, "State Court Evasion of the U. S. Supreme Court's Mandates," 156 *Yale Law Journal* (Feb., 1947), 574.

UNSIGNED NOTE, "The Substance of the Right to Counsel," 17 *University of Chicago Law Review* (Summer, 1950), 718.

WILKINSON, VERNON L., "The Federal Bill of Rights and the 14th Amendment," 26 *Georgetown Law Journal* (Jan., 1938), 439.

ANNOTATIONS

"Accused's Right to Assistance of Counsel," 84 *Lawyer's Edition* 383.

"Duty to Advise of the Right to Counsel," 3 *American Law Reports* 2d 1003.

"Plea of Guilty without Advice of Counsel," 149 *American Law Reports* 1043.

"Relief in Habeas Corpus for Violation of Accused's Right to Assistance of Counsel," 146 *American Law Reports* 369.

"Right of Accused to Discharge or Substitute for Appointed Counsel," 157 *American Law Reports* 1225.

"Right of Defendant in Criminal Cases to Conduct Defense in Person," 17 *American Law Reports* 266.

"Right of Defendant to Waive Jury When without Counsel," 143 *American Law Reports* 445.

TABLE OF CASES

(The superior figures indicate footnotes on the pages specified.)

LOWER FEDERAL COURT CASES

Commonwealth ex rel. Hice v. Ashe, 166 Pa. Super. 35, 70 A. 2d 479 (1950):
103
Commonwealth ex rel. McGlinn v. Smith, 344 Pa. 41, 24 A. 2d 1 (1942): 106
Commonwealth ex rel. Piccerelli v. Smith, 150 Pa. Super. 105, 27 A. 2d 484
(1942): 103
Commonwealth ex rel. Quinn v. Smith, 144 Pa. Super. 160, 19 A. 2d 504
(1941): 106
Commonwealth v. Ashe, 149 Pa. Super. 423, 26 A. 2d 217 (1942): 123
Commonwealth v. Bryant, 367 Pa. 135, 79 A. 2d 193 (1951): 127
Commonwealth v. Jester, 256 Pa. 441, 100 A. 993 (1917): 120
Commonwealth v. McNeil (Mass.), 104 N.E. 2d 153 (1952): 128
Commonwealth v. Millen, 289 Mass. 441, 194 N.E. 463 (1935): 81
Commonwealth v. Polichinus, 229 Pa. 311, 78 A. 382 (1910): 119
Commonwealth v. Portner, 92 Pa. Super. 48 (1927): 91
Commonwealth v. Strada, 171 Pa. Super. 358, 90 A. 2d 335 (1952): 90[51]
Commonwealth v. Thacker, 328 Pa. 402, 194 A. 924 (1938): 119
Commonwealth v. Thompson, 367 Pa. 102, 79 A. 2d 401 (1951): 125
Commonwealth v. Valerio, 118 Pa. Super. 34, 178 A. 509 (1935): 98
Cook, Ex parte, 84 Okla. Cr. 404, 183 P. 2d 595 (1947): 113
Cook v. State, 48 Ga. 224, 172 S.E. 471 (1933): 82, 102, 112
Cooper v. State, 106 Fla. 254, 143 So. 217 (1932): 119
Cornell, Ex parte, 87 Okla. Cr. 2, 193 P. 2d 904 (1948): 112, 114[143]
Crawford v. State, 112 Ala. 1 (1895): 119, 120
Crisp v. Hudspeth, 162 Kan. 567, 178 P. 2d 228 (1947): 99
Cruthirds v. State, 190 Miss. 892, 2 So. 2d 145 (1941): 118
Cutts v. State, 54 Fla. 21, 45 So. 491 (1907): 102
Dane, County of, v. Smith, 13 Wis. 585 (1861): 137
Daugherty v. State, 33 Tex. Cr. 173, 26 S.W. 60 (1894): 116
Davis v. Hudspeth, 161 Kan. 354, 167 P. 2d 293 (1946): 110
Davis v. O'Grady, 137 Neb. 708, 291 N.W. 82 (1940): 104
Dearing v. State, 229 Ind. 131, 95 N.E. 2d 832 (1951): 127
Dearo, Ex parte, 96 C. 2d 141, 214 P. 2d 585 (1950): 128
Delk v. State, 99 Ga. 667, 26 S.E. 752 (1896): 123
Dietz v. State, 149 Wis. 462, 136 N.W. 166 (1912): 93
Dille v. State, 34 Ohio St. 617 (1878): 119, 120
Downs v. Hudspeth, 162 Kan. 575, 178 P. 2d 219 (1947): 110
Dunfee v. Hudspeth, 162 Kan. 524, 178 P. 2d 1009 (1947): 108, 114
Egan, In re, 24 C. 2d 323, 149 P. 2d 693 (1944): 125
Elam v. Rowland, 194 Ga. 58, 20 S.E. 2d 572 (1942): 109
Elliott, In re, 315 Mich. 662, 24 N.W. 2d 528 (1946): 83
Ellis v. State, 149 Tex. Cr. 583, 197 S.W. 2d 351 (1946): 129
Fairce v. Amrine, 154 Kan. 618, 121 P. 2d 256 (1942): 99
Ford v. State, 114 Tex. Cr. 77, 24 S.W. 2d 55 (1930): 83, 90, 91
Frazee v. State, 79 Okla. Cr. 224, 153 P. 2d 637 (1944): 113
Gallagher v. Municipal Court of City of Los Angeles, 31 C. 2d 784, 192 P.
2d 905 (1948): 128
Garner v. State, 97 Ark. 63, 132 S.W. 1010 (1910): 114

INDEX

(The superior figures indicate footnotes on the pages specified.)

127; at arraignment, 127–128; at contempt proceedings, 128; at coroner's inquest, 127; at courts-martial, 126; at hearings for removal of public officers, 126; at preliminary examination, 127; at sanity proceedings, 128; at *voir dire* examination, 128; attempted waiver of counsel by incompetent defendants, 110–115; attempted waiver of counsel by ignorant defendants, 110–112; attempted waiver of counsel by youthful defendants, 112–113; before grand jury, 127; before legislative committees, 126; conflicts of interest, 124–125; constitutional provisions, 80–84; consultation with counsel, 120–121; continuances to obtain counsel, 91; defendants as own counsel, 93; defendants who must receive counsel, 114–115; duty to advise of right in absence of statute, 94–98; duty to advise under statutes, 98–101; early state constitutional provisions, 18–22; examination of defendants in regard to counsel, 205–207; express waiver of counsel, 109–110; failure of trial records to show advice, 98–99; failure to comply with court rules concerning advice, 98–99; failure to request counsel as statute requires, 101–104; in civil cases, 126; in misdemeanor cases, 126; incompetent defendants, 114–115; ineffective counsel, 121–123; limitation of counsel's preparation for trial, 115–121; limitation on counsel's presentation at trial, 119–121; motion for continuance, 116–117; motion for new trial, 130; motion in arrest of judgment, 130–131; narrow construction of right, 83; need for counsel at arraignment, 108–109; objection to appointed counsel, 125; payment of counsel, 135–137; reform efforts, summary of, 232–234; right of out-of-state counsel to appear, 92–93, 190; right on appeal, 128; right to retain counsel and defend in person, 89–93; rules concerning counsel, 87–89; rules respecting counsel, need for, 197; states without statutory provision for noncapital cases, 94; statutory provisions, 85–87; trial record showing advice, 99–100; waiver of counsel implied from failure to request, 106; waiver of counsel implied from plea of guilty, 106–109; writ of *coram nobis*, 131; writ of error, 132; writ of habeas corpus, 133–134. *See also the individual states.*

Stephen, Sir James F., cited on criminal-trial practice after 1750, 10

Story, Joseph, on meaning of counsel provision of Sixth Amendment, 28–29

Supreme Court: alignment of justices on counsel issues, 193; application of due-process clause to noncapital state cases, 170–188; application of rule of *Powell* v. *Alabama* 1932–1942, 157–160; decision in *Betts* v. *Brady*, 160–164; decision in Scottsboro cases (*Powell* v. *Alabama*), 154; "double standard" of, 1; exhaustion of state remedies, 181–182; intervention in state criminal cases, 157; precedents for interpreting counsel provision of Sixth Amendment, 33–36; reaction to decision in *Betts* v. *Brady*, 163–164; reversal of state-court decisions, 182. *See also* Due-process clause; Federal courts.

Survey of the Legal Profession, attention to indigent defendants, 201

Sutherland, George, Justice: cited on English rule in colonies, 21; opin-